"Once again Erwin Lutzer has given us a challenging, inspirational, and provocative work that will call all serious Christians to clearly represent our God and His Word in the public square. He has strategically balanced biblical authority, cultural relevance, and spiritual sensitivity in this must-read book. You will be both righteously provoked and personally convicted not to be a silent secret agent Christian after being confronted by the truth in this excellent resource."

Dr. Tony Evans, president, The Urban Alternative
Senior pastor, Oak Cliff Bible Fellowship

"What's behind the current 'unraveling of America'? And how should we respond? In his magnificent book *We Will Not Be Silenced*, my friend Erwin Lutzer has the vital answers, exhorting us to boldly and courageously witness about our faith, come what may!"

Eric Metaxas, #1 *New York Times* bestselling
author of *Bonhoeffer* and *Martin Luther*
Host of the nationally syndicated *Eric Metaxas Radio Show*

"My dear friend Erwin Lutzer has given us an insightful framework in which to think through and approach the challenges we face during this moment in history. You will find *We Will Not Be Silenced* thought-provoking and helpful. At times you may even wrestle with a few of his insights and conclusions. That's a good thing. Thank you, Erwin, for addressing these matters, including racism, Marxism, and capitalism against the backdrop of the cross and the transforming truth of the Word of God."

Dr. Crawford W. Loritts Jr., author, speaker, radio host
Senior pastor, Fellowship Bible Church, Roswell, Georgia

"*We Will Not Be Silenced* explains a number of trends growing at frightening speed that endanger the liberties of people everywhere. This book is a worthy investment of your time. As always, Lutzer provides keen analysis and presents numerous insightful conclusions. He is one of the few authors of whom I make a point to read *everything* they release. Why? Because regardless of the topic he's addressing, his analysis will be factual, artfully presented, and beneficial."

Alex McFarland, Christian apologist
Truth For A New Generation

"Erwin Lutzer has written a timely and important book that calls the church to face the challenges of our society from a Christ-honoring, Scripture-driven, and gospel-saturated perspective. In *We Will Not Be Silenced*, he offers the simple yet radical solution to the manifold problems that plague the culture we live in: Let the church be the church! Read this book carefully. Share it as widely as possible. Refuse to be silent in your witness for Christ!"

H.B. Charles Jr., senior pastor,
Shiloh Church, Jacksonville, Florida

"Sooner or later, we all have to take a stand. Erwin Lutzer says the time has come for Christians to stand up for the truth. With pastoral wisdom and deep insight, he exposes the lies that have brought Western culture to the brink of destruction. But he doesn't stop there. This book shows how we can reclaim the church (which is the key to the culture) if we will once again speak God's truth without fear or favor. I can only hope millions of believers will read this book and be moved to take action."

Dr. Ray Pritchard, president,
Keep Believing Ministries

"*We Will Not Be Silenced* is, in my view, the most important book my friend Erwin Lutzer has written. This is a book for generations. A manifesto for Christians and churches. I love the courageous stand for truth and the bold declaration of faith that is clearly delivered within its pages. No doubt about it—this book is light shining brightly in the darkness."

Dr. Jack Graham, pastor, Prestonwood
Baptist Church & PowerPoint Ministries

"I have longed to see pulpits blaze with passion as they did during the American Revolution. I've longed for powerful teaching that applies God's Word to the chaos we are experiencing. Erwin Lutzer's deep understanding of history, culture, and God's Word blend powerfully in *We Will Not Be Silenced* to do just that as he refreshingly challenges us to hold fast, be bold, and finish well!"

Sandy Rios, Director of Governmental Affairs for AFA
(American Family Association), host of *Sandy Rios in the Morning on
AFR Talk*, former president of CWA (Concerned Women for America)

"We are living in desperate days that pose unique challenges to the proclamation of Jesus Christ. In such days, we need faithful voices to guide the way. Erwin Lutzer is a faithful man who addresses a challenging and crucial topic with biblical clarity and conviction. I am thankful for this book and believe it deserves your attention."

Dr. Heath Lambert, senior pastor,
First Baptist Church in Jacksonville, Florida

"Based on decades of successfully defending religious leaders, churches, and seminaries in the body of Christ in litigation all across America, if the body of Christ hopes to survive in the public forum and have the impact on this culture Jesus has commanded in the Great Commission, the message of this book must be heeded."

J. Shelby Sharpe, Constitutional lawyer

"After working as an actress in Hollywood and seeing how Marxism is taking over the entertainment industry and the public school system from within, this book is A MUST READ to know what battle we are up against. Knowledge is power. I can say this book not only exposes the enemy but gives us the wisdom and tools to get God back in our country, community, and home. The time is NOW!"

Tina Marie Griffin,
www.CounterCultureMom.com

"Thinking about the climate dominating our culture today, Erwin Lutzer gives insight into a number of key issues facing the church. I highly recommend this volume be read by those interested in being a part of the solution to today's volatile issues."

Milton E. Kornegay,
Central Baptist Church, Syracuse, New York

"Biblical prophecy and history instruct us on how great nations collapse from within before ever being conquered from without. In this book, Erwin Lutzer reminds us of our enemy's 'Game Plan' and how we should respond to it."

Cal Thomas, syndicated columnist
Author, *America's Expiration Date*

We Will
Not Be
SILENCED

Erwin W. Lutzer

HARVEST HOUSE PUBLISHERS
EUGENE, OREGON

Editing by Steve Miller

Cover design by Studio Gearbox

Cover photo © imagehub / Shutterstock

Interior layout by KUHN Design Group

For bulk, special sales, or ministry purchases, please call 1-800-547-8979.
Email: Customerservice@hhpbooks.com

We Will Not Be Silenced
Copyright © 2020 by Erwin W. Lutzer
Published by Harvest House Publishers
Eugene, Oregon 97408
www.harvesthousepublishers.com

ISBN 978-0-7369-8179-8 (pbk)
ISBN 978-0-7369-8180-4 (eBook)

Library of Congress Control Number 2020946074

Printed in the United States of America

21 22 23 24 25 26 27 28 29 / BP-SK / 10 9 8 7 6

To all who are committed to carrying the cross of Christ into a needy and confused world and consider opposition to be a badge of honor—to such fellow travelers this book is prayerfully dedicated.

> *"If anyone would come after me, let him deny*
> *himself and take up his cross and follow me.*
> *For whoever would save his life will lose it,*
> *but whoever loses his life for my sake will find it."*
>
> MATTHEW 16:24-25

Contents

Why You Should Read This Book

Dr. David Jeremiah

Recently, while sitting at the breakfast table, I told my wife that I felt like I was living through the dismantling of America. We talked about the horror of watching the news each night and seeing this country that we love being destroyed before our very eyes. How could this be happening? What does it mean? Where is it leading? What can we do?

These are the cultural questions that are being asked in almost any setting you visit today. Unfortunately, almost no one is providing any answers.

But Erwin Lutzer, in *We Will Not Be Silenced*, is responding. And what he has written about what is happening in our nation is the most complete, the most honest, and the most understandable explanation I have encountered.

I agreed to write this foreword because I believe you need to read this book—not just the first few pages but every page, every paragraph, every word.

If I could, I would put *We Will Not Be Silenced* into the hands of every Christian in America. But it is already in your hands, and I want to tell you why you should read it.

This book *examines* every cultural issue we are facing. Nothing is left out. It addresses diversity issues, racial issues, gender issues, social justice issues, media issues, issues of free speech, and issues rooted in socialism and Marxism. Most importantly, it covers issues related to the church and how it is responding to all of this.

We Will Not Be Silenced examines all the above and much more. But it doesn't just examine them, it *explains* them. Why are these things happening? How did we get to where we are without noticing where we were headed? Recently we have watched as criminal mobs have ravaged our cities, burned down buildings, and declared war on the police. What has been most troubling has been the attempt of these organized rioters to tear down moral and spiritual values as well. Why are they doing this? It is not just random civil disobedience. Nor is it lawful protests gone awry.

Erwin Lutzer explains that behind all this destructive behavior is the determination of the Marxists to destroy America's history so that it can be replaced by a new Marxist "history" that is being inculcated into our children's minds from kindergarten through graduate school. They're not just tearing down monuments, they're trying to destroy the very foundation upon which our nation was founded. They understand that "he who controls the past controls the future."

This book traces every secular cultural expression back to its roots. These things are not just "happening"; they have been orchestrated. They are not random individual occurrences; they are all part of a carefully scripted and produced overture to the destruction of America.

Finally, this book does not just examine what is happening and explain why it is happening. It *exhorts* us to respond to what is happening. Lutzer asks, "How do we live courageously in a culture where people who shout the loudest win the argument? How do we live during a time when Christianity is openly being remade to blend more comfortably into a secularized culture?"

Here is Lutzer's hopeful answer for you, for me, and for all who call upon the name of the Lord:

> I want to inspire us to have the courage to walk toward the fire and not run away from the flames. God has brought us to this cultural moment, and our future cannot be taken for granted. As has been said, "In a time of universal deception, telling the truth is a revolutionary act."

I want to encourage you to prayerfully—and carefully—read this book. Take good notes, highlight the key passages, write in the margins. And when you have finally wrapped your mind and heart around these truths, don't be silent!

Dr. David Jeremiah
Senior Pastor, Shadow Mountain
Community Church, El Cajon, CA
Founder and President,
Turning Point Ministries

The Surprising Response of Jesus

The disciples asked Jesus an interesting question: "Lord, will those who are saved be few?" (Luke 13:23).

Haven't we all wondered how many people will be saved and how many lost? We know that in the end there will be a multitude of the redeemed from every tribe and nation that no one can number (Revelation 7:9). But this multitude represents only a fraction of the human race. We would like to know more specific numbers and percentages.

Jesus, as was often His custom, did not answer the question directly. Rather, He chose to give a warning.

> Strive to enter through the narrow door. For many, I tell you, will seek to enter and will not be able. When once the master of the house has risen and shut the door, and you begin to stand outside and to knock at the door, saying, "Lord, open to us," then he will answer you, "I do not know where you come from" (Luke 13:24-25).

The same frightening truth appears in the Sermon on the Mount. Jesus affirmed that many who expected to be saved would in fact be lost and that the gate leading to the heavenly kingdom was narrow; the way to destruction was broad and "those who enter by it are many" (Matthew 7:13). Clearly, more people—many more people—will be lost than will be saved.

Yet today there are calls for evangelicals to remake Christianity into a more inclusive religion. There are widespread efforts to make the narrow door wider and to even affirm the salvation of well-meaning people of other religions. So-called progressive Christians advance their causes under the banner of love and compassion. In the process, the hard truths of Christianity are either redefined or ignored.

Let me be clear that I am opposed to a form of judgmental Christianity that holds to truth without compassion and righteousness without humility. I am opposed to a form of Christianity that judges without listening and sees the faults of others without seeing our own. As a pastor, my heart breaks for those who hurt, who are confused, and who don't know where to turn for help. Our churches should be sanctuaries for the downtrodden, the oppressed, and the lonely. They should be hospitals for the soul.

But I see much of contemporary Christianity submitting to the culture in many areas of life, especially in matters of sexuality. The only way to make Christianity appealing, we are told, is to move the markers—to be more inclusive, more affirming. I fear we are allowing culture to inform our thinking and even raise our children. We no longer are submissive to "the whole counsel of God" (Acts 20:27). We think we must accept or acquiesce to culture in order to redeem it.

Pastor Alistair Begg told a story about how he and his wife were driving on an expressway when he remarked to her that the sun was going down in the wrong direction. For a moment he didn't know how to interpret this strange phenomenon—until he realized they had missed a turn and were on an expressway headed east instead of south. Today, many people use their own judgment as their point of reference; they feel so right about their direction that they are deaf to calls for them to rethink their approach to culture. They are making progress on the wrong road.

Too often, compassion is used to override our better judgment and approve of ungodly lifestyles. We tell ourselves that we don't witness about our faith because we fear offending someone; we are silent in the face of political and moral decline because we want to be thought of as nice and not judgmental. We don't want to let people know that the way into the kingdom is narrow and there is a cost to following Jesus. The Christian poet Vasily Zhukovsky wrote, "We all have crosses to bear and we are constantly trying on different ones for a good fit."[1]

We are all trying to find a lighter cross.

I dedicate this book to those who seek to stand for the truth and still be loving—to those who are willing to be identified with the cross of Christ despite the possible vitriol and consider it a badge of honor. I dedicate this book to all who are convinced that how we are perceived on earth is not as important as how we are perceived in heaven. I dedicate this book to all who believe that the day of casual commitment to the gospel must come to an end.

We must pray that our light
might shine more brightly than
ever in our darkening world.

Will few or many be saved? Jesus asks us to make sure we are on the narrow road even though it may not have as many travelers. Let's not spend our time looking for a lighter cross. Someone has said that "a Christianity without courage is cultural atheism."

In this book I shine a light on several cultural trends that I see working against us, including the divisive issue of racism that dominates much of our national discourse. I also try to encourage the church to keep its focus and understand that the gospel we believe also has implications for how we view culture and how we treat one another. And no matter the headwinds, we must keep rowing toward the heavenly shore.

What a special privilege it is to be called to represent Christ at this pivotal moment of history! We are called for such a time as this. And we must pray that our light might shine more brightly than ever in our darkening world.

CHAPTER 1

How We Got Here

The secular left does not believe that America can be fixed; they say it must be destroyed.

On the rubble of America's Judeo-Christian past a new America will emerge, which they say will be free of poverty, racism, and white supremacy. The secular left's goal is a future in which everyone will be equal on *their* terms and the disparities of the past will be read about only in history books. Those who resist this utopian vision are to be vilified, bullied, and shamed until they admit to the mistakes of the past and embrace the secular left's great hope for the future.

Take a moment to reflect on what has happened in America in the last 20 years. Consider the increasingly sexually explicit curriculum in our public schools; listen to the racial rhetoric of the self-appointed social justice warriors who are committed to enflaming racial division; and look at the new laws forcing Christian colleges to compromise their biblical stance about marriage and surrender to the LGBTQ agenda.

Who would have ever believed the day would come when men would say that they too can bear children and menstruate and thus must fight for "period equity"? Or that drag queens would be allowed to read fairy tales to very young children in public libraries? This kind of sexualized thinking and behavior is spreading rapidly in a nation obsessed with its overblown emphasis on individual rights for a select few at the expense of others.

It's difficult to even have a real conversation on the many social issues of our day, such as policies advocating unrestricted immigration and sweeping proposals to combat climate change. Or issues regarding racism. To merely question the viewpoints of secular left radicals on social issues is denounced as hateful, bigoted, and racist. We who are Christians are told that if we want to be known as good citizens, we should keep our antiquated views to ourselves. We are made to feel embarrassed about defending traditional marriage and a sane understanding of gender. Like a deer caught in the headlights, we don't quite know what to do and whether we are willing to pay the price of fidelity to Scripture. We are shamed into silence.

To summarize the late Dr. Haddon Robinson: In the past, we, as American Christians, always had home-field advantage. We knew that in the crowd there were those from the other team who were opposed to us, but the larger stadium crowd was either on our side or indifferent to our witness as Christians. All that has changed. Now we play all our games on enemy turf. A minority is on our side while the wider culture sits in the stands shouting hateful epithets at us, rejoicing at our losses. And the elitists in the skyboxes cheer them on.

But here is the good news! *Praise be to God we are on the playing field.* And we invite all those who are on the bench to join us for some great fourth-quarter plays! We are more prepared for this moment than we realize.

But we must better understand the home team that opposes us.

Cultural Marxism's Growing Shadow

A powerful cultural stream has fed this river of political correctness—the curbing of free speech, increased government control, growing racial conflict, and hostility toward Christianity. Leading these attacks against traditional American values is a form of Marxism that is widely taught in many universities and assumed by elitists as the theory that best explains the inequities of our society and our best hope for curing them.

Yes, incredible as it may seem, Karl Marx still rules from the grave.

Marx introduced a theory of state supremacy that necessitated economic and social controls that were imposed in Russia after the revolution of 1917. After this revolution, during which millions of people were killed, the state abolished private property and set out to bring "equality" and "justice" to an oppressed people. State supremacy necessitated religious suppression and the curbing of individual rights.

Today we face what is known as *cultural* Marxism. It is not being imposed on people on war battlefields; instead, it's a form of Marxism that wins the hearts and minds of people incrementally by the gradual transformation of the culture. Bombarded with exaggerated and illusionary promises, people accept it because they *want* to; they welcome it because they are convinced of its "benefits." It promises "hope and change," income equality, racial harmony, and justice based on secular values rather than Judeo-Christian morality. It is known for professing inclusion rather than exclusion and promoting sexual freedom rather than what they view as the restrictive sexual ethics of the Bible. It is not stifled by allegedly narrow religious traditions but espouses progressive ideas that are deemed worthy of an enlightened future. It promises "social justice," a term with various meanings that we will discuss later in this book.

Cultural Marxists seek to capture five cultural institutions: the social, political, educational, religious, and most importantly, familial life of a nation. And as we observe what is happening in our culture, we can say that they are succeeding in frightening ways—all in the name of progress.

To better interpret what is happening in our culture, we must understand more about Marx himself and his original vision. He knew certain foundational pillars must be torn down before a nation could rebuild a new economic, racial, and moral culture.

The Destruction of the Nuclear Family

Standing in the way of these changes is the nuclear family with a father, a mother, and children. Marx taught that families based on natural law and Judeo-Christian values breed inequality and feed on greed and systemic oppression. Such families had to be dismantled if the Marxist vision of equality was to be realized. (In legal history, natural law means divine principles imposed on the creation that govern its functioning, including that of humans, so that obedience brings benefits while disobedience brings consequences.[1])

One reason the nuclear family is an obstacle to Marxism is because of the tendency for the children of the rich to inherit wealth and the children of the poor to pass along their poverty. Marx was determined to change this. The solution: If the state owned all the wealth, it could be distributed more evenly among all its citizens. Gone also would be disproportionate salaries and unequal economic opportunities.

Frederick Engels, who along with Karl Marx wrote *The Communist Manifesto*, said that the monogamous nuclear family emerged only with capitalism. Prior to capitalism, tribal societies were classless, children and property were community owned, and people enjoyed sexual freedom. Marxists claimed that the restrictions limiting sexual intimacy to a man-woman relationship within the marriage covenant were invented by religion to maintain the dominance of men. Belief in God and the Bible—with its teaching about social institutions such as marriage—was the source of multiple forms of oppression.

And there is more.

In Marxism, the family is perceived as a unit in which wives are suppressed by their husbands and children are suppressed by their parents. These clusters of oppression have to be broken up; mothers have to leave their homes and join the workforce. So, as Marx put it, "Anybody who knows anything of history knows that great social changes are impossible without the *feminine ferment*. Social progress can be measured exactly by the social position of the fair sex (the ugly ones included)."[2]

So "feminine ferment"—or feminine upheaval—is said to be the key to liberating the family from multiple forms of oppression and the capitalistic pattern of passing on wealth from one generation to another. Mothers have to be encouraged to leave their children for others to raise; after all, stay-at-home moms live in servitude to their husbands and are too easily satisfied. If their grievances—many of which are legitimate—can be exploited, they will then be willing to stifle their motherly instincts and step outside the home and enter the workforce. This can be sold as a step toward liberation and equality.

Marxists believe one of the benefits of mothers joining the workforce is that their children must then attend state-sponsored day care centers and schools where they can be taught about the errors of creationism, the church, and, of course, the Bible. Children can also be indoctrinated about the evils of capitalism and the benefits of socialism and "economic equality." For this to become a reality, the education of children has to be taken out of the hands of the parents and surrendered to the state.

Government assurances are designed to create a dependency on the state that is essential for Marxism to thrive. Here in America, a boost to such dependency took place when trillions of dollars were created electronically for the massive government bailouts in the wake of the COVID-19 pandemic. Going forward, we can expect calls for more government intervention, more government control, and increased redistribution of resources. As of this writing, the US government has not taken over the businesses of the nation, but we are incrementally accepting and making our way toward a socialist view of the economy.

Marxism proposes that the government take permanent control of the economy and provide financial security with cradle-to-grave benefits. Healthcare, guaranteed wage and price controls, free college tuition, and assured comfortable retirement are all part of its larger agenda. Marxism proposes a government-planned economy and, in the end, says that state rights should supplant God-given rights.

Oppression Is the Key to History

Enter victimology.

Marxists know they need to exploit the existing and often very real grievances of the proletariat (the working class) and, yes, even the grievances of oppressed mothers in their homes. Women are told they are victims—victims of the past, of social norms, of traditions, and of men. Only victimhood will make them willing to break out of their Judeo-Christian past and enter the Marxist ideal of a world where everyone is equal. If mothers want to achieve their potential, they should reject restrictive traditional roles and prove their equality by earning a living and enjoying the prosperity that a Marxist state will bring.

As will be shown in a later chapter, this emphasis on victimhood also applies to race—not with the intention of bringing about reconciliation, but instead, to keep the races in conflict with each other. Upheaval, with various factions fighting each other, is necessary for the larger goal of bringing about a cultural revolution that will destabilize the existing order and usher in a new era of government control and Marxist values. Impossible demands are made to hinder progress in race relations rather than searching for common ground and commonsense solutions.

Please understand that Marx was right in pointing out that oppression exists, often in horrible ways. But his solutions are entirely wrongheaded and destructive. By locating the problem as only the external systemic oppression between classes and by ignoring the biblical doctrine of original sin and individual responsibility, he sent his followers on a path of endless and unresolved conflict. Historically, when Marxism has won victories, it has done so at the expense of millions of lives and then set up its own system of oppression—a system with far worse oppression than the oppression it promised to alleviate. Later in this book, we will discuss such failure in more detail.

Many people who know nothing about Karl Marx nevertheless advance a Marxist agenda. For example, rather than simply insisting on fairness in policing and weeding out "bad cops," the movement seeks to neuter the police force altogether to destabilize the existing social order; they know that anarchy is an important step toward destroying capitalism and Western culture.

Marxists insist schools must change their curricula to reflect this alternate view of society. Works written by Western writers must be rejected, bizarre behavior must be normalized, the need for socialism must be emphasized, and contrary views must be shamed. The hope is that future generations, controlled by political correctness and pro-Marxist politicians, will embrace the Marxist vision. Freedom from sexual taboos, traditional gender roles, and natural law will result in racial and economic equality that will eventually liberate an otherwise complacent and oppressed population. Once their leaders are in charge, these reforms will be ushered in.

And today there are organizations dedicated to this agenda.

We all agree that yes, black lives matter—in fact, *all* black lives matter, but the organization that was formed using this slogan hides its real agenda, which is fueled by Marxist ideologies. For example, its website says, "We disrupt the Western-prescribed nuclear family structure requirement by supporting each other as extended families and 'villages' that collectively care for one another…We foster a queer-affirming network."[3] And one of its cofounders admitted, "We are trained Marxists."[4] Obviously the organization Black Lives Matter does not speak for all black Americans, but after the brutal murder of George Floyd, it has gained widespread national and political support. Those who don't support it are frequently denounced as racist.

Various changes are demanded in the name of *equality* and *justice*, terms that we will discuss later in this book. Meanwhile, let's pause for a moment to trace the influence of someone who helped to break down the family structure.

Margaret Sanger Advances the Agenda

Margaret Sanger, influenced by the ideals of cultural Marxism, was a revolutionary who intended to transform the American family so she could change the world. In March 1914, she launched a newspaper called *The Woman Rebel*, which promoted moral and political anarchy. Her motto was "No Gods, No Masters." In the paper she touted the virtues of single motherhood, contraception, and asserted that women have the right to face the world "with a go-to-hell look in the eyes; to have an ideal; to speak and act in defiance of convention."[5]

In her 1920 book *Women and the New Race*, she predicted that the rebellion of women would remake the world. She believed in evolution and that the fit should have more children than the unfit. She endeavored to liberate women by affirming "reproductive freedom," which would give women the ability to be promiscuous and still be able to decide whether they wanted to bear children or not. "Even as birth control is the means by which woman attains basic freedom, so it is the means by which she must and will uproot the evil she has wrought through her submission."[6]

Don't miss what she said: A woman must overcome "the evil she has wrought through her submission." In other words, submission to her husband was evil; to stay at home to rear children was servitude. The home would no longer consist of a father, a mother, and children. Liberation meant equality of roles, equality of income, and equality of sexual freedom. The biblical roles of marriage and faith in God were deemed obsolete and harmful.

Illegitimacy would serve the Marxist cause well because out-of-wedlock children would be less likely to be devoted to their homes and their parents or church. Children without family roots can be more easily directed toward secular values and state benefits. The state can do for them what their parents failed to do. Freed from the constraints of sexual fidelity, along with promises of income equality, society could finally be liberated.

From these basic premises, feminism flourished, as well as abortion, the sexual revolution, homosexual marriages, and more recently, transgender euphoria. Incredibly, in 1969, Judy Smith, a member of Students for a Democratic Society, predicted our future when she wrote, "We in Women's Liberation deny any inherent differences between men and women...All of us are trapped by the society that created our roles. We are questioning the ideals of marriage and motherhood...[and] the very society that has created these roles and values must be questioned."[7]

Natural law would, of course, have to be abandoned in this quest for equality. This quest would become the overriding mantra that would bring about the destruction of the family so necessary to achieve the Marxist vision. Today, we know that same quest for equality has led to the notion that two men or two women can have sexual relations and these "unions" should be normalized. And yes, two homosexual men can adopt and care for a baby just as well as a traditional mother and father.

The doctrine that men and women are alike in all respects (in fact, we are now told that even a man can give birth to a child) is now an article of faith that permeates the minds of many progressives. Those who celebrate the differences between femininity and masculinity are said to be old school and out of touch with the world as it is supposed to be. They are "on the wrong side of history."

Woe to those who challenge the orthodoxy that the roles and aptitudes of men and women are interchangeable. Even back in 2005, at an academic meeting, Harvard University president Larry Summers was asked why so few women had been receiving tenure in mathematics and the hard sciences. Summers had the temerity to say that the reason might be because of the variant abilities of men and women. "In the special case of science and engineering, there are issues of intrinsic aptitude, and particularly of the variability of aptitude...these may cause the different availability of aptitude at the high end."[8]

The fuse was lit.

MIT biology professor Nancy Hopkins, who heard the remark,

said, "My heart was pounding and my breath was shallow…I just couldn't breathe because this kind of bias makes me physically ill." She went on to say that if she had not left the room, "I would have either blacked out or thrown up."[9]

Later, Summers was subjected to a "no confidence" vote and forced to resign. So far as I know, no one has produced hard data that proved him wrong. But as we will see later in this book, when it comes to cultural Marxism, science, history, biology, and reason must be cast aside to maintain the current orthodoxies. Freedom of speech and diverse opinions are strictly forbidden—or else.

The trans movement (which we will also look at later in this book) has further broken down gender distinctions and ushered in a whole new range of gender options. And as we will see, reason, civility, and science would again be discarded in favor of the Marxist vision of a classless and genderless society.

And we have not yet seen the end. New barriers will be crossed, new ideologies developed, and new laws adopted that Christians will be expected to gratefully accept. This is what progress is said to look like; and from a biblical perspective, it is progress in the wrong direction.

The Benefits of the Women's Movement

This is a good place for me to say that not all the changes brought about by the women's movement have been negative. It is hard for some of us to realize that although some states had already given women the right to vote, the Nineteenth Amendment, which codified that right, was adopted in 1920, nearly 150 years after the United States became a nation. In 2020, we celebrated the one-hundredth anniversary of this milestone. Like many reforms for women, this right was long overdue.

Women who join the workforce should receive equal pay for equal work. And we agree that women have often been victimized not just by their husbands but by their employers and others in society. Certainly the #MeToo movement, though occasionally misused, was long overdue. I rejoice that many lecherous men are finally being held to account for their abuse of women. Thankfully, the church is waking up to the reality that in many homes there is abuse that should neither be overlooked nor somehow tolerated. It's time that women have their say. And we as Christians had best listen.

The Bible teaches that the genders are equal in value but different in roles. The creation mandate specifies unique and complementary roles for men and women as it relates to marriage and the family. The exact nature of these roles has been and continues to be debated, but it's clear that mothers and fathers should rear their children together. The ideal, biblically speaking, is for the father to work and provide as the mother cares for and nurtures the children, but with today's significant economic pressures and in the case of single parents or other difficult family scenarios, that's not always possible.

There was a time when those who desired to follow the biblical pattern could do so peacefully, but today, those who seek to adhere to this ideal are mocked.

The Media: Leading the Culture

The Agenda

The media not only *reflects* the culture but *directs* the culture; it is out front and we are expected to follow.

We should not be surprised that the focus of the cultural Marxist revolution would center on sex and gender and race. After all, these themes play dominant roles in our lives and are especially impressionable on young people. Sexuality promises pleasure and fulfillment; its transcendent feelings of connection and value are the source of enduring hope and fantasy. It is the basis for our identity as male or female, as men or women. Sexuality gives us the privilege and responsibility of reproduction and the guarantee of future generations. We are all sexual beings.

However, if the biblical teaching about marriage can be redefined, then the social order can be transformed. Homosexual activists learned early on that the advancement of their agenda can be achieved through bullying, threats, and when necessary, violence. But their agenda can also be presented as the high moral ground by cloaking it in the language of love, acceptance, and inclusion. In doing this, activists emphasize the word cultural Marxists repeatedly use: *equality.*

The Power of Media Images

You may have missed it—I sure did—but if you had watched the 56th Grammy Awards program on January 26, 2014, you would have heard the song "Same Love" sung as an ode to same-sex relationships. Afterward, Queen Latifa invited 33 diverse couples onto the stage—gay, straight, multicultural, and multiracial. They were asked to exchange rings and she pronounced them legally married as "the white outlines in the backdrop burst into a rainbow of colors, gleaming like windows of a cathedral."[10]

Madonna entered the stage to sing "Open Your Heart" as the couples were seen hugging, crying, and singing along as the crowd rose to a standing ovation. Then a choir sang the opening words of 1 Corinthians 13, interspersing it with Mary Lambert's chorus from "She Keeps Me Warm." Of course, this was an attack against the biblical prohibition of same-sex relationships. As Robert P. Jones described the event, "It was a direct challenge to religious opposition to gay rights mounted in front of 28.5 million American viewers on a Sunday night."[11]

That evening, nearly 30 million Americans saw what appeared to be a display of love that clearly attempted to make a mockery out of Christian morality. Never mind the implications for the family or society in general.

In one of the lyrics, the Bible was dismissed as a book written long ago, yet the same book was conveniently embraced by emphasizing its references to love. This serves as a wonderful example of how today's culture believes it can cherry pick the parts of the Bible they like and dismiss the parts they don't. That mentality is a danger for all of us.

The mainstream media is the handmaiden of the sexual revolution. It will never, under any circumstances, expose the dark side of the same-sex movement—its commitment to unrestrained sexuality, its unnatural physical relationships, and the deep regret and confusion that exist among those who want to leave same-sex relationships or have had gender-reassignment surgery. This same media does not want to present the benefits of natural law and why the traditional family is to be preferred.

In fact, television programs such as *Will and Grace* have humored secular culture by depicting those who oppose same-sex relationships as being bigoted, uninformed, and nasty. *Modern Family*, which had a successful 11-year run on television, sought to destroy any vestige of the traditional family with clever scripts and humor. Who could possibly object to two men who are in love with each other having sex? Don't we need more love, not less?

The sexual revolution is not the only challenge that the church faces today but is surely one of the most important. In this book we will address social justice, racism, socialism, propaganda, and the like. But the pressure to accept our society's sexual transformation is on our doorstep. Or more accurately, it has invaded our homes.

The Ominous Choice We Face

Will we confront or compromise?

Robert P. Jones, in his book *The End of White Christian America*, describes the challenge facing Conservative Christians:

> What's at stake isn't just the outcome of political debates. Conservative religious groups' very future hinges on how willing they are to navigate from the margins toward the new mainstream…To move away from strong opposition to same-sex marriage would spark a profound identity crisis and risk losing support from their current—albeit aging—support base. Refusing to reevaluate, on the other hand, may relegate conservative religious groups into cultural irrelevancy and continued decline, as more and more young people leave church behind.[12]

Basically, Jones is saying that those who hold to biblical teachings about marriage appear to be forced "into cultural irrelevancy," and proof of this is declining church attendance as the younger generation leaves the church. In the above quote, Jones lays out for us the challenge today's Christians face.

Secularists are not content to "live and let live." They are not satisfied with pluralism and the exchange of ideas. They seek not just to be equal but to dominate. That which was at one time condemned must not simply be tolerated, it must be celebrated. And that which was at one time celebrated must be condemned. Only then will these crusaders see their vision of utopia come to pass. Their goal is the total capitulation of the culture to *their* point of view. Dissenting voices are shamed into either submission or silence.

Some believe that if the church does not get on board with the same-sex agenda, its schools will have to close and the church will become obsolete. Already Christian colleges are facing legal and economic pressures to revise their biblical stances, particularly on sexual issues.

So, must we choose to join the revolution lest we become obsolete? That's what some pundits are telling us. We are warned that if we as a church do not bow to the powerful cultural currents of our era, we will find ourselves a relic in a cultural museum, an object of historical curiosity without influence and without a voice.

The other possibility is to stand for historic, biblical Christianity and face the consequences. Are we up to the task?

The Silent Church

It is time for the church to step to the plate and seize the high moral ground.

Those of us who have been witnesses to the rapid transformation of our country—we who are members of the church—have been strangely silent. And with good reason. To our shame, we are afraid of the secular left. We fear being misquoted by the press, vilified by the special-interest groups, and threatened by the radicals. There is no joy in being called racist, hateful, bigoted, homophobic, or accused of imposing our religious views on others.

I'm personally glad that I have seldom, if ever, been asked to comment on these matters on secular television. In 1982, I was part of a group of Chicago pastors who held a news conference to protest a gay ordinance that was up for debate in city hall. We experienced the usual criticism and, in the end, lost our battle. Later, one of our secretaries at The Moody Church received a phone call intended for me. The caller wanted to remind me that we had lost and they had won. He chided me for getting into the fray. We who are Christians have been told to stay in our corner, pay homage to the left's revolution, and, at best, keep our mouths shut.

When I wrote a book *The Truth About Same-Sex Marriage*, demonstrators came to the steps of The Moody Church and shouted curses as they tore up a copy the book. One of the demonstrators shouted, "I would like to throw a brick through one of the windows."

Who needs this kind of publicity?

There is another reason we have been silent. We want to be nice, welcoming, and grace-centered. We want to present Jesus as Savior to the greatest number of people possible. If what we say and believe about the secular left's agenda becomes public, we will be called haters, grace-deniers, and legalistic. We will be scrutinized with even the smallest offenses magnified. We cannot shout as loudly as the radicals, nor should we. So we retreat into silence.

We, as evangelicals, are expected to stay in our small cubicles and keep out of the issues that pertain to secular culture. To speak beyond the leftist-approved boundaries risks humiliation and vilification. As one atheist told me, "The church is fine as long as it stays in its corner."

I write this book with a heavy heart. Never before have I felt so much like Jehoshaphat, who called a fast when several vicious armies united and came against Israel. He prayed a desperate prayer of repentance, pleading with God and saying, "We are powerless against this great horde that is coming against us. We do not know what to do, but our eyes are on you" (2 Chronicles 20:12). But when the choir began to sing praises to God, the victory was won.

Clearly, the sovereign God who knows all things and plans all things has prepared us for this moment. We are more ready than we realize to represent Christ in our fragmenting culture. We might not know exactly what to do, but we say with Jehoshaphat "our eyes are upon you."

The Purpose of This Book

How do we live courageously in a culture where the people who shout the loudest win the argument? How do we live during a time when Christianity is openly being remade to blend more comfortably into a secularized culture? How do we fight against legitimate injustices when we are asked to bow a knee to a larger destructive agenda?

I write not so much to reclaim the culture as *to reclaim the church.*

The purpose of this book is not to inspire us to "take America back." We have neither the will nor the clout to reverse same-sex marriage laws or to halt culture's obsession with destroying sexual norms and erasing our shared history. It's highly unlikely we will ever reverse the laws that restrict religious freedom in the military or return public education back to the control of the parents rather than school boards that proudly adopt the most recent "sexually liberalized" curriculum. We have crossed too many fault lines; too many barriers have proven too weak to withstand media-driven cultural streams that have flooded our nation. The radicals know how to make themselves look good and make Christians look bad.

I write not so much to reclaim the culture as *to reclaim the church.*

This book has several purposes. Most importantly, I want to inspire the church to courageously stand against the pressures of our culture that seek to compromise our message and silence our witness. This is not a time for us to hide behind our church walls, but rather, to prepare ourselves and our families to stand bravely against an ominous future that is already upon us. We must interact with groups and individuals giving "a reason for the hope" that is within us, and doing it with "gentleness and respect" (1 Peter 3:15).

I write this book for anyone who has a burden to "strengthen what remains," as Jesus told the church in Sardis (Revelation 3:2). I write this book so that families will know what their children are facing in the public schools, colleges, and in the broader culture. I write this book with the hope that we will remain strong and joyfully defend "the faith that was once for all delivered to the saints" (Jude 3). We must separate the true from the false and reality from desire-driven delusions.

Most critically, this book is also a call to prayer accompanied by deep repentance. This is a Daniel moment when we call on God, confessing our sins and the sins of our churches and nation. We cannot move forward with words alone but with our deeds, our resolve, and a renewed dependence on God. This book is intended to clarify the threats the church faces today, but this information will be of no value apart from an earnest desire to desperately seek God with accompanying obedience and compassion.

Americans are spending $2.1 billion on the "mystical services market" trying to find meaning by looking at themselves, trying to hear a voice from the heavens that would give them some hope and direction.[13] If we think we can fight against this deceived culture by winning the war of ideas, we are mistaken. The best ideas do not win very often in a culture obsessed with empty utopian promises.

It's vital for us to understand that behind the headlines is a raging spiritual battle that can be confronted only by prayer and repentance followed by action in keeping with repentance. Only then can we hope to be a powerful voice in this nation. I am skeptical about our willingness to stand against the headwinds we face. We are so much a part of our culture that it might be difficult for us to know where to begin in our resolve to remain firm. We are like a fish swimming in the ocean wondering where the water is. Perhaps we have lost our capacity to despise sin, whether it be our own or the sin prevalent in our culture.

A Wasp, a Knife, and a Horrid Discovery

In one of George Orwell's essays we are given a graphic image of human lostness. He describes a wasp that was "sucking jam on my plate, and I cut him in half. He paid no attention, merely went on with his meal, while a tiny stream of jam trickled out of his severed esophagus. Only when he tried to fly away did he grasp the dreadful thing that had happened to him. It is the same with modern man."[14]

Everything might seem normal among us. We have our homes, our vocations, and our salaries. Like the wasp, we are content because we still have elections, we still have courts. We still have a congress and a president. We are still able to preach the gospel in our churches. But recently we have faced a health pandemic, an economic crisis, and heightened racial conflict amid political wrangling and increased polarization. The underbelly of our nation is being eaten away and, like Orwell's wasp, we might not recognize our true condition until we wake up and realize our wings have been severed. The America we thought we knew is no more. And our churches have accepted these changes with little more than a whimper.

We are in a firestorm for the future of America. But more importantly, we are in a firestorm within our churches, some of which have already substituted culture in the place of the gospel. I want to inspire us to have the courage to walk toward the fire and not run away from the flames. God has brought us to this cultural moment, and our future cannot be taken for granted. As has been said, "In a time of universal deception, telling the truth is a revolutionary act."[15]

> Only repentance and faith will enable us
> to stand against our cultural headwinds.

Let us determine that we will not be shamed into silence or inaction. We will speak, and like Shadrach, Meshach, and Abednego in the book of Daniel, let us resolve that we will not bow.

The Layout and Language of This Book

As you glance through the table of contents at the front of this book, you will see that the next eight chapters discuss how the cultural left seeks to remake America. Each chapter ends with a personal word about our response as believers to these moral and spiritual attacks.

The last chapter is based on the words of Jesus to the church in Sardis: "Wake up! Strengthen what remains!" (see Revelation 3:2). This, I believe, is what Jesus is saying to the church today.

In most instances, I prefer to use the term *radical secularism* rather than the *radical left* because of the latter's political implications. My concerns are not really about the right or left politically, but about the cultural transformations that are being imposed upon us from a variety of political viewpoints. My preference, then, is to use the term *radical secularists*, or another familiar term, *humanists*. When I do use the term *radical left*, it is because in those instances I see it as interchangeable with the other two terms. The underlying philosophies and attitudes advocated by radical secularists are so dominant in our society that they must be identified and seen as a threat to our freedoms and the strength of our churches.

Thank you for joining me on this journey. I pray that you will become better informed, more challenged to speak up for your faith, and more willing to act on the conviction that the day of complacent Christianity must come to an end.

Each of the following chapters in this book has a brief prayer that is to serve as an example of what we should be praying both for ourselves and for our collective witness; let these brief prayers be a springboard for extended repentance and intercession. We know that only God can rescue us from coming destruction. We must call on Him as never before.

Let us hear the words of the Lord to Joshua: "Do not be frightened, and do not be dismayed, for the LORD your God is with you wherever you go" (Joshua 1:9).

CHAPTER 2

Rewrite the Past to Control the Future

"W ho controls the past controls the future," said George Orwell when he described the totalitarian state.[1] Orwell, who wrote during the rise of Communism, pointed out that if you can rewrite or even erase the past, you can help people forget who they are and forge a new future.

In his book *1984*, Orwell described the "Ministry of Truth," whose duty it was to make the past consistent with the present. Winston Smith's assignment was to make the truth look like a lie and vice versa. If Big Brother made a prediction that didn't come to pass, the past was to be rewritten to harmonize with whatever Big Brother had said.

Revising history lies at the heart of all social and political revolutions. Perhaps the best example is the bloody cultural revolution in China (1966–1976). Mao Zedong decreed that China was to rid itself of all traces of capitalistic Western influence. The Red Guards took to the streets and monuments were destroyed, Western literature was burned, and buildings renamed along with new designations given for cities and streets to reflect contemporary heroes. Churches were either destroyed or repurposed. Either you sided with the new Marxist standard of justice and equality or you did not. Those who didn't get on board were jailed or killed.

Thankfully, we are not there yet in America. But the point to be made is that when revolutionaries want to remake a country, they vilify the past to give legitimacy to their vision of the future. It is obvious that the "Ministry of Truth" is busily at work transforming America by rewriting the past. They say their purpose is "to root out racism," but a look at what they're doing reveals a much more sinister goal. They are using racism to attack America at its core. It's not about making America better; it's about destroying the past to build America on an entirely different foundation.

Arthur Schlesinger, a historian and former confidant to President John F. Kennedy, observed, "History is to the nation much as memory is to the individual. The individual who loses his memory doesn't know where he came from or where he's going and he becomes dislocated and disoriented."[2] I might add that an individual who has lost his memory can be manipulated into believing he is whoever someone else says he is.

The Destruction of Monuments

I can understand why Confederate monuments are offensive and even demeaning to the black community. In some sense, their reaction to the removal of these monuments might be likened to how the people of Iraq rejoiced when a statue of Saddam Hussein was toppled to the ground. There is nothing sacred about a monument, no matter whose it is. I'm glad that lawmakers in Mississippi chose to retire the state flag that bore the image of the Confederate flag on it, which was adopted back in 1894.

But the radicals have moved beyond the destruction of Confederate monuments, directing attacks against our Founding Fathers. Their underlying sinister intention is to destroy this country's Judeo-Christian heritage. This forces the rest of us to ask: Is America's past history of slavery reason to discard its Judeo-Christian values?

The destruction of monuments is part of a larger attempt to destroy what it means to be an American. It's an attempt to remove not just racism, but to discredit all else that was done by those who created our nation's founding documents and established the foundational principles that led to making America what it is. In the minds of many people, America is so terrible that it cannot be fixed; it must be destroyed and rebuilt according to a radical socialist agenda that will be free of racism and free of capitalism, which they claim makes the rich richer and the poor poorer. They ignore the fact that capitalism has given countless people the opportunity to create their own success—to the extent that those who live in America enjoy a higher standard of living than most, if not all, nations.

At the George Washington High School in San Francisco there are those who insist that a mural of George Washington be covered because some complained that it was offensive and demeaning to Native Americans and African Americans. Board members say the art "traumatizes students and community members." The mural, painted in 1936, consists of 13 panels intended to depict some of the incidents in Washington's life. One image portrays Washington gesturing toward a group of explorers who are walking by the body of a deceased Native American. Another features Washington standing next to some slaves.[3]

Not one board member advocated keeping the mural, reported the *SF Weekly.* However, only a few denounced it, complaining that it was painful and demeaning. To put it all in perspective, one person said that the complaints were few, "but a small group of outside busybodies joined with a few students to ensure that it would be removed from the public's sight. Once the words 'racist' or 'white supremacist' are attached to something, no matter how inaccurate, liberals will not risk their reputation by defending it."[4]

In keeping with the secularists' commitment to deconstructing American history, political commentator Angela Rye said this:

> We have to get to the heart of the problem here. The heart is the way many of us were taught American history. American history is not all glorious...George Washington was a slave owner. We need to call slave owners out for what they are. Whether we think they were protecting American freedom or not, he wasn't protecting my freedoms. I wasn't someone—my ancestors weren't deemed human beings. To me, I don't care if it's a George Washington statue or Thomas Jefferson, they all need to come down.[5]

The statues of Washington and Jefferson all need to come down!

As of the writing of this book, the Washington and Jefferson memorials are still standing in Washington, but the George Washington statue in Portland has already been toppled.[6] The Tomb of the Unknown Soldier was vandalized and defaced in Philadelphia's Washington Square[7] and the police watched as Christopher Columbus monuments were destroyed in several cities. In Boston, his monument was "beheaded" for the whole world to see.[8] The monument to Francis Scott Key, who wrote our national anthem, "The Star-Spangled Banner," was also vandalized in California.[9] Incredibly, rioters in Madison, Wisconsin, destroyed a statue of Hans Christian Heg, an immigrant and leader of the abolition movement![10] And as I am writing this, incredulous though it sounds, there are calls to topple a monument of Abraham Lincoln, who freed the slaves! The list of desecrated monuments is long and continues to grow.

All of this was significantly precipitated by the murder of George Floyd in Minneapolis. We can definitely understand the anger this horribly unjust incident generated. When I saw the video, I wanted to shout, "No! You can't do that!" In response, we all wanted justice and reasonable police reform. Many African Americans who for years have felt unfairly targeted by the police found this a rallying cry to push for meaningful changes, and I totally support the peaceful demonstrators who wanted to let their outrage be known. But the riots that followed were not about police reform; the mayhem wasn't about *racism* but *revolution*.

The mobs could not have asked for more. In some cities, our elected officials told the police to stand down, so there was no end to the mobs' thirst for vengeance against their perceived oppressors, whether real or imagined. As the police themselves scurried to abandon their precincts in submission to the radicals in Minneapolis and later in Seattle, our elected officials shrugged. In the minds of the mobs, the destruction of businesses (many in the poorest minority communities that the mobs professed to want to help) was justified. They were on a sacred mission to destroy "white supremacy," and in its place, a just society would emerge when they (the radicals) would finally bring about the transformation of society they sought.

Here in the city of Chicago, police and protestors clashed at a statue of Christopher Columbus in Grant Park. Protesters threw frozen water bottles, rocks, and fireworks at the police, injuring at least 18 officers. When 1,000 of these "peaceful protesters" showed up at the mayor's home, demanding that the police be "defunded" and that two Christopher Columbus statues in the city be removed, she submitted to the demands of the mob. At 3:00 a.m. the next morning, a city crew removed both statues. This, of course, only emboldened the mob, and soon they insisted other demands be met.

What's next? Your church? When a mob mentality overtakes a country, apparently no one can stop them. On June 22, 2020, activist Shaun King wrote on his Twitter page, "All murals and stained glass windows of white Jesus, and his European mother and their white friends should also come down. They are a gross form [of] white supremacy. Created as tools of oppression. Racist propaganda. They should all come down."[11] His tweet has since been deleted, but screenshots exist in many different places. Yes, murals and pictures of Jesus just might be next to come down.

The silence of some of our elected officials in the face of the looting and arson shows that we might be losing the battle for civilization itself. The word on the street is that America cannot be good unless she is perfect. And because it's clear that she is not perfect, her social and cultural and legal structures should be destroyed. And on the other side of the revolution, there will be justice and equality. The revolutionaries see themselves as innocent of all the sins and evils that they see so clearly in others.

The radicals know exactly what they are doing, even if a compliant media does not. We are witnessing the unraveling of America.

Milan Kundera, a well-known Czech writer and historian who opposed the Soviet takeover of Czechoslovakia 1968 and author of the book *The Velvet Revolution of 1989*, wrote about a conversation he had with a friend. He writes,

> My all but blind friend Milan Hübl, came to visit me one day in 1971 in my tiny apartment on Bartolomejska Street. We looked out the window at the spires of the Castle and were sad. "The first step in liquidating a people," said Hübl, "is to erase its memory. Destroy its

> books, its culture, its history. Then have somebody write
> new books, manufacture a new culture, invent a new
> history. Before long the nation will begin to forget what
> it is and what it was."[12]

Yes, once the past has been destroyed, we can expect that a new culture and a new history will emerge. We will forget who we once were. And who we are.

Robin West, in her book *Progressive Constitutionalism*, writes, "The political history of the United States…is in large measure a history of almost unthinkable brutality toward slaves, genocidal hatred of Native Americans, racist devaluation of nonwhites and nonwhite cultures, sexual devaluation of women…"[13] For her, this sums up America's past. Of course, all of us know that we can do better in race relations. But is the path forward to learn from the past, or to simply vilify it? Before our eyes, our shared history is being erased.

Visualize yourself stepping out the door of an impressive sixteenth-century building and walking along the street. When you look back, you can clearly see where your trip originated. But suppose you turn a corner; now when you look back, you see a twenty-first century building that bears no resemblance to where you came from. The secularists are insisting that we turn a corner so that we lose sight of the Judeo-Christian influence of our past. And if we do choose to look back, they want us to see our religious history as a blotch, not a blessing. They want us to substitute their worldview in the place of our historic religious roots. They know that if we lose our history we will lose our future, a future they wish to control.

Let's pause and agree that slavery is an abomination, but there is much more to be said about the founding of America than a litany of evils. Allan Bloom, in *The Closing of the American Mind*, foresaw what lay ahead when he wrote, "We are used to hearing the

Founders charged with being racists, murderers of Indians, representatives of class interests…weakening our convictions of the truth or superiority of American principles and our heroes."[14]

The secular radicals have a goal: deny us the knowledge of who we are, thus destroying the principles upon which this nation was built. The strategy is to accentuate America's crimes and sins, destroy the reputations of her heroes, and use our history to divide us rather than to teach and unite us. Above all, ignore the fact that the United States has achieved the greatest civilization in history and is the envy of the world. Just ask where most migrants wish to go, and some will mention some Western European nations, but for the majority, America tops the list.

The radical secularists believe that it's not enough to acknowledge the ways in which America's founders were flawed and then learn how we can move on, inspired to do better. The secularists want to purge America's entire legacy and create a new America altogether. They believe this is the only way that all the wrongs of the past will be rectified. Only then can America be ruled by people who are free of greed and exploitation and injustice and racism. But they say that cannot happen until our memory of who we are is vilified and left behind.

Milan Kundera's friend (quoted above) was right: Before long, our nation will forget what it was. And who we are.

A Marxist History of the United States

If your children return from school hating America, the reason could be due to reading textbooks like *A People's History of the United States* by Howard Zinn, an avowed Marxist who believes America was founded in tyranny and for profit. He writes, "The American revolution…was a work of genius, and the Founding

Fathers deserve the awed tribute they have received over the centuries. They created the most effective system of national control devised in modern times…"[15]

Zinn goes on to say that the Declaration of Independence "was not a revolutionary statement of rights, [it was] a cynical means of manipulating popular groups into overthrowing the King of England to benefit the rich."[16]

His book despises the United States at its very core. He says nary a word about America's achievements, its enviable scientific progress, and the many great inventions that have made people's lives so much more satisfying worldwide.

Very conveniently, this textbook omits any recounting of the brutality of Communism and its failure to deliver on the promise of utopia. He judges America by its highest ideals and would never dare compare it to other countries and cultures because he knows— or at least he should—that America would shine brightly against the oppression, poverty, and backwardness of many other countries of the world.

As we will see in a later chapter, the freedom Zinn had to publish a textbook advocating Marxism is the very freedom Marxism takes away from others.

Was America Begun in 1619?

The New York Times Magazine has completed a project that seeks to "reframe" America's history to mark 1619 as its true founding. This is when the first slaves arrived in Jamestown, which they see as the central event in the founding of America. They conclude that slavery is foundational to America's beginning and, along with it came the plantation, the beginning of capitalism.

According to *The New York Times Magazine*, these two evils show that "our democracy's founding ideals were false when they were written."[17] In other words, the authors of the Declaration of Independence, who wrote that "all men are created equal, that they are endowed by their Creator with certain unalienable Rights," did not believe what they were writing.

The editor of the project, Nikole Hannah-Jones, wrote an essay back in 1995 in which she said that the white race "is the biggest murderer, rapist, pillager, and thief of the modern world." The white race is comprised of "barbaric devils, bloodsuckers" and Columbus was no different than Hitler.[18] Clearly, the project she oversaw was intended to reflect her views.

Is this a fair or accurate reading of American history? Again, I repeat that slavery is an abomination. I have read stories about the slave trade that should cause a stone to weep. No person should own another, and America's history of buying and selling slaves should be documented and denounced in all its horrible aspects. And certainly, only the black community knows experientially the continuing impact of slavery on their history.

It is true that slavery did not end the moment the Declaration of Independence was signed. It continued for many years with some victories and many defeats. But that declaration began America on a journey that few other countries have undertaken. And no nation has worked as hard as America to make right the wrongs of the past. Yes, absolutely there is more that we can do, but we must do it together, not by vilifying our Founding Fathers but learning from them, separating the good from the bad, and learning how we can do better.

Sadly, slavery is as old as civilization itself. By the time the slaves arrived in Jamestown, the Spanish and the Portuguese had been enslaving people for more than 100 years. Slavery was widespread in ancient times, and sadly, today there are still 40 million slaves in the world, primarily in India and Africa. In August 2017, CNN captured on video slaves being auctioned off in Libya.[19]

Forty million slaves still exist in other countries of the world!

To hear the radicals speak, you would think that the West invented slavery. We forget, as Pat Buchanan has pointed out, that "the West did not invent slavery; the West ended slavery."[20] And it was committed Christians such as William Wilberforce who worked tirelessly to end the slave trade in England.

Will *The New York Times Magazine* rewrite the history of other countries based on when they began to permit ownership of slaves? You can be sure they won't. The 1619 Project is a targeted effort intended to show that the United States is to be hated because it's a racist and capitalistic nation whose roots must be destroyed and rebuilt upon a cultural Marxist foundation that will bring equality and justice to all.

The people behind The 1619 Project know, all too well, that *you can't get people to hate America if you compare it with other countries.* The fact is, America brought an end to slavery more than 150 years ago, whereas it is still practiced today in many places around the world. At the same time, we are not yet where we want to be in race relations; the failures of the past must be acknowledged, and forgiveness and reconciliation are the way forward.

At the risk of being accused of repetition, let me say again that we should not gloss over the vices, scandals, and crimes that have dotted America's early history. But the dark periods of that history are not the whole story. The memory of specific wrongs in our past should not cancel the victories that have been won and the good that has been accomplished. We have made great strides in overcoming our past and look forward to more such gains in the future. Virtually every country has begun with aggression, wars, or slavery. The radical secularists are judging America by an impossible standard, condemning the good with the bad.

The blotches on America's past should not be minimized, but

neither should we ignore the American Constitution with its Bill of Rights, the religious convictions of our Founding Fathers, and the Judeo-Christian principles upon which our freedoms are built. The faults of America do not give the radical secularists the right to exclude God from the public square and prevent those who wish to exercise their faith in the public square from doing so.

Don't lose sight of the radicals' goal: to delegitimize the Founding Fathers and America's Judeo-Christian heritage. And, for that matter, delegitimize all of Western history and condemn those who brought us the civilization we enjoy today.

Denouncing Western Civilization

As the secularists promote their version of history, the great works of Western civilization are being denounced with increasing frequency. For example, a long-standing requirement for English majors at Yale University was to take a course covering Chaucer, Spenser, Milton, and Wordsworth. In 2016, a student petition called for ending that requirement. The complaint was that reading these authors "creates a culture that is especially hostile to students of color."[21] This expresses the modern contempt for the contributions of Western culture to the arts, literature, and history.

All historians select what they believe is most important about the past and what should be ignored. But it's unfair to approach history with an agenda to prove when the facts say otherwise. Racism and various other sins are rather equally distributed among all the peoples of the world; we must distinguish the positive contributions from the negative and the victories from the losses regardless of which group or race we are discussing.

Let us remember that the Germany that gave us Hitler is also the Germany that gave us the moveable-type printing press. This same Germany gave us the Reformation that was the seed from which freedom of conscience grew. When Martin Luther said, "My conscience is held captive by the Word of God. I cannot and will not recant," he broke with 1,000 years of religious oppression. Until then, it was unthinkable that a man could say his conscience superseded the pope or tradition. Luther awakened awareness of the priesthood of the believer and the rights of individual conscience, which eventually resulted in freedom of religion. The Germany of the Holocaust is also the Germany of Goethe and Schiller, the fathers of the German Enlightenment.

The England that is so widely criticized for its imperialism is the country that gave us the Magna Carta, which presented the novel idea that even the king should be subject to the law. It is England that gave us John Wycliffe, who insisted that the Bible be translated into English and available to all who wanted to read it. It is England that gave us the writings of John Locke, who is acknowledged as the father of the English Enlightenment and whose views are reflected in the American Constitution. It is England that gave us William Wilberforce, whose efforts to end slavery in England and beyond were successful.

The America whose history is tarnished by the evils of slavery, the America whose Founding Fathers kept slaves—*that* America also gave us the Constitution, the Bill of Rights, and inventions such as the telephone, pacemakers, lightbulbs, the first electronic digital computer, and the Internet. It is America that sent 12 men to walk on the moon and further space exploration and scientific progress. It is America that has made possible a civilization that has positively affected many others around the world through advancements in education, technology, medicine, and even philanthropy.

The mixture of good and evil found in nations also applies to individuals. Many people who have made great contributions to Christianity and civilization have had blind spots that serve as warnings to us. Consider, for example, Martin Luther, who began the Reformation and gave Germany the Bible in its own readable dialect. *This* man, this same Luther, wrote hateful screeds against the Jewish people. Thomas Jefferson, who penned the wonderful words "all men are created equal," owned slaves.

Our textbooks should be balanced with the contributions of black history and its heroes, who were involved in civil rights, music, the military, science, and more. Then there are women like Bessie Coleman, a mathematician who was barred from flight training in the United States because of her race and gender. She traveled to Paris, where she was allowed to study aviation and become the first woman to receive an international aviation license. When she returned to the United States, she participated in air shows, performing tailspins and other stunts such as banking and looping the loop. As a brilliant mathematician, she contributed greatly to the field of aviation. The contributions of black Americans to other disciplines such as entrepreneurship, preaching, and sports are, of course, legendary.

My plea is that we work together for a "more perfect union," but this cannot be done as long as we refuse to put our past in perspective and take personal and collective responsibility to move on to a better future. Most of us who live in America originated from different countries. We have different skin colors, different expectations, and different gifts and skills to offer. We must listen to each other as we talk about the injustices of our shared history, acknowledging that both repentance and forgiveness are necessary. But then we must move on, or we will never be able to make progress in race relations.

In the eyes of the radical secularists, America has systemic racial, economic, and political disparities that only cultural Marxism can solve. To build America on a better foundation, religion must be replaced with humanistic values. After all, they say, religion—particularly Christianity—is used as an instrument of oppression and social control, and white privilege is said to be the source of our systemic ills.

Rewriting the Constitution

Standing in the way of the secularist agenda is the US Constitution, the founding document that guarantees our basic freedoms, the separation of powers, and due process. Whenever there is a vacancy in the courts, particularly the US Supreme Court, the battle lines are drawn. Why the hyperpartisanship? The debate is whether the new appointee will follow the Constitution or have the liberty to vote for laws that are in keeping with changing cultural norms. Secularists are angry because there are some constitutional judges who have recently been appointed to the US Supreme Court who don't hold to the secularist worldview.

The radical secularists have a proposal to establish a permanent grip on power in the government. In January 2020, the prestigious *Harvard Law Review* published the article "Pack the Union: A Proposal to Admit New States for the Purpose of Amending the Constitution to Ensure Equal Representation."

We read:

> An "easier" way to amend the Constitution would be for Congress to admit a large number of new states whose congressional representatives would reliably ally with the existing majority in sufficient numbers to propose and ratify new amendments fixing the problem of unequal representation. Because Congress can admit new states with a simple majority, this would provide a more attainable political threshold.[22]

The article explains that 127 new states would be created within the District of Colombia to offset any conservative majority in Congress.

The purpose of this is not subtle, but the secularists' agenda is clearly stated. One reason these new states should be created within the District of Columbia is because "every measurable subdivision of D.C. voted overwhelmingly for the Democratic party in the 2016 election, so the Democratic caucus in Congress could be confident that new states created within the District would elect like-minded delegations to Congress."[23]

Once this new "Congress" is in place, the Constitution would be amended. The Senate's role would be changed to resemble the House of Lords in England, a more or less ceremonial upper chamber that could review legislation passed by the House but unable to prevent it from becoming law. And the Electoral College, which helps to ensure that all 50 states have a voice in the national political arena, would be abolished.

What else? For starters, illegal residents would be allowed to vote and the Second Amendment (the right to bear arms) would be repealed. After that, other changes could be made as needed. The secularists could be assured that America's religious history would finally be sufficiently vilified to make room for their new progressive agenda. Judges could be appointed who would not have to bow to the Constitution; they could propose laws of their own liking that adapt to the culture and secular values. Although not stated in this article, private property could be abolished and state rights would be substituted for the rights granted by God. At long last, the radicals' vision of a thoroughly socialistic state would become a reality.

The Constitution, it is said, is outmoded; it was written by slave owners as an instrument of "white privilege." The radical proposal outlined in the aforementioned *Harvard Law Review* article would liberate us from our Judeo-Christian past and free us to rebuild on a purely secular foundation.

The Secularists' Foundation

Years ago, I read *The Humanist Manifesto* but until recently had forgotten that it was a Marxist, globalist document. The original version was written in 1933, but here I quote from the second version (1973), edited by Edwin H. Wilson and Paul Kurtz. Many regard Kurtz as the father of secular humanism.

As you might expect, the document denies supernaturalism in all its forms. "Promises of immortal salvation or fear of eternal damnation are illusionary and harmful." The human species "is an emergence from natural evolutionary forces"[24] and there is no credible evidence that life survives the death of the body. The universe is considered to be self-existent.

The Humanist Manifesto strongly advocates globalism:

> We deplore the division of humankind on nationalistic grounds. We have reached a turning point in human history where the best option is to transcend the limits of national sovereignty and to move toward the building of a world community...Thus we look to the development of a system of world law and a world order based upon transnational federal government.[25]

Connected to this is cooperation about climate change: "The planet earth must be considered a single ecosystem...It is the moral obligation of the developed nations to provide...massive technical, agricultural, medical, and economic assistance...to the developing portions of the globe."[26]

So a country like the US must provide massive assistance to other countries to fight climate change. The goal of globalism is world citizenship so that universal freedom and human rights can be fostered for all mankind. The humanists argue that the economies of countries must be intertwined so these goals can be achieved. Article Fourteen in the original 1933 document says simply, "Humanists demand a shared life in a shared world."[27] Ponder that for a moment.

Keep in mind that in the eyes of the radical secularists, those who acquire wealth do so on the backs of the poor, and social justice requires that their wealth be redistributed. And if you think globally, America allegedly has become wealthy to the detriment of other nations; thus, America owes the rest of the world. How better to redistribute this wealth but through giving other nations the resources to fight climate change?

No wonder patriotism must be denounced. You can't achieve a globalist agenda as long as "American exceptionalism" is alive and well. Perhaps now we understand why the secularists see the US flag as a symbol of racism, oppression, white privilege, and corrosive nationalism and capitalism. In one Minnesota city, a move was made to ban the Pledge of Allegiance because it fosters patriotism and is too hurtful to minorities.[28] In Australia, some Muslims say that singing the national anthem is nothing short of "forced assimilation."[29] How long before we hear that in the United States?

America must be dethroned.

To overcome these obstacles to globalism, the humanists push for what amounts to open borders because even the concept of national citizenship must be erased. To have a secure, controlled border is not conducive for developing a world community. That's why humanists long for a borderless world.

Acheiving open borders advances two of the humanists' most prized objectives. The first is that the presence of millions of people from different countries will eventually counterbalance the continuing influence of the white and allegedly racist culture that has dominated America since its founding.

The second benefit of uncontrolled immigration is that millions of people will end up being government-dependent, a great boon for those who strive toward a socialist state. As we will see in a future chapter, socialism can only be advanced by government dependency. By giving all who enter our borders free housing, free health care, and other free benefits, such people will always vote for the political party that promises the most government incentives. All of this is sold under the banners of compassion and justice.

Of course, as we might expect, virtually nothing is said about the gangs, drugs, sex trafficking, and criminals who use open borders to enter our country. Without border control as a deterrent enforced with stiff penalties, we find ourselves playing host to people who take advantage of our kindness. In return, the criminals who cross illegally into our country perpetuate crime and are parasites on our civilization. And they damage the reputation of the legal, hardworking immigrants we gladly welcome to America. A sensible policy of legal immigration is long overdue. (For a more detailed discussion of immigration, I suggest the chapter "Islam, Immigration, and the Church" in my book *The Church in Babylon*.)

As a side note, I reject the notion that those of us who believe in secure borders are racist and lack compassion. We gladly welcome the mother who comes to us with a baby in her arms (contrary to the open border zealots who are determined to paint us as uncaring). I wish we could take in all the desperate mothers and children of the world, though that is impossible. But without enforced border control, we have, in effect, lost our country. The long-term consequences are devastating.

But here we are.

Our calling and privilege is to represent
Christ at this turbulent moment in history.

Learning from History

Hard questions, no easy answers.

What do we as Christians do when the history of our country is being rewritten or even deleted? And how do we respond when the cultural ground beneath us is shifting? Our calling and privilege is to represent Christ at this turbulent moment in history.

We are faced with questions: Will we honestly confront our past? Or will we only react to what is happening around us? Will we still have freedom, or will we be pressured to bow to the impossible demands of the radicals? What kind of a country do we want our children and grandchildren to inherit? Will America continue to be a beacon of hope and freedom for the world?

Let me paraphrase Arthur Schlesinger's comment that if a person loses his memory, he does not know who he is. When a nation loses its history, it becomes whatever people say it is. And usually the loudest and most angry voices win.

This is not a time for us to deny the negative parts of our history and paint a picture that ignores the sins and racism of the past. We can learn from history without needing to destroy it. America has proven willing to learn from its history. How many children will get a better education in our schools because stores have been looted and monuments destroyed? How will opioid addiction, which kills more than 70,000 people each year, be better addressed if Confederate statues in our nation's capital are removed, as one of our congressional leaders proposed? These monuments are a part of our history and should serve as teaching opportunities that both warn and instruct us. The good and the bad.

We also have to ask the radicals some questions. How will we keep crime in check if we defund the police? This is not a theoretical question. Here is a headline: "Deadly weekend in Seattle, Chicago,

Minneapolis as New York City reports uptick in shootings." The article goes on to say, "Major cities in the U.S. reported bloody weekends amid increased calls to defund and disband police departments in the wake of George Floyd's death in police custody."[30] That weekend, 104 people were shot in Chicago, 15 people were killed.[31]

Yes, of course we should weed out those police officers who have abused their power and shown themselves unworthy of wearing their badge. Those who have committed crimes should be prosecuted. But the vast majority leave their homes every day and put their life on the line to "serve and protect." They are our last line of defense against anarchy. How did we come up with the idea that the police forces across the country are the real agents of oppression, but anarchists aren't? On May 31, 2020, when gangs were looting stores and businesses lost millions of dollars of merchandise, Chicago experienced its most bloody weekend in 60 years. Eighteen people were shot to death in a 24-hour period.[32] Do the radicals have a solution to the growing problem of inner-city crime?

Don't ALL black lives matter?

We are in a crisis. America cannot continue to give hope to the world unless we have shared basic values. The kind of ordered liberty we enjoy can only be kept if Americans are, on the whole, a virtuous people. John Adams, the second president of the United States, speaking to the first Brigade of the Third Division of the Militia of Massachusetts in 1798, warned about those who assume "the Language of Justice and moderation" while practicing "Iniquity and Extravagance" and he ends with this famous statement: "*Avarice, ambition, revenge or gallantry, would break the strongest cords of our constitution as a whale goes through a net. Our constitution was made only for a moral and religious people. It is wholly inadequate to the government of any other.*"[33]

Radical secularism accompanied by illusionary promises will always seek to eliminate free speech and the free exercise of religion. "Men fight for liberty," says D.H. Lawrence, "and win it with hard knocks. Their children, brought up easy, let it slip away again, poor fools. And their grandchildren are once more slaves."[34]

When we say goodbye to freedom, we welcome tyranny.

But what about the church? Do we run and hide?

America, the Church, and Our Future

This is not a time to surrender America to the radicals. God has brought us to this hour and it is time for us to take the high moral ground and say with Martin Luther, "Here we stand; we cannot do otherwise!"

The Bible teaches us, as Christians, to love our enemies (Matthew 5:44), and as someone has pointed out, that means we must love our ideological enemies too. To lash out in anger is only to enflame more anger in return. We must remember that for some people, emotions trump reason and civility, so it might be difficult to have a rational discussion of these issues.

And yes, we should respect people who disagree with us. We must use these disagreements to evaluate our own arguments and interpretations of history; we need the humility to admit that we might be wrong about some of our perspectives. We must also listen to those who say they are trying to make the world a better place, albeit in ways that we see as destructive. And much as we disagree with their views, we must lead bravely, but differently; we must stand for truth but not succumb to the name-calling we can expect to receive. We must fight for freedom yet remember that "the anger of man does not produce the righteousness of God" (James 1:20).

That said, we cannot stand by and surrender to the radicals out of fear of being called racists. I was both heartened and saddened by the headline, "Pastors vow to 'defend' houses of worship, 'not allow Christian heritage to be erased.'"[35] I was gratified that pastors in Seattle had banded together to defend their churches; I was saddened to think that such a headline would ever appear in America.

The article stated that Brian Gibson, pastor and founder of the Peaceably Gather movement, met with other pastors across racial lines to say, "The call from Black Lives Matters leaders to destroy images of Christ and deface houses of worship is nothing less than a terroristic threat to people of faith...Christians across America must stand against this violent religious discrimination and stand to protect sacred ground." Pastor Kedrick Timbo of Evangel World Prayer Center in Louisville agreed, saying, "Next they'll go for the crosses."[36]

The pastors agreed to prosecute any who damaged their churches. They also know that if they call the police—and I'm sure they will if it's necessary to do so—they risk being called racists. We pray that the time will not come in America when we the people (including pastors and their congregations) will have to defend our property. We can be thankful that as I write these words some of the anarchists and protestors behind the riots that took place after George Floyd's death are belatedly being brought to justice. But hundreds more will never be prosecuted for their crimes.

How should we as Christians respond to these issues if they divide us?

As fellow believers, we must separate the legitimate concerns of our black brothers and sisters from the allegations of radicals who have highjacked protests and seek to destroy our history. We must carefully listen to the way secularists interpret our history and discuss differences with fellow believers in light of biblical truth as we strive for the unity we have in Christ. This is a time for displaying the multinational community that God has called us to be.

Many books have been written about racial reconciliation, so it's not my intention to deal with that here. But the church *must* lead the way toward reconciliation and not away from it. I like what Eric Mason, the founder and pastor of Epiphany Fellowship in Philadelphia, wrote: "We don't have to look alike. There's beauty in the variations of our skin color. But we can rejoice that on the inside we're all trying to look like the same person. We're all trying to look like our elder brother, Jesus, because we're family, and we're holy."[37]

Yes, seeking to look like our elder brother, Jesus, is not easy. It involves listening, understanding, repenting, and action. Those are our privilege and our calling.

Frequently throughout history, the church
has thrived in the midst of the opposition and
persecution that arise in a disintegrating culture.

But how should we answer the larger questions about the trajectory of our nation and the destruction of our history? We need to get back to bedrock here.

"If the foundations are destroyed, what can the righteous do?" (Psalm 11:3).

First, a word of hope, then a dire warning.

The word of hope is that we must relearn what we already know: The church of Jesus Christ was not built on the US Constitution. The church was launched 18 centuries before the Constitution and the Bill of Rights. The church is not Americanism; it is not built upon the foundations of our Founding Fathers, however important their contributions are. There is no doubt that Christianity in America has benefited from the nation's Judeo-Christian roots, but we must learn to survive without this support. If we respond correctly, the church can grow stronger even as our cultural supports grow weaker. Frequently throughout history, the church has thrived in the midst of the opposition and persecution that arise in a disintegrating culture.

When Jesus made the statement "On this rock I will build my church, and the gates of hell shall not prevail against it" (Matthew 16:18), He was standing in Caesarea Philippi, the center of pagan worship. So, standing on pagan ground, Jesus predicted that He would build a multinational community. This church would be neither black nor white, Western nor Eastern. Jesus was, and still is, building a community where cultures and races meet at the foot of the cross. We must intentionally return to the church's own independent foundation.

So far, so good.

Now the warning: Repent, or else...

Does the future of the church rest solely with Jesus, with us, or with both? Recently, a news service article carried this headline: "Church of Canada May Disappear by 2040."[38]

Yes, a news report forecast that there will be neither attendees nor givers in the Anglican Church in Canada by 2040. The Anglican Church is in a freefall financially and numerically, and if the trend continues, it will vanish from the country.

Who or what is responsible for this demise? Decades ago, the major branches of the Anglican Church turned from the gospel to social justice issues to become more acceptable to the mainstream culture. Its leaders were too sophisticated to believe in the miracles of the Bible, so they were reinterpreted to fit the mindsets of people in the twentieth and twenty-first centuries. Having been absorbed by the culture, it had nothing eternal and transcendent to present to its members. There apparently is little reason for it to survive.

But one rector, in responding to this dire report, took solace from the words of the former Archbishop of Canterbury, Rowan Williams, who once said, "The church is not ours to save." The rector observed, "We are only called to be good stewards of what we have been given. God will do what God will do."[39]

The church is not ours to save.

Really?

On one level, this comment is completely true. As indicated, Jesus established the church 2,000 years ago, and it is His to save. As a firm believer in the sovereignty of God, I agree that only God can save the church. It is in His hands, not ours.

But—and this is critical—we as Christians play a role in the survival and continuing impact of the church of Jesus Christ. Consider what Jesus wrote to the church in Ephesus—He commended their commitment to truth, their works, and their endurance, then said, "I know you are enduring patiently and bearing up for my name's sake, and you have not grown weary" (Revelation 2:3). What a glowing report—good works, good doctrine, and standing up to the pressures of their culture! Any church consultant would give them an A+.

Then comes this bombshell:

> But I have this against you, that you have abandoned the love you had at first. Remember therefore from where you have fallen; repent, and do the works you did at first. If not, I will come to you and remove your lampstand from its place, unless you repent (verses 4-5).

I will come to remove your lampstand!

Whether or not their lampstand would be removed was conditioned on their repentance. The church wasn't theirs to save, yet its continuation was dependent on whether they returned to their first love through repentance and good deeds. Apparently they did not and their lampstand was removed, for there has not been a church in Ephesus for many centuries.

We in America have been blessed with the ordered liberty that has helped maintain the church: a government that has permitted the adherents of Christianity to freely observe their faith, a shared belief in constitutional freedoms, widespread and generally accepted Christian moral values, etc. But as these supports are being dismantled, can the church in the United States survive without them?

Perhaps yes. Perhaps no.

How tragic that in this time of increasing darkness, some lampstands are flickering while others are being blown out. Too often we are coasting on our past blessings, unwilling to repent of our worldly values and passionless response to Christ. Jesus predicted, "Because lawlessness will be increased, the love of many will grow cold" (Matthew 24:12).

Whether we will only talk about repentance or actually repent depends on how desperate we are about the shifting foundations beneath us. Are we willing to not just read the words of Jesus but actually *heed* them?

In his day, David pondered, "If the foundations are destroyed, what can the righteous do?" (Psalm 11:3). Thankfully, he answers his own question in the next verse: "The Lord is in his holy temple; the Lord's throne is in heaven; his eyes see, his eyelids test the children of man. The Lord *tests* the righteous" (verses 4-5).

God remains in control even as He *tests* the righteous. If we pass the test, our lampstand can still be lit and show a confused nation the way back to God and sanity. But the price is sustained repentance and personal sacrifice. And that might be more than some of us are willing to pay.

> Even as we have seen major cultural
> shifts taking place, let us know that the
> kingdom of God remains unshaken.

Augustine loved the city of Rome. When he was told that vandals had trashed it, he is reported to have said, "Whatever men build, men will destroy. So let's get on with building the kingdom of God." Even as we have seen major cultural shifts taking place, let us know that the kingdom of God remains unshaken.

God is asking us to join with Him in returning to our first love and lighting many lampstands throughout our country. We need to remain diligent about sustaining the church as a beacon of light that shines in the darkness of today's secularism and humanism. If we throw ourselves at the feet of Christ in humility and faith and with renewed courage obey Him, then our lampstand will remain and not be removed.

> The church's one foundation
> Is Jesus Christ, her Lord;
> She is His new creation
> By water and the Word:
> From heav'n He came and sought her
> To be His holy bride;
> With His own blood He bought her,
> And for her life He died.[40]

The church is not ours to save. But without repentance and personal sacrifice, our lampstand might be removed. History confirms this has often been so.

Corrie ten Boom said, "The wonderful thing about praying is

that you leave a world of not being able to do something, and enter God's realm, where everything is possible."[41]

A Prayer All of Us Must Pray

Our Father, we come to You today in the name of Jesus for mercy and grace. We thank You that when Jehoshaphat was told that a great army was coming against him that he "set his face to seek the LORD, and proclaimed a fast throughout all Judah" (2 Chronicles 20:3).

Teach us to seek Your face on behalf of our churches and our country. Help us to be agents of reconciliation and hope in a time of strife and conflict. Cause us to see our great need for repentance and wisdom. We know that behind the scenes of history cosmic battles are being fought between good and evil, God and Satan. We acknowledge our dependence upon You, for like Jehoshaphat, we confess, "We are powerless against this great horde that is coming against us. We do not know what to do, but our eyes are on you" (verse 12).

We thank You that after Jehoshaphat and his people fasted and prayed, You gave him the assurance, "Do not be afraid and do not be dismayed at this great horde, for the battle is not yours but God's" (verse 15). As they sang praises to You, You brought deliverance to Your people. Help us to face the future with optimism and joy, for we are Yours.

We pray that Your church, comprised of all races and backgrounds, may unite in singing Your praises and giving thanks to Your name. Teach us to love one another and to display the oneness for which our Savior prayed.

Today, let us not be overwhelmed by the sins of others but by our own sins, our own needs and failures. Let us not use prayer as a cop-out, but rather, may we speak with author-ity and confidence—and face our challengers with a listen-ing ear.

Let us listen, learn, and stand!

In Jesus' name, amen.

CHAPTER 3

Use Diversity to
Divide and Destroy

D on't solve problems; use them!

That's how a coworker of Saul Alinsky described the philosophy of the famous radical community organizer in Chicago. Alinsky is the author of the book *Rules for Radicals,* which he dedicated to "Lucifer...the first radical...who rebelled against the establishment and did it so effectively that he at least won his own kingdom."[1] Alinsky died in 1976, but his handbook is still followed by the radical left in their quest to fundamentally transform America.

I happened to meet one of Alinsky's coworkers while my wife and I were vacationing in Colorado. In the early 1970s, this man joined Alinsky with a desire to help impoverished communities in Chicago. He said Alinsky blocked any such plans because he saw such problems as opportunities to push his political and economic agendas.

According to David Horowitz, when Alinsky would ask community organizers why they were joining him, they would say "to help the poor and the oppressed." Then Alinsky would scream, "No! You want to organize for power!" Alinsky agreed with the leftist organization Students for Democratic Society, which affirmed, "The issue is never the issue. The issue is always the revolution!"[2]

Let's hear it in Saul Alinsky's own words:

> An organizer must stir up dissatisfaction and discontent...He must create a mechanism that can drain off the underlying guilt for having accepted the previous situation for so long a time. Out of this mechanism, a new community organization arises.[3]

Stir up discontent. Use problems. Create guilt.

Alinsky made no secret of the fact he was a committed Marxist who believed that the conflict between the oppressed and the oppressors must be continual, unending, and without a satisfactory resolution—unless, of course, there is a revolution that brings about the "equalities" of a Marxist state. He spoke of what could be described as "the paradise of communism."

For Karl Marx, the conflict was primarily between the capitalists and the proletariat, the rich and the poor. Alinsky saw this conflict not only through the eyes of economics, but race as well. Racism would be used to foment the revolution he sought. So the call for change is never really about race, gender, or economic status, but revolution—and *power*.

Earlier, I made the point that the riots that ensued after the tragic murder of George Floyd by a Minnesota police officer demonstrated that, for some, the issue was not race or even police brutality. The gangs who looted the stores and shouted, "No justice, no peace!" were simply following Saul Alinksy's dictum that race was the pretext, power was the goal. And thousands of sincere people bowed their knee to express their solidarity against racism, probably unaware of the larger destructive agenda behind the riots.[4]

There was a time when racial reconciliation was a search for common ground, seeking understanding between the races, minimizing our differences, and focusing on our similarities and shared commitments. We believed that progress was made by including the various ethnic and racial groups in businesses, educational institutions, and churches. We were committed to honoring one another.

God loves diversity, especially
when it is brought together into
a mosaic of unity in Christ.

At The Moody Church in Chicago, where I served as senior pastor for 36 years, we were grateful that more than 70 countries of origin were represented in the congregation every Sunday morning. We always knew we were not where we wanted to be, but we were on our way. The Moody Church continues to be a church that reflects our city's diversity. We look forward to the day when all will give praise to the Lamb, "for you were slain, and by your blood you ransomed people for God from every tribe and language and people and nation" (Revelation 5:9).

God loves diversity, especially when it is brought together into a mosaic of unity in Christ. Racial and ethnic animosity is sinful and denies the inherent dignity of all persons, and it is particularly sinful within the body of Christ. We as Christians should be on the forefront of giving leadership to unity in the midst of diversity, and we should work toward love and acceptance rather than racial division and suspicion.

But despite the many gains made in the last generation or two, the racial divide in America is becoming wider, not narrower. Certainly one reason is the heightened political rhetoric in our national discourse. We grieve at the name-calling, the distortions, and the heated accusations on all sides of the political spectrum. Some politicians are driven not by reason and civility but by ego and slogans. Another key reason for the growing racial divide is due to the widespread acceptance of cultural Marxism, which encourages racial division, not unity.

Though Communism has failed in every country in which it has been instituted, the Marxist vision of a society in which all men and women are, by law, forced to be "equal" hasn't died. In America, this has been rebranded as *social justice* and *political correctness*. We can even add the words *diversity* and *equality*. These terms have been pressed into service to ensure that conflict between the races will continue without any hope of meaningful reconciliation.

We live in what is known as the "woke" generation. For some, that's a positive term that means you are enlightened and you understand how history, racism, and economics all merge to explain the injustices of our society. For others, it means you see layers of oppression almost everywhere, even in rigorously scientific disciplines such as mathematics. Injustice and oppression abound, even in our Pledge of Allegiance.

To make sure we understand what's at stake here, let's take a closer look at this concept of equality.

The Many Faces of Equality

A good starting point is this oft-quoted text written by Thomas Jefferson in the preamble to the Declaration of Independence: "We hold these truths to be self-evident, that all men are created equal."[5] Abraham Lincoln echoed these words in his famous Gettysburg Address, saying that this nation was "conceived in liberty, and dedicated to the proposition that all men are created equal."[6] All human beings are created with equal value before God and are entitled to life, liberty, and the pursuit of happiness.

Some, however, tell us that *equality* means we should seek equality in all aspects of life and use persuasion, laws, intimidation, and shaming to bring it about. But neither Jefferson nor Lincoln stated that everyone was expected to be equal in ability, education, opportunity, income, etc. They believed in equality with regard to God-given rights—namely, life, liberty, and the pursuit of happiness. Equality in value before God, yes; equality of gifts, ingenuity, intelligence, and income, no.

Today the word *equality* is applied to every social cause imaginable. We have "marriage equality" (same-sex marriage), "economic equality" (socialism), "reproductive equality" (abortion), and "healthcare equality" (free/socialized healthcare), "gender equality" (legal protection for trans persons); and the positive goal of "racial equality," which must, however, be carefully defined.

The Hallmark Channel featured a commercial with two women kissing each other and then pulled it when viewers reacted with criticism. But when the commercial was pulled, a backlash came from the LGBTQ lobby. The company whose ad was pulled insisted that all kisses and couples are equal and yanked all their advertising from the Hallmark Channel. Hallmark ended up reversing its decision.[7] According to the secularists, this is what "equality" requires. Perhaps more concerning, the Equality Act, passed by the House of Representatives in 2019 but not yet in the Senate, would destroy all freedom of religion in hiring practices; it would allow trans boys to use girls' bathrooms and vice versa.[8]

Let me repeat that God created all men and women in His image and therefore they are equal in value. But in Scripture, men and women have distinctive places and roles in the world.

God does not dispense blessings and favor equally. God did not treat Hammurabi like he did Abraham. He did not treat the Assyrians like He did the Jews. Jesus had twelve disciples but gave special privileges to three of them (only Peter, James, and John were with Him on the Mount of Transfiguration, and only these three were invited to pray with Him in Gethsemane). Certain kinds of inequality are built into the nature of the world and human nature.

What the Bible *does* teach is equal responsibility based on the gifts and talents we are given. "Everyone to whom much was given, of him much will be required" (Luke 12:48). Greater gifts mean greater accountability. "Not many of you should become teachers, my brothers, for you know that we who teach will be judged with greater strictness" (James 3:1). And again, "Who sees anything different in you? What do you have that you did not receive? If then you received it, why do you boast as if you did not receive it?" (1 Corinthians 4:7).

Jesus told a parable in which a man went on a journey and entrusted his property to three different stewards. "To one he gave five talents, to another two, to another one, to each according to his ability" (Matthew 25:15). The five-talent man and the two-talent man both doubled their investments and heard their master say, "Well done, good and faithful servant. You have been faithful over a little; I will set you over much. Enter into the joy of your master" (verses 21, 23).

But the one who was given one talent refused to invest it. Instead, he hid it in the ground, unwilling to use what had been entrusted to him for the good of the master. The master was angry and said, "You wicked and slothful servant!...you ought to have invested my money with the bankers, and at my coming I should have received what was my own with interest" (verses 26-27). The rest of the story did not go well with the lazy servant, and he was severely judged.

Jesus didn't expect the one-talent man to gain five talents; he, like the others, should have simply doubled the investment. God's fairness is not seen in the distribution of talents but in the expectation of our faithfulness with what we have. We will be judged for what we *have*; we will not be judged for what we don't have.

The Jews were given privileges the Gentiles did not have, but along with these privileges they had the responsibility to be a light to other nations. They failed, and for this they were judged. Those who are privileged have a responsibility to help those who are less privileged. If they don't, they are accountable to God for it. However, we should not live with the illusion that we will ever achieve equality in income, lifestyle, or achievements.

Marx insisted on equality of income, status, and power through state control. This is the dream of utopians who understand neither history nor human nature. But freedom necessitates inequality of outcomes. Theories about imposing economic equality stamp out freedom in ingenuity, heritage, and gifting.

Years before the Soviet Union collapsed, my wife and I visited a Communist country in which everyone was paid essentially the same wage. Doctors were paid only a little more than those who cleaned the rooms of the hospital. Thanks to the state, everyone had income equality. Is it any wonder that there was a shortage of doctors in this country? As Winston Churchill said, "The inherent vice of capitalism is the unequal sharing of blessings. The inherent virtue of Socialism is the equal sharing of miseries."[9]

In our context in the United States, many university professors teach that everyone must be equally rewarded regardless of their achievements. Some educators even resist the use of exams because those who fail will be seen as less than equal to those who succeed. And if you don't succeed as others do, you're told it's not your fault because you are entitled to equality. Allegedly someone else's success was gained at your expense. The theory is that because all people are inherently equal, if you are poor, it is because someone else was made rich on your back. If you aren't successful, the responsibility rests with your oppressors.

It is true that oppression exists and leaves many minorities with a higher (and sometimes impossible) hill to climb. That's why, as Christians, we should vigorously defend the oppressed and seek for a level playing field of opportunities. But equality of *opportunity* cannot guarantee equality in *outcomes*.

Jude Dougherty, dean emeritus of the School of Philosophy at Catholic University, was right when he said, "Men differ in strength, intelligence, ambition, courage, perseverance and all else that makes for success. There is no method to make men both free and equal."[10]

There is no method to make people both free and equal.

As we will see, we as Christians have a responsibility to fight for laws that are just and to help those who are oppressed. But we should not expect the state to impose an artificial equality that, of necessity, stifles our freedoms (in a later chapter on socialism we will discuss this in more detail). Nor should we advocate the many different kinds of forced equality secularism is demanding.

The Quest for Social Justice

When people tell you that they are working toward social justice, you need to ask what they mean. We must not be quick to judge, but quick to listen and slow to speak. If they define social justice as being advocates for the poor, helping the sick, giving voice to the marginalized, and working for equal opportunity, these are the responsibilities of all Christians. Seeking justice is repeatedly taught in Scripture, especially for the widows, the victims of injustice, and the poor. The Good Samaritan went beyond justice and showed mercy. Strictly speaking, he did not owe the wounded man time and money, yet he was generous on both counts and was commended for showing mercy (see Luke 10:37). As Christians, we should go beyond justice and show mercy to the needy even at great personal cost.

Biblically, justice means that we insist on equality under the law—that we oppose oppression and take the side of the needy and the poor (see Isaiah 10:1-2). Martin Luther King Jr., in his "Letter from Birmingham Jail," gave us a succinct definition of a just law. He wrote, "How does one determine whether a law is just or unjust? A just law is a man-made code that squares with the moral law or the law of God. An unjust law is a code that is out of harmony with the moral law. To put it in the terms of St. Thomas Aquinas, an unjust law is a human law that is not rooted in eternal and natural law."[11] Well said.

King's fight against segregation and for equal rights for black Americans was just, for this is the kind of equality and justice that was the original vision of our Founding Fathers, and such equality and justice aligns with the biblical teaching that all persons are created in the image of God. Sadly, some in the evangelical church opposed King's vision of racial equality, which was based on the biblical teaching that all human beings have equal worth. He fought for what we must all fight for, and that is equality under the law. And as far as possible, equality of opportunity.

But—and this is where we must speak carefully—this is not the understanding of justice that prevails in many of our universities and in popular culture. Today, justice has been separated from the divine law and, like the word *equality*, it is attached to many different agendas. *Justice* has become a bloated term; as mentioned earlier, we have politicians and activists calling for environmental justice, gender justice, educational justice, immigration justice, economic justice, and reproductive justice. We dare not take the word *justice* and apply it to values that are sinful or evil.

I've heard so-called social justice warriors quote the famous text from Micah 6:8: "What does the LORD require of you but to do justice, and to love kindness, and to walk humbly with your God?" Then they use the phrase "do justice" as a springboard to speak about their own views about what justice requires, often based more on Marxism than the Bible.

Today, social justice is most often defined as the redistribution of resources and power to oppressed minorities; the oppressors must be identified and blamed for the failures of others. In a single word, social justice can be defined as a form of socialism. This kind of justice is built on what is known as Critical Race Theory (CRT), which teaches that race is a social construct created by the dominant group to maintain its superiority. It proposes that white supremacy and racial power lie at the root of our society's ills. These dominant groups use law, language, and various forms of power to keep minorities subordinate and oppressed.

Neil Shenvi, whose careful analysis of these matters should be read by all of us, puts it this way: "Contemporary critical theory views reality through the lens of power, dividing people into oppressed groups and oppressor groups along various axes like race, class, gender, sexual orientation, physical ability and age."[12]

In CRT, people are classified by groups with little or no distinction between individuals. If one group underachieves, it's the fault of the achievers; if one group is poor, it's the fault of the wealthy. Remember, the goal is not to foster unity or common ground but to assign blame and ensure that people will be put into categories so that tensions between the groups can be enflamed and maintained.

This has spawned a whole litany of classes in our universities that stress oppression and victimization. As Heather Mac Donald put it, "Students specializing in critical race theory play the race card incessantly against their fellow students and their professors, leading to an atmosphere of nervous self-censorship."[13] Opponents to these social justice theories are called racist, homophobic, bigoted, or worse.

Enter Diversity Studies

I have no doubt that many students in our universities who enroll in social justice classes not only mean well but often benefit from such studies to help bring about racial reconciliation. But I'm equally convinced that many courses in the classroom and discourses on the Internet are designed to fuel differences, enrage those said to be oppressed, and target the supposed oppressors. The victims are told they must confront the victimizers. No common ground is allowed because that would diminish the extent to which some groups have been oppressed. And no concessions are ever enough.

The German-American Marxist philosopher Herbert Marcuse had a strategy for destroying the influence of Christianity and traditional morality. He sought what we might call a coalition of victims.[14] He would exploit groups that were being oppressed, then blame Christianity and capitalism for their oppression. This, he believed, would hasten the demise of the enemies of Marxism and help establish the Marxist state. In all of this, God was seen as the ultimate oppressor.

Entire fields of study have been given over to the matter of diversity—issues of race, ethnicity, sexuality, and gender identity. Who you are depends on the group you belong to, whether you are among the oppressed or the oppressors. And because we are "trapped by a society that created our roles,"[15] we must study ways that some groups have been oppressed to the benefit their oppressors. We are told that bigotry is ubiquitous, even in the most subtle ways.

And, in a fallen world, everyone is victimized by somebody.

Social justice's theoretical goal is the emancipation of minorities by attacking the power and supremacy of the dominant group. CRT advocates for social justice by stressing how whites have oppressed black Americans, how men have oppressed women, how heterosexuals have oppressed homosexuals, how Christians have oppressed Muslims, and so on. This is all sold under the banner of "seeking justice for those who are oppressed."

Studies have been done to prove that you might be the victim of microaggression—that you've been oppressed by people who mean well but are nonetheless making you feel inferior. For example, if you meet someone who speaks with an accent and ask, "Where are you from?," that person might claim to be offended and made to feel as if they don't belong. As Heather Mac Donald writes, "In the process, they are creating what tort law calls 'eggshell plaintiffs'— preternaturally fragile individuals injured by the slightest collisions with life. The consequences will affect us for years to come."[16]

In this atmosphere, it is said that oppressors must be confronted and told it is their turn to sit down and listen. And if need be, the victimized must shut down a school or business so that their grievances can be heard. Advocates of this approach say that if you oppose such ruthless tactics it only proves you are siding with the oppressors. And if you are an oppressor (usually a white, cisgender heterosexual), it is said the only way you can survive is to confess your bigotry and judgmentalism, and admit you are guilty of the sin of being a person of privilege.

The victimized are told that when they are exposed to what they perceive to be oppression, they should demand a "safe place" where they can deal with the resultant anxiety and hurt feelings (this is called safetyism). This is not a matter of physical safety, but emotional support and healing because of the harm that is said to have been done to them. This stance even determines which guest speakers are or aren't allowed to speak on a university campus. If students claim a speaker might say something considered "offensive" or "triggering" to someone else, then that speaker is disinvited or told not to come. (We will deal with this more fully in the next chapter, which has to do with free speech.)

Intersectionality

The concept of intersectionality was developed through the work of leftist law professor Kimberlé Williams Crenshaw. As Robbie Soave puts it, intersectionality is "a philosophical framework that has come to dominate progressive activist thinking."[17] In brief, there are multiple sources of oppression in connection with race, class, gender, sexual orientation, etc. These can intersect in a person's life in ways that put them at risk for multiple layers of oppression. All this, Crenshaw tells us, is about power; it is time for the oppressors (predominately the whites) to listen to the oppressed. "It's not about asking, it's about demanding…it's about changing the very face of power itself."[18] Studies have been invented to prove "unconscious bias," which means that you might be bigoted and not know it. Accusations, whether real or imagined, against the "oppressors" abound.

Val Rust, an award-winning education professor at UCLA, was a pioneer in the field of comparative education and spent his time mentoring students from around the world. His students praised him for his compassion and integrity. But in a graduate-level class on dissertation preparation, he became the target of student protests. He was criticized for the political implications of what he deemed to be proper punctuation, insisting that the students follow the *Chicago Manual of Style* for formatting their papers.

This eventually resulted in radical students entering his classroom, and among other things, accusing him of racial microaggressions that have been "directed at our epistemologies, our intellectual rigor and to a misconstruction of the methodological genealogies that we have shared with the class."[19]

In all of this, neither the administration nor his colleagues defended Rust. Even when the dean announced that Rust would not be allowed to teach for a year, this was not enough for the radicals. The school pressured him to resign, and the administration pandered to the students.

Nothing was said about the unwarranted displays of narcissistic victimhood, but a committee was formed to discuss the matter. Its final report stated, "Recently, a group of our students have courageously challenged us to reflect on how to enact [our] mission in our own community. We owe these students a debt of thanks."[20] The lesson is clear: You can be called a bigot and lose your job for correcting a student's grammar and spelling.

Contrary to what you might think, this is not an isolated, extreme example. Incidents like this occur with some regularity in some (but not all) of our universities. Fearing the accusation of bias, racism, or hate, both professors and students take great pains to self-censure themselves lest they might say a word that will brand them as racist or bigoted.

CRT in the Church

In the world of political correctness, arguments are resolved by social force and shaming, not by discussion, evaluating evidence, or civility. This kind of hysteria is hardly conducive to racial reconciliation. Social justice theories have also infiltrated some churches, especially those of a liberal bent that say they are inclusive, meaning that they accept same-sex marriage and the like.

I agree with Neil Shenvi, who is distressed about the acceptance of CRT even in some evangelical churches. Some Christians apparently do not understand that these theories are antithetical to Christianity on virtually every point. CRT teaches that a person's identity cannot be separated from the group to which they belong. If you are born white, you are labeled an oppressor regardless of your character or personal attitude; individuality is lost within the group you belong to. And if you are born white and you choose to defend yourself against the charge of racism, this only proves that indeed you are racist! Wealthy black Americans are not considered persons of privilege, but a white person born into abject poverty is considered a person of privilege. There is no room for individuality, kindness, forgiveness, or meaningful reconciliation.

Even more importantly, in the purely secular application of CRT, redemption is viewed as separating a group from oppressors, not as the need to be freed from sin by the gospel of God's saving grace. Salvation, in the radical view of CRT, is to gain power over your oppressors. Until the oppressed triumph over their oppressors, the conflict must continue. Pure Marx.

As Shenvi points out, CRT also agrees with Marx that lived experience is much more reliable than objective truth; the oppressed are said to see reality in a unique way that is not open to oppressors. This, we are told, is why we must submit to a member of an oppressed group to interpret the US Constitution or the Bible. Behind all this is Marx's idea that truth is only that which is used by the oppressors to keep the oppressed in submission. So, there is no objective truth that we can strive toward to encourage unity. The oppressed have a unique perspective, and the oppressors must sit and listen.[21]

We've all heard the pejorative expression "dead old European white males." They are said to be oppressors in at least three ways. They were European, they were white, and they were males. They must be disparaged regardless of any contributions they might have made to science, medicine, education, or anything else related to people's well-being. This explains why many of the great accomplishments and works of Western civilization are being denounced these days.

That said, those who are white need to be sensitive to the concerns of their brothers and sisters from other ethnic backgrounds. I've had black seminary students tell me that their courses in church history were dominated by the white theologians of Europe, and they longed to have a book written by someone who they could identify with—someone of their cultural background who shares their life experiences. We should listen to these concerns and make sure that black history and writers are included in discussions of the history of Christianity going all the way back to the early theologians of North Africa. Without rejecting the past, we can be more inclusive and balanced in our seminaries and churches.

But CRT is not the answer.

There is growing evidence that wokeness and social-justice theories have infiltrated the Southern Baptist Convention (SBC). In 2019, a resolution that was intended to denounce CRT was actually modified or changed by progressives to advocate that CRT be given at least some credence. The delegates adopted the rewritten Resolution 9, which stated that CRT/intersectionality is "an analytical tool" though not a worldview. In the minds of many delegates, this was further proof that CRT was gaining broad support not just in SBC churches but in SBC seminaries.[22]

Later, Dr. Albert Mohler, president of the Southern Baptist Theological Seminary and a key leader in the SBC, who voted against the resolution, felt the need to clarify where he stands:

> Both critical race theory and intersectionality are a part
> of the continuing transformative Marxism that is now so
> dominant in higher education and increasingly in policy.
> Critical race theory emerged from worldviews, and from
> thinkers who were directly contrary to the Christian faith.[23]

We must speak carefully here, but I have noticed that blatant racial attacks against "whiteness" and "white privilege" are often disguised under the banner of "racial reconciliation." But soon it becomes clear that there is little interest in actual reconciliation, but simply the blaming of one race in favor of the other. Individual differences and individual responsibility are ignored.

And we are not yet finished with this analysis. We must now turn our attention to another facet of CRT—namely, the issue of white guilt.

The Controversy About White Guilt

Coming from Canada, my first introduction to the black American experience under segregation was reading the book *Let Justice Roll Down,* written by John Perkins. He is, by all accounts, one of the great heroes of racial reconciliation, a dear brother whom I invited to speak at The Moody Church. I marveled at his large-hearted forgiveness despite the injustice and victimization he experienced growing up in the Deep South during the Jim Crow era. You would also benefit from his most recent book, *One Blood: Parting Words to the Church on Race and Love.*

We can be thankful that segregation is largely a matter of the past, but we should not be blind to the reality that certain forms of racism still exist. To give but one example: Many black communities in Chicago have been exploited by white landlords who buy properties and charge high rent yet never reinvest their profits back into the community. Talk to our black brothers and sisters, and they will give you multiple examples of racism, often unseen and even less understood by those in the white community.

Yet at the same time, in recent years, those who are white have been stigmatized with "white guilt"—that is, white people as a group are told they should not only feel guilty about the past but also about the present. They inherently have "white privilege," which is said to be a detriment to black progress in jobs, education, housing, and more.

I agree that people who are white do have an advantage in our culture. I have never had to worry whether I'd be accepted in a church or any other setting because of the color of my skin. Racism explains many of the inequities in our culture that must be addressed. But there is also another side to this story.

Black leader Shelby Steele wrote the book *White Guilt: How Blacks and Whites Together Destroyed the Promise of the Civil Rights Era*. Although not everyone would agree with Steele, he is widely praised for his works. The *Chicago Sun-Times* endorsed the book, saying, "Anyone concerned with the endless standoff that is black-white relations in this country has a duty to read Shelby Steele."[24]

Steele also experienced the racial injustices of white supremacy, but he believes that the transition from white supremacy to white guilt has not been good for the black community. In brief, he argues that during segregation, black Americans had responsibility but no rewards; now with the advances made in civil rights, black Americans have sometimes sought rewards without responsibility. Although black Americans have been victimized by the white supremacy of the past, he now chides some black American leaders and warns them that they are using white guilt to promote continuing black victimization as an identity.

Speaking of what happened after the Civil Rights legislation, he writes,

> The litmus test for being black required one to accept racial victimization not as an occasional event in one's life but as an ongoing identity. When victimization is identity, then the victim's passionate anger can be called out even where there is no actual victimization...White

guilt was the power, and this identity was the leverage militant leaders used to access that power. Unfortunately, all this gave blacks a political identity with no real purpose beyond the manipulation of white guilt.[25]

Whether we agree with Steele or not, he contends that white guilt is being used by some black Americans (though by no means all) as a means to achieve rewards without responsibility. We recall the directive of the late Marxist Saul Alinsky, who told his followers that they should exploit "latent guilt." Some would say that guilt is used as a means by which minorities can insist on unearned privileges. *This encourages victims to feel entitled.*

What keeps much of the black community in systemic poverty? Black pastor Reverend Bill Owens, who marched with Martin Luther King Jr. in the battle for civil rights, would probably agree with Steele. In his book *A Dream Derailed: How the Left Hijacked Civil Rights to Create a Permanent Underclass*, Owens, after presenting what he believes is documented evidence that the welfare state was begun to keep black Americans as a permanent underclass, argues that it is liberal social policies that have, in effect, stolen pride from black Americans.

> For black Americans...the more the federal government provides so-called "free" services and hand-outs paid for by taxpayers, the more blacks are incentivized to be dependent on the government. With this system, fewer blacks are likely to get an education, work hard for their families, and become entrepreneurs, professionals, and business leaders. With this system, fewer blacks will stand with pride and dignity. Again, look at our inner cities. Do you like what you see?[26]

In all the debates regarding white guilt and white privilege, we would do well to remember the words of Martin Luther King Jr., who reminded us that we should not judge one another by the color of our skin but by the content of our character. What could be more racist than to judge an entire group of people simply by the color of their skin? We cannot change the color of our skin, but we can listen to each other and ask how we can move forward in race relations and not be needlessly sidetracked by debates that attempt to raise up one group of people at the expense of another.

When I asked one of our members at The Moody Church (he calls himself a true African-American because he was born in Ghana but grew up on Chicago's South Side) what he thought of the social justice curricula on many university campuses, he said, "We are being separated further and further each day and being told that there can be no reconciliation unless whites meet certain demands. And since these demands are impossible, the impasse persists."

I hope that after the demonstrations and riots of 2020, needed changes will be made to combat what is often referred to as systemic racism, which is variously defined. But I am also convinced that for the diehard progressives, nothing done will ever be enough. Their goal is endless retaliation, not reconciliation.

Arithmetic Gets Woke

Social justice is spreading to disciplines we normally would have thought were immune from racism. Surely the so-called hard sciences like math are objective, not subject to the social justice and race theories that are applied to disciplines such as sociology, history, and politics. But no more; these theories are now being applied to mathematics.

"Seattle Public Schools Will Start Teaching That Math Is Oppressive" is the headline written by Robby Soave on October 22, 2019. "A new ethnic studies curriculum will teach students that 'ancient mathematical knowledge has been appropriated by Western Culture.'" Math is accused of fostering "a litany of more serious crimes: imperialism, dehumanization, and oppression of marginalized persons."[27]

The proposed mathematics curriculum is infused with social justice issues, focusing on "power and oppression" as well as the "history of resistance and liberation." Again, let me state that this is in the field of *mathematics*. So far, the curriculum isn't mandatory; however, it is offered as a resource to those teachers who want to introduce ethnic studies into the math classroom. The goal is to "infuse ethnic studies into all subjects across the K–12 spectrum."

Soave says the proposed framework is "chock full of social justice jargon that sounds smart but is actually vapid. What does it mean when it says...it will 're-humanize mathematics through experiential learning' and facilitate learning 'independently and interdependently'?"[28]

The proposal itself states that students will be able to "identify the inherent inequities of the standardized testing system used to oppress and marginalize people and communities of color" and "explain how math dictates economic oppression."[29]

Can't we all agree that 2 + 2 = 4 without having an argument about race? Apparently not.

Like an arsonist who is also a firefighter sent to douse the flames of a fire he started, so the social justice warriors purport to seek solutions to problems they created. Indeed, not even Saul Alinsky could have hoped for a better scheme to keep the races in perpetual, unresolved conflict. We can almost hear him shouting from the grave, "*Create* problems! Then *use* them!"

The Critical Role of Families in Our National Struggles

Does systemic racism exist? Yes, there are systems in place that throughout the years have favored inequities and marginalized black communities. And even when we declare that there is equality under the law, racism can exist in many ways—sometimes visibly, sometimes subtly. Only our black brothers and sisters can say what it is like to experience this. And we should do all we can to right the wrongs done against various peoples and groups no matter who they are.

But—and this is critical—I believe there are serious issues within cultures that cannot be solved from the outside. Even if all the issues of systemic racism that we hear about were adequately addressed, this will not eliminate the root problems in our culture. There are systemic problems within cultures that can only be addressed from within those cultures. And within our homes.

Without meaningful changes within our homes, no university courses or national social programs can remedy our nation's racial and economic ills. We are constantly told that white people must change, and they should. But *every* community, including the black community, must be held accountable for its own internal systemic issues. Ultimately the solving of these "within culture" problems comes down to individual responsibility within each of our families, no matter the race or ethnicity.

Regardless of your political leanings, take the time to read former president Barack Obama's Father's Day speech at the Apostolic Church of God in Chicago on June 15, 2008. He was speaking predominantly to the black community, but what he said applies to us all. Here, I have just excerpted a couple paragraphs:

> If we are honest with ourselves, we'll admit that what too many fathers also are is missing—missing from too many lives and too many homes. They have abandoned their responsibilities, acting like boys instead of men. And the foundations of our families are weaker because of it. You

and I know how true this is in the African-American community. We know that more than half of all African-American children live in single-parent households, a number that has doubled—doubled—since we were children. We know the statistics—that children who grow up without a father are five times more likely to live in poverty and commit crime; nine times more likely to drop out of schools and twenty times more likely to end up in prison. They are more likely to have behavioral problems or run away from home or become teenage parents themselves. And the foundations of our community are weaker because of it...

But we also need families to raise our children. We need fathers to realize that responsibility does not end at conception. We need them to realize that what makes you a man is not the ability to have a child—it's the courage to raise one.[30]

Well said.

Let me emphasize that the white community has its growing share of single-parent homes, divorce, rampant drug abuse, and crime. What the former president said applies equally to all cultures, races, and ethnic communities.

Psychiatrist Theodore Dalrymple, in his book *Life at the Bottom: The Worldview That Makes the Underclass*, shows that the most powerful influence that holds people down as an underclass is not race, but moral relativism. For the record, Dalrymple's father was a Communist. Dalrymple himself is an atheist but argues that socially liberal, progressive views minimize individual responsibility and produce an underclass afflicted by violence, sexually transmitted diseases, welfare dependency, and drug use.

So what causes a permanent underclass? He says,

> Of nothing is this [social pathology] more true than the
> system of sexual relations that prevails in the underclass,
> with the result that 70 percent of the births in my hos-
> pital are now illegitimate (a figure that would approach
> 100 percent if it were not for the presence in the area
> of a large number of immigrants from the Indian
> subcontinent).[31]

According to him, the foremost perpetrator of the underclass is
uncommitted sexual relations. People from the Indian subconti-
nent (southcentral Asia) get married, stay together, get an education,
and work hard so most are not part of the underclass.

Dalrymple continues:

> The connection between this loosening [of morals] and
> the misery of my patients is so obvious that it requires
> considerable intellectual sophistication (and dishonesty)
> to be able to deny it. The climate of moral, cultural, and
> intellectual relativism—a relativism that began as a mere
> fashionable plaything for intellectuals—has been suc-
> cessfully communicated to those least able to resist its
> devastating practical effects.[32]

I suspect that immorality, sexual freedom, and unmarried teenage
parents—along with opioid and other addictions such as alcohol-
ism and gambling—will always ensure that we have what Dalrymple called a "permanent underclass," and it will include all races,
cultures, and ethnicities that will not face the internal moral issues
that hold them captive to their plight. If a person is being held down
by a problem that can only be fixed by taking responibility, it is time
for that person to stop blaming others for the problem.

Blessed are those who give their lives
and fortunes to pick up the pieces of our
broken culture and show a better way.

In the midst of this brokenness, the church must step up to the plate and be the church. I greatly admire those pastors in our most under-resourced communities here in Chicago (and other cities) who are in the trenches working with families, sharing resources, and maintaining gospel ministries to give hope to people trapped in cycles of poverty and utter despair.

In what follows, I will give an example of a ministry that is speaking directly to this need by giving children and families the vision that things can be different. This is challenging but it must be done; blessed are those who give their lives and fortunes to pick up the pieces of our broken culture and show a better way. I rejoice when I see the church be the church where the need is the greatest.

The Church in a Toxic Culture

What does the church do in the midst of this cacophony of angry voices, each clamoring for their "rights" and the "justice" they think they deserve? Marxism is not the answer, the gospel is. We must not merely react to the culture but be proactive and lead the way.

First, we must not allow social justice theories to keep us divided; the social justice or CRT teachings have made it more difficult for us to have honest conversations about race and gender because they insist that we stereotype one another based on what group we belong to. Denny Burk, a professor of biblical studies and director of the Center for Gospel and Culture, agrees and writes,

> Intersectionality is the most unforgiving, unsparing, and unmerciful system of legalism that I have ever seen. If you cross the line, there is no absolution or redemption. There is no expiation of the original sin of privilege. There is only a black hole of shame and disgrace.[33]

CRT rhetoric can be so intimidating that fear of being misunderstood can tempt us to retreat into the safety of silence. This would be a mistake. Thankfully, most black leaders welcome honest discussion without prejudging people because of the color of their skin. And that should be true of all of us.

And now for some great news!

At the foot of the cross we confess that there is common ground between all the racial and ethnic diversity in the world.

The gospel does what CRT cannot do. The church has an advantage that CRT does not have: We believe that the root cause of evil is not only external systems, but rather, the sin that lies within every human heart. Therefore, we strive for commonality among the races, not accentuating our differences. At the foot of the cross we confess that there is common ground between all the racial and ethnic diversity in the world. We stand together as sinners confessing our common need of personal redemption. We see the source of evil not outside of us, but within us. We acknowledge, as someone has said, that we don't have a *skin* problem, but a *sin* problem.

We confess that we have received God's forgiveness and the transformation of our hearts, also known as the new birth. We confess that the gospel is not what we can do for Jesus but what Jesus has done for us. Martin Luther put it simply: "Thou, Lord Jesus, art my righteousness, but I am thy sin."[34]

Then what? The evangelical church must repent of its passivity, its indifference to racial disparities. I like what Tony Evans says: We must begin with friendships with people who are different from us; we must intentionally connect as families and partners. We must demonstrate that we are willing to disadvantage ourselves for the sake of others. Jesus laid aside privileges and power to redeem us. He is our example of humility and sacrifice. A good starting point is to ask: How can I personally put the needs of my brothers and sisters above my own?

We do not have to shout at each other across racial fences. We can sit down, talk, listen, and help one another mirror the unity that has already been established by Christ. This humble acknowledgment is the core of all meaningful reconciliation.

In the first century AD, the animosity between Jews and Gentiles ran deep. But remarkably, Christ changed all that. "For he himself is our peace, who has made us both one and has broken down in his flesh the dividing wall of hostility…that he might create in himself one new man in place of the two, so making peace, and might reconcile us both to God in one body through the cross, thereby killing the hostility" (Ephesians 2:14-16). In Christ, we agree with Martin Luther King Jr. that we should not be judged by the color of our skin but by the content of our character.

Killing the hostility!

Christ created something new: The church is not a collection of individuals with a common interest, but a group of people who share a common *life*. In Colossians, Paul lists people with racial, ethnic, cultural, and societal differences. However, rather than dividing them into different categories, he sees them as united in Christ. "Here there is not Greek and Jew, circumcised and uncircumcised, barbarian, Scythian, slave, free; but Christ is all, and in all" (Colossians 3:11). Truly radical.

For the sake of space, I will resist the temptation to expound on the rest of Paul's teaching about the unity brought about by the gospel. It is enough to say that we not only have the same Savior, but we share the same life and are stones in the same temple (1 Peter 2:5).

Now that Christ has reconciled us, we have to ask: How can we help one another? We begin by listening. Black Americans see things that white Americans miss; each of us looks at life through our own lens, our own background, our own family experiences, and certainly, our own perceptions. As a white man, I cannot adequately put myself in the shoes of my black brothers and sisters and understand what it is like to be black in a white-dominated society. Only honest conversation, without fear of being labeled, will enable us to get past stereotypes and misunderstandings. We have a lot to learn *from* each other and *about* each other.

We must leverage whatever privileges we have for the benefit of those who were not born into the same economic, racial, and cultural opportunities as others. We ask: What can we do to work together to bring about more equality and opportunity?

Of the many ministries I could reference that are getting past the racial vitriol of our communities, I would like to introduce you to one that is making a permanent and strategic difference in four of the most-needy neighborhoods of Chicago. It is a marvelous example of what can happen when people who are blessed with means invest their resources to change the lives of thousands of children and make a lasting impact on the next generation.

D.L. Moody is long gone, but God has raised up a new generation that carries on his legacy in the city of Chicago. One of our members, Donnita Travis, volunteered through The Moody Church to help students from a notorious housing project with their homework. Struck by a love for the kids, she felt led to start a holistic after-school program with the vision of helping children from Chicago's high-risk, inner-city neighborhoods to experience the abundant life Jesus promised (John 10:10). In 2001, she launched what is now known as By The Hand Club For Kids. Beginning with 16 students, the ministry has grown to nearly 1,600 kids from four of the most under-resourced and crime-ridden neighborhoods.

Donnita and her staff, along with hundreds of volunteers, literally and figuratively take kids by the hand and walk alongside them from the time they enroll all the way through college. By The Hand takes a holistic approach to child development, caring for the children mind, body, and soul. Each child is mentored and tutored. The ministry is so successful that 83 percent of By The Hand freshmen have gone on to graduate from high school. And 87 percent of its high school graduates have enrolled in a college or technical school, compared to 68 percent for Chicago students overall. Many have come to trust Christ as their Savior and Lord. Please become acquainted with this incredible ministry by going to their website, https://bythehand.org.

During World War I, some French soldiers brought the body of a comrade to a cemetery for burial. The priest gently told them that this was a Roman Catholic cemetery, so he needed to ask whether the victim was a Catholic. They answered no, he was not. The priest was very sorry, but if that was the case, he could not permit burial in the churchyard. So the soldiers sadly took the body of their friend and buried him just outside the fence of the cemetery.

The next day they returned to mark the grave, but to their astonishment, they couldn't find it. They knew they had buried him just next to the fence, but the freshly dug soil was not there. As they were about to leave, the priest saw them and said that his conscience had troubled him about telling them that they could not bury their friend within the cemetery. So troubled was he that early in the morning, he had the fence moved to include the new grave within the parameters of the churchyard.

I tell this story not to minimize the differences between Protestants and Catholics, but rather to show that we as the church must be willing to "move the fences" that so easily separate us. Not the doctrinal fences that define our faith (indeed, removing such fences is one of our most serious problems), but those cultural and racial fences that keep the body of Christ divided.

Edwin Markim, in his poem "Outwitted," wrote:

> He drew a circle that shut me out—
> Heretic, rebel, a thing to flout.
> But Love and I had the wit to win:
> We drew a circle that took him in!

The weak must be protected. The abused healed. The rejected accepted. And the greatest of sinners must be invited to receive Christ's forgiveness. Only through the cross can we show what reconciliation looks like to the world. The world can do anything the church can do except one thing: It cannot show grace. And I will add that it cannot show grace because it does not bow before the cross, where grace is given to sinners. The world can have union but not unity; self-interest but not selflessness.

Christ has called us to show the way.

A Prayer All of Us Must Pray

Father, teach us the full meaning of Jesus' words in John 17:20-22:

> *I do not ask for these only, but also for those who will believe in me through their word, that they may all*

*be one, just as you, Father, are in me, and I in you,
that they also may be in us, so that the world may
believe that you have sent me. The glory that you
have given me I have given to them, that they may
be one even as we are one.*

*We thank You that You have already united us; teach us
what this means for us as individuals and for us as the
church. And may no sacrifice be too great to bring Your
words to a more visible reality.*

In Jesus' name, amen.

CHAPTER 4

Freedom of Speech for Me, but Not for Thee

Many of us have been critical of the church in Nazi Germany. We have asked why the Christians did not rise in opposition to the propaganda of the Third Reich. But after the riots that followed the murder of George Floyd, we now must be more understanding of the silence of the church. It is difficult to speak up in a culture carried away by a mob mentality: Submit, or else.

How do revolutions begin?

Revolutions begin with a cultural moment, a pretext that will hide the real agenda to justify the revolution. You need (1) the triumph of an ideology over science, reason, and civil liberties. Then you (2) recruit people who are willing to advance the revolution of anarchy in the name of justice and equality. And finally, (3) you must silence all dissident voices. Submission to the ideology is enforced either by shaming, by laws, or simply by exclusion, such as firing opposing voices from the workplace.

Because this is a chapter on free speech, I will comment only on the last of the three factors I have mentioned above: In a revolution, dissident voices must be silenced.

Consider this news headline from June 6, 2020: "Stan Wischnowski resigns as *The Philadelphia Inquirer*'s top editor."

We read:

> Stan Wischnowski, the top editor of *The Philadelphia Inquirer*, has announced his resignation, days after discontent among the newspaper's staff erupted over a headline on a column [published June 2] about the impact of the civil unrest following the police killing of George Floyd in Minneapolis.[1]

What was his infraction? He allowed an article to be published titled "Buildings Matter, Too," written by the paper's architecture critic. The author began by saying that lives are more important than buildings, but then she went on to describe some of the looting that occurred in Philadelphia during the riots and the defacing of architecture. The paper received so much pushback that it wrote an apology and changed the title of the article to "Black Lives Matter. Do Buildings?"[2] and yet again to "Damaging buildings disproportionately hurts the people protesters are trying to uplift."[3] But that was not sufficient for the radicals. The very suggestion that somehow the riots were illegitimate because of the physical destruction they created was too much for the mob spirit that prevailed throughout the country. Their top editor of 20 years had to go. All in the name of diversity.

Drew Brees, quarterback for the New Orleans Saints, made this statement to Yahoo Finance:

> I will never agree with anybody disrespecting the flag of the United States of America or our country. Let me

just tell you what I see or what I feel when the national anthem is played and when I look at the flag of the United States. I envision my two grandfathers, who fought for this country during World War II…Both risking their lives to protect our country and to try to make our country and this world a better place. So every time I stand with my hand over my heart looking at that flag and singing the national anthem, that's what I think about.[4]

The fuse was lit…

What Brees said provoked such a backlash he decided to further clarify his remarks on ESPN: "I love and respect my teammates and I stand right there with them in regards to fighting for racial equality and justice."[5] His conviction that the flag should be respected was a bridge too far for the thought police. He apologized for that statement not once but twice; independent thought and freedom of speech were not allowed.

I could list several more examples like this that have come to my attention. I'm sure you have read about the many people being fired or called out because they voiced an opinion that was different from the mob's. The radicals have little interest in rational discussion. Free speech is what they grant themselves, but not to others. They seek uncontested cultural dominance.

Here is the way the cancel culture works: It says yes, you have the First Amendment. You can exercise your freedom of speech. But if you do, we will make sure that you are fired. You will be vilified and ostracized. Cancelled.

Does the cancel culture sound like it's part of a country that is on its way to greatness, or a country in decline? Remember, mobs are only able to destroy; they cannot build. And every victory spurs them on to more demands. Many politicians and businesses came out in support of the radicals and funneled millions of dollars into their cause, no doubt virtue signaling that they were free of racism and hoping that the mob would not come after them. Churchill is credited with having said, "An appeaser is one who feeds a crocodile hoping it will eat him last."

And what if you remained silent, not wanting to bow to the mob spirit? The signs said it all: "Silence Is Violence." Bow the knee, or else.

How did we get here? The great bastions of tolerance have become more intolerant than any religious fundamentalist could ever dare to be. Intolerance from radical left secularists is not a new phenomenon.

In 1997, psychologist Nicholas Humphrey gave the Oxford Amnesty lecture for that year, the purpose of which was "to argue in favor of censorship, against freedom of expression"; specifically, it was to censor "moral and religious education," especially the education a child receives at home.

> Children have a right not to have their minds addled by nonsense. And we as a society have a duty to protect them from it. So we should no more allow parents to teach their children to believe, for example, in the literal truth of the Bible, or that the planets rule their lives, than we should allow parents to knock their children's teeth out or lock them in a dungeon.[6]

Really?

To teach children the truth of the Bible is equivalent to knocking their teeth out? Or locking them in a dungeon? The harshest critics of free speech are the secular leftists who pride themselves on their alleged tolerance. Supposedly they are the ones who are in favor of inclusion and not exclusion, pluralism and not bigotry. That is true, of course, only if you agree with their worldview.

The Value of Free Speech

Let's remind ourselves of what the First Amendment says:

> Congress shall make no law respecting an establishment
> of religion, or prohibiting the free exercise thereof; or
> abridging the freedom of speech, or of the press; or the
> right of the people peaceably to assemble, and to peti-
> tion the Government for a redress of grievances.[7]

Free speech was, at one time, a right that the radical left applauded. The Free Speech Movement, as it was called, was a considerable and lengthy protest on the campus of the University of California, Berkeley, during the 1964–1965 school year. Students protested an administrative ban prohibiting on-campus political activities and demanded that the university acknowledge their right to free speech. This movement was supported by the left-leaning social activists of the day and gave impetus to both the civil rights and antiwar movements.

My wife and I lived in Skokie, Illinois, back in 1977 when the National Socialist Party of America wanted to march in this suburb where hundreds of Jews who survived Hitler's concentration camps lived. At first these Nazi advocates were denied a permit to march and spew their hatred against the Jews. But they were defended by the ACLU, which insisted that free speech was free speech no matter how offensive. The US Supreme Court rendered their verdict in what is known as the *National Socialist Party of America v. Village of Skokie* dispute, stating that the Neo-Nazis had a right to demonstrate and speak.[8] This free speech case is often taught or cited in constitutional law classes.

That was then; this is now.

Institutions that once favored free speech are now limiting speech, arguing that this right is unfair, unjust, and insensitive. They say that free speech should be allowed for some groups but not others. Nearly one-half of millennials believe that hate speech should be banned.[9] These days, however, hate speech is often defined as the speech of a political opponent with which one does not agree. For example, if you're for securing US borders, that can be considered racist hate speech by those who believe the US should have open borders. Or to state that there are only two genders is considered offensive and therefore deemed hate speech (more about this in the next chapter).

The slogan of those who want to silence speech they disagree with is "If you can't beat them, ban them."

Arguments for Banning Free Speech

Let's begin with the Marxist philosopher we've already been introduced to, Herbert Marcuse, who was very influential during the 1960s and whose legacy continues. He attributed all the evils of society to capitalism because he believed that a few wealthy elite controlled the means of production. The workers employed by the capitalists worked harder than they needed to; knowingly or unknowingly, they were simply feeding the greed of the capitalists.

Marxism, he believed, would remedy these inequities. But how is Marxism to be brought about? Not by freedom of speech, which he said "is loaded and dominated by existing elites, who skew the debate to favor their position."[10] It is not a level playing field, he said, because the capitalists have the advantage of deluding the masses with their rhetoric, which has resulted in violence, racism, and oppression of various kinds. As long as capitalism survives, people will lack the discernment to know what is really true.

What is to be done?

Marcuse lamented, "Tolerance is extended to policies, conditions, and modes of behavior which should not be tolerated because they are impeding, if not destroying, the chances of creating an existence without fear and misery"[11] (that is, the utopian Marxist state).

To put it simply: Freedom of speech allows capitalists to stay in power; therefore, freedom of speech should not be tolerated. To allow non-Marxists free speech is to delay, if not prevent, the possibility that Marxism will prevail.

What restrictions did Marcuse think should be placed on free speech?

> They [the restrictions] would include the withdrawal of toleration of speech and assembly from groups and movements which promote aggressive policies, armament, chauvinism, discrimination on the grounds of race and religion, or which oppose the extension of public services, social security, medical care, etc.[12]

If you believe in armaments (patriotism) and discrimination on the grounds of religion and race, you are not entitled to free speech to defend your views. Once Marxism is firmly in place, freedom may be restored, but some restrictions will continue. Marcuse wrote,

> Moreover, the restoration of freedom of thought [after Marxism is firmly in place] may necessitate new and rigid restrictions on teachings and practices in the educational institutions which, by their very methods and concepts, serve to enclose the mind within the established universe of discourse and behavior.[13]

What should we conclude?

Jeffery A. Tucker, editorial director at the American Institute for Economic Research, comments,

> Marcuse says that if you oppose policies like social security or Obamacare, you should be denied the freedom

of speech and assembly. You should be shut up and beat up. The path toward true freedom is through massive real-world oppression. *If you have the wrong views, you have no rights.*[14]

Let's recap. Marcuse was frustrated that Marxism had not yet prevailed and blamed capitalistic opposition. Therefore, capitalists had to be denied freedom of speech. Tucker, with a hint of sarcasm, comments, "Given that he and his friends are part of a priesthood of truth, shouldn't they just be declared the winners and contrary views suppressed?"[15] After all, as Marcuse said, "Suppression of the regressive ones [policies and opinions] is a prerequisite for the strengthening of the progressive ones."[16]

What about the liberalism that championed freedom? Marcuse wrote that we must put an end to "the liberal creed of free and equal discussion" and to be "militantly intolerant."[17] Liberalism's policy of freedom of speech must be denounced.

The radical left should be militantly intolerant!

Who should make the distinction between the progressive views of Marxism and the repressive views of capitalism? The answer is the properly enlightened intellectuals like Marcuse and his friends. Marcuse describes the person who should decide who is permitted to speak as someone who should be "in the maturity of his faculties as a human being."[18]

Did you get that? Those of us who aren't Marxists are immature; it follows that the ones who determine what can and can't be said are those who "have maturity of faculties." Let me say it again: Marcuse believed that Marxists should have freedom of speech, and capitalists should not. Marxists are mature thinkers; therefore, we should not argue with them. When the radical left speaks, they want only to hear the echo of their own voice.

Ideas have consequences.

Most of the faculty and students at our universities have probably never read Herbert Marcuse. But his influence has worked its way into academia. To quote Jeffrey Tucker one more time, "It doesn't mean that people are literally reading Marcuse or even that their professors have done so. Philosophy works this way. Bad ideas are like termites: you can't entirely see them and suddenly the whole house falls in."[19]

Tucker is right. Repressive termites are everywhere in academia, allowing only for progressive ideas. Just think of how difficult—or even impossible—it is to have a conservative speak at a university. We humbly acknowledge that Herbert Marcuse won the argument. And he used free speech to do it.

Shutting Down Free Speech

Now, I have no objection to universities having reasonable speech codes so people can't just say anything. The old adage that you can't shout "Fire!" in a crowded theater unless there actually is a fire is but one example of where free speech is restricted. Universities might have speech codes that forbid insults, name-calling, taunting others, etc., but these codes should not be so restrictive that so-called offensive speech is banned because the term *offensive* can be interpreted so broadly as to include anyone who merely disagrees with the secularists' agenda regarding race, gender, and politics. Ours is a generation where many are offended simply by legitimate opposing viewpoints.

Social justice professors steeped in Critical Race Theory are ready to give a contemporary application to the views of Marxists such as Herbert Marcuse. Like George Orwell's Thought Police, they are the gatekeepers, keeping score and determining who can speak and who must listen. In the eyes of the radicals, the oppressors should not be given sympathy. As David Horowitz describes the radical left,

"To respect oppressors' rights is to support the injustices they commit. If social justice is to be achieved, one must suppress the perpetrators of injustice by depriving them of their rights. That is why progressives—cultural Marxists—are so intolerant and seek to suppress the free speech of those who oppose them."[20]

Let me introduce Stanley Fish, the author of *There's No Such Thing as Free Speech, and It's a Good Thing, Too.* He writes,

> Individualism, fairness, merit—these three words are continually in the mouths of our up-to-date, newly respectable bigots who have learned that they need not put on a white hood or bar access to the ballot box in order to secure their ends.[21]

Reread that if you have to. Those of us who believe in free speech are compared to the Ku Klux Klan and called bigots. Stephen R.C. Hicks sums up the idea this way: "So in order to equalize the power imbalance, explicit and forthright double-standards are absolutely and unapologetically called for in the postmodern Left."[22]

Double standards are absolutely and unapologetically called for!

This is why the radical left has changed its position from championing free speech to banning it and allowing only "oppressed" groups to speak. The argument is that minorities, such as those in the LGBTQ communities, have been discriminated against, and therefore, to level the playing field, we must curb the social power of the dominant group that for too long has used free speech to uphold their position of power. Racism and sexism must be attacked vigorously,[23] and one way to do that is to deny certain groups the right to speak. They only have the right to remain silent.

Philosopher Stephen Hicks believes in free speech and helpfully summarizes the contemporary arguments against freedom of speech this way: "Speech is a weapon in the conflict between groups that are unequal."[24] Therefore, the radical left argues, it is necessary to protect the weaker groups from the dominant groups (whites, males, and capitalists) who will use the power of speech to their advantage at the expense of minorities and women.

To explain further, "The postmodern argument implies that if anything goes, then that gives permission to the dominant groups to keep on saying the things that keep the subordinate groups in their place. Liberalism [freedom of speech] thus means helping the silencing of the subordinate groups."[25] So from the radical left's perspective, speech codes designed to censor conservative voices are not censorship but "forms of liberation" for the oppressed groups because their voice will be the only one heard. Contrary views on social justice issues are not up for discussion; they must be silenced. In other words, *the more oppressed I am, the greater my right to shut you down.*

Some argue against free speech on the basis of the "emotional well-being" of oppressed groups. "Offending rhetoric" includes "racist" books such as those of Plato, Aristotle, John Locke, etc. These books that belong to the Western tradition are said to cause minorities to feel oppressed. That is why they have been deleted from many courses in literature or philosophy. Recently, Yale University abandoned its highly rated course "Introduction to Art History: Renaissance to the Present" because it put European art on a pedestal at the expense of other art traditions. In its place the school will teach mini-classes on "'art and politics'; questions of 'gender, class and race'; and the relationship of art to capitalism and climate change."[26]

Gone are the rich traditions and contributions of European history, including those of Leonardo da Vinci, Michelangelo, and Rembrandt. And dozens of others.

And the consequences are far-reaching.

Intimidation on Campus

According to the radical secularists, unapproved speech has to be shut down—even with violence, if necessary. In March of 2017, a mob at Middlebury College in Vermont refused to allow social scientist Charles Murray to speak. The protesting students shouted, pounded on the walls, and even activated fire alarms. They assaulted a professor, giving her a concussion, and Murray himself came close to being beaten. His research reached conclusions about race, the welfare system, and the American experience that did not meet the criteria of the thought police.

I have not read Murray's writings, so it is not my intention to defend his view. My only point is that he should have been allowed to share his research, especially because he was invited by a group of students to do so. Why not at least be willing to debate his views?

Just in case you think that the Middlebury event was an isolated instance of violence against free speech, 177 professors nationwide signed an open letter blaming Middlebury College, not the students, for the mayhem. The presence of Murray was a "threat to the students." And the protest was described as "active resistance against racism, sexism, classism, homophobia, transphobia, ableism, ethnocentrism, xenophobia, and all other forms of unjust discrimination."[27]

My view is that if you disagree with Murray, why not let him speak for himself and then rebut his arguments with alternate research? Those who objected to what he had to say could have chosen to stay away and even warn others of his views. Or even better, they could have invited another speaker to respond to his presentation. But no—Murray's speech had to be shut down by violence. No rebuttal of his proposed theories is needed; violence is deemed to be an acceptable substitute for rational thought.

In incidents such as these, the college or university usually issues a statement that begins, "We believe in the right of free speech, but…" and then gives a list of reasons for banning free speech. Then the administration almost always panders to the students' protests, no matter how outrageous, by stating that "we need to have a further conversation."

The loss of our freedoms can take an unusual twist. The lawsuit *Christian Legal Society v. Martinez* arose when University of California, Hastings College of the Law insisted that the Christian Legal Society could not require its leaders to adhere to a certain set of beliefs and behaviors, but had to be open to all students, without discrimination. This means, among other things, that an atheist could become president of the Christian Legal Society on that campus. This action on the part of the university was a denial of freedom of association and the free exercise of religion. The notion that student groups at the university can have no religious, political, or moral requirements for leadership defies common sense and defeats the very purpose of such groups.

What lies at the center of campus intolerance? Heather Mac Donald writes, "At its center is a worldview that sees Western culture as endemically racist and sexist. The overriding goal of the educational establishment is to teach young people within the ever-growing list of official victim classifications to view themselves as existentially oppressed. One outcome of that teaching is the forceful silencing of contrarian speech."[28]

You will recognize that the arguments against free speech are basically the same ones that the Communists used during their reign of terror in Russia and Eastern Europe. The argument is simple: Free speech would undermine the rights of the oppressed and the poor, whom the state desires to help. Free speech must be outlawed for the good of the people—that is, so that the rights of *all* the people would be equally represented. Capitalists should not be allowed to argue against the socialists; Christians should not challenge atheism. And free thinkers do not have the right to argue that there are ways the state might do a better job of serving the populace. Free speech would disrupt the Communist vision of bringing "equality" to all groups and would disrupt the unity of the body politic.

Please hear me when I say that students *should* be taught to be respectful of different races and different views of race, sexuality, and political affiliations. Free speech should not mean that we can call people names, demean them, and use obscenities. But nor should people be coddled to the point that their egos are so fragile that an alternate point of view, even if legitimately and thoughtfully presented, should never be given a fair hearing.

Too often, shaming and blaming have replaced listening and reasoning.

The Effects of Intolerance

Since the 1970s, the radical movement has been establishing a political base in our universities, purging conservative faculty and texts and transforming scholarly disciplines into political training courses. These leftist indoctrination programs were described in the previous chapter as oppression studies, social justice studies, feminist studies, whiteness studies, and the like.

Seldom do I agree with Andrew Sullivan, a principled liberal and prominent activist who recently felt impelled to sound an alarm. He pointed out that this radical movement posed an existential threat to the American order of pluralism and individual freedom:

> When elite universities shift their entire worldview away from liberal education, as we have long known it, toward the imperatives of an identity-based "social justice" movement, the broader culture is in danger of drifting away from liberal democracy as well. If elites believe

that the core truth of our society is a system of inter-locking and oppressive power structures based around immutable characteristics like race or sex or sexual orien-tation, then sooner rather than later, this will be reflected in our culture at large. What matters most of all in these colleges—your membership in a group that is embed-ded in a hierarchy of oppression—will soon enough be what matters in the society as a whole.

Sullivan went on to describe how this notion constituted an assault on the fundamental American principle of the freedom and equal-ity of individuals:

The whole concept of an individual who exists apart from group identity is slipping from the discourse. The idea of individual merit—as opposed to various forms of unearned "privilege"—is increasingly suspect. The Enlightenment principles that formed the bedrock of the American experiment—untrammeled free speech, due process, individual (rather than group) rights—are now routinely understood as mere masks for "white male" power, code words for the oppression of women and nonwhites. Any differences in outcome for various groups must always be a function of "hate," rather than a function of nature or choice or freedom or individual agency. And anyone who questions these assertions is obviously a white supremacist himself.[29]

It is strange indeed that in this century we would have to actually defend freedom of speech, a right that has been hard won even to the point of bloodshed. If the Enlightenment taught us anything, it is that freedom of speech came about through a willingness of those who held opposing viewpoints to engage in argument, discussion, and heated debate.

Arguments in Favor of Free Speech

We live in an "offended generation." We are being told that everyone's right to free speech should be curtailed so as not to offend anyone. Offensive speech, no matter how politely or reasonably spoken, is to be shut down.

Islam takes this to an extreme and represses free speech wherever it prevails. Ever since 2008, The Organization of Islamic Countries (OIC) has wanted to pass legislation through the United Nations that would make all criticism of Islam a crime. So-called "blasphemy laws" in many Muslim countries criminalize all criticisms of Islam, often treating such criticisms as a capital crime.[30] Even to be a silent Christian is to be blasphemous because Christians believe in the Trinity and the Sonship of Jesus Christ. No religion in all the world is as repressive as Islam. Sadly, even in Western nations, being critical of Islam is politically incorrect and condemned.

No one knows more about the intolerance of Islam than Salman Rushdie, the novelist who was put under a fatwa—that is, a Muslim sentence to death. His crime: writing about what are called "the Satanic Verses" found in the Qur'an. Ten years after the fatwa was announced, it was lifted, but to this day Rushdie shows up in public with a heavy guard.

Rushdie's defense of free speech is a classic; he rightly argues that freedom of speech means the right to offend others. "The idea that any kind of free society can be constructed in which people will never be offended or insulted is absurd."

He continues:

> A fundamental decision needs to be made: do we want to live in a free society or not? Democracy is not a tea party where people sit around making polite conversation. In democracies people get extremely upset with

each other. They argue vehemently against each other's positions.

Notice his clarity of thought:

> People have the fundamental right to take an argument to the point where somebody is offended by what they say. It is no trick to support the free speech of somebody you agree with or to whose opinion you are indifferent. The defense of free speech begins at the point where people say something you can't stand. If you can't defend their right to say it, then you don't believe in free speech. You only believe in free speech as long as it doesn't get up your nose.[31]

This statement should be written across the entry hallway of every college and university: *You don't believe in free speech unless you give others the right to offend you by what they say.*

The arguments in favor of free speech go back to the Reformation, when Martin Luther stood against some 1,000 years of church control and asserted his right to disagree with popes and councils. The biblical doctrine of the priesthood of the believer opened the door to freedom of conscience and expression. These ideas were expanded in the Enlightenment. Men like John Locke argued that reason is essential for knowing reality and is part of who we are as individuals. The freedom to think, interact, criticize, and discuss issues is essential for the common good. And when you consider those studies that are especially intended to further knowledge—the scientific, philosophical, and religious studies—freedom of speech is essential. Free speech is the basis for our other freedoms.

George Orwell, whom all of us should be reading, said it best: "If liberty means anything at all, it means the right to tell people what they do not want to hear."[32] That is worth repeating: *If liberty means anything at all, it means the right to tell people what they don't want to hear.*

Clearly, the radical left despises liberty. The possibility that they might hear something that is offensive or that does not conform to their cherished beliefs makes them retreat into "safe places" where they can deal with what they view as their marginalization and unappreciated victimhood. They long for an echo chamber where they hear only the sound of their own voices and grievances.

Here is the irony: The censurers—the radicals who are all too ready to deny freedom to those who disagree with them—are perceived in our culture as being tolerant, while those who desire to adhere to Christian or traditional views are considered intolerant. In other words, the philosophy of the left is this: *Preach tolerance, but practice inflexible intolerance against anyone who has the courage to express a different point of view.*

Herbert Marcuse and Stanley Fish both took advantage of freedom of speech when they wrote their books against freedom of speech. The very freedom they enjoyed was won at high cost. They wanted to deny to others the very right that allowed them to express their perspective via their writings and lectures.

Free speech has always been one of the most hallowed freedoms in America. Frederick Douglass declared in 1860 that "slavery cannot tolerate free speech. Five years of its exercise would banish the auction block and break every chain in the South."

Douglass said these words at a time when newspapers were supporting a ban on abolitionist speech. After he was attacked by a mob, Douglass warned that "liberty is meaningless where the right to utter one's thoughts and opinions has ceased to exist. That, of all rights, is the dread of tyrants. It is the one right which they first of all strike down."[33]

Free speech is the dread of tyrants!

The Response of the Church

This is not a moment for timid souls.

Boldness comes easily when you are in the presence of those who agree with you; it is difficult when you are standing alone in the midst of people who seek your demise. Boldness behind a pulpit is one thing; boldness in a city council meeting is another. Boldness is seen most clearly when you have burned the bridge that would have enabled you to retreat to safety.

There are two ways culture attempts to intimidate Christians. One is to criminalize what they say or do, and the other is to shame them. Many Christians will not be *talked* out of their faith, but they will be *mocked* out of it. Shame will cause many Christians to retreat into silence.

Hate speech legislation will effectively make our witness illegal. For Christians to speak against the culture will be defined as hate, and hate has no place in a civil debate. Canada already has hate speech laws. Christian pastors are forbidden to preach against same-sex marriage on television, and one man, Mark Harding, was sentenced to 340 hours of sensitivity training by an imam for speaking out against Islam.[34]

Is free speech important?

Obviously, free speech laws in Western nations have supported Christians in spreading the gospel throughout the world. Free speech is a special gift that is underappreciated by all of us. But historically, for most of 2,000 years, the church has had to survive without freedom of speech. Opposition to free speech began early in the history of the church. Shortly after the church was birthed, to preach in the name of Jesus was considered forbidden speech; it was hate speech that carried the penalty of imprisonment and sometimes even death.

Take time to reread Acts 4. Peter and John performed a miracle in the name of Jesus. But the authorities were not pleased. For this the two were arrested. When asked to defend themselves, Peter boldly proclaimed that the miracle was performed in the name of "Jesus Christ of Nazareth, whom you crucified…for there is no other name under heaven given among men by which we must be saved" (Acts 4:10, 12).

No political correctness here. "By your agreement, you let Jesus be crucified, and if you don't believe in Him, you have no salvation!"

The martyrs before us have shown
that it is not necessary to have free
speech in order to be faithful.

When Peter and John were threatened and warned to no longer speak in the name of Jesus, they answered, "Whether it is right in the sight of God to listen to you rather than to God, you must judge, for we cannot but speak of what we have seen and heard" (verses 19-20). Take it or leave it—your threats will not keep us from preaching the gospel!

The martyrs before us have shown that it is not necessary to have free speech in order to be faithful. Richard Wurmbrand, in *Tortured for Christ*, wrote about parents who taught their children the Christian faith. "If it was discovered that they taught their children about Christ, their children were taken away from them for life—with no visitation rights."[35]

God is humbling us. In the 1980s, we looked to the Moral Majority to halt America's moral and spiritual toboggan slide. We looked to the courts and to the White House. But bit by bit, our culture is silencing our witness. Students in today's universities face challenges that previous generations have never had. I attended university at a time when we could share our faith freely, when various political and religious groups could meet on campus. I attended at a time when you could either ignore those with whom you disagreed or dialogue with them. There was a general willingness to discuss points of disagreement. The adage "I may disagree with what you say, but will fight to the death for you to have the right to say it" was accepted as the norm.

Those days are gone—not just in our universities, but also in the workforce, in the military, and sadly, even in our churches. And where laws are not yet in place to limit free speech, we are tempted to self-censor what we say. Or at least there are many who stand ready to accuse us of being guilty, unloving, and intolerant.

Of course, our speech must be with grace seasoned with salt. We don't shout at passersby (as I saw an angry evangelist do in Zurich, Switzerland, years ago). Free speech does not mean that we speak judgmentally to our nation as if we are free from our own weaknesses and sins. We give reason for the hope within us with respect, meekness, and fear (see 1 Peter 3:15).

One of my heroes is the sixteenth-century Reformer Hugh Latimer. When asked to preach in front of King Henry VIII, he struggled with exactly what to say. You'll recall that Henry had the reputation of chopping off the heads of his enemies, including two of his wives.

As he spoke, Latimer struggled within himself, "Latimer! Latimer! Do you remember that you are speaking before the high and mighty King Henry VIII; who has the power to command you to be sent to prison, and how he can have your head cut off, if it please him? Will you not take care to say nothing that will offend royal ears?"

He paused for a moment, then continued, "Latimer! Latimer! Do you not remember that you are speaking before the King of kings and Lord of lords; before Him, at whose throne Henry VIII will stand; before Him, to whom one day you also will have to give account yourself? Latimer! Latimer! Be faithful to your Master, and declare all of God's Word."[36]

Latimer did declare God's Word, and although Henry spared his life, Henry's daughter, Queen Mary (Bloody Mary), had him burned at the stake in Oxford. As he was dying amid the flames, he called out to Bishop Ridley, who was also consigned to the flames with him, and is quoted as saying, "Master Ridley, play the man; we shall this day light such a candle, by God's grace, in England, as I trust shall never be put out."[37]

The secret of boldness? Fear God more than the flames. Fear Him more than your reputation. Let us be done with fainthearted, tepid leadership. Ours is the day to "play the man" with bold, uncompromising truth and love, risking it all for God.

We can expect views that differ from those of the thought police will be boycotted, shamed, and outed. But we will not be silenced. We will endure the shame, the ridicule, and the penalties.

We will be heard, and we pray that the church will speak with one voice.

A Prayer All of Us Must Pray

Father, we pray words taken from a prayer meeting held in the early church:

> *Sovereign Lord, who made the heaven and the earth and the sea and everything in them...for truly in this city there were gathered together against your holy servant Jesus, whom you anointed, both Herod and Pontius Pilate, along with the Gentiles and the peoples of Israel, to do whatever your hand and your*

plan had predestined to take place. And now, Lord, look upon their threats and grant to your servants to continue to speak your word with all boldness *(Acts 4:24, 27-29).*

Let us give a reason for the hope within us with meekness and fear (1 Peter 3:15). Let us humbly stand for truth and leave the consequences in Your hands. Teach us when to speak and when to be silent; may we be as "wise as serpents and innocent as doves" (Matthew 10:16).

Let us not shout, but let us speak.

In Jesus' name, amen.

CHAPTER 5

Sell It as a Noble Cause

Propaganda can change the direction of a nation.

In Oceania, George Orwell's chilling totalitarian state in the novel *1984*, we have a compelling description of how the so-called Ministry of Truth used a subtle, sinister language, Newspeak, to brainwash the people. The slogan of Oceania is "War is peace; freedom is slavery; ignorance is strength."[1] The Thought Police were able to control the ideas that determined the political and moral views of the culture.

The withdrawal of individual freedoms was sold to the population as a plus. Slavery to the state was presented as the gateway to freedom and prosperity. Conquest was sold as liberation. Everything done was always for "the good of the people." I personally remember visiting several of Adolf Hitler's concentration camps, described as freedom camps. The entry gates bore the slogan *Arbeit macht frei*—"Work sets you free."

Newspeak, Doublethink, Thought Police, Big Brother—all of these words and phrases have entered our vocabulary thanks to

George Orwell. His writings, perhaps like no other, exposed how propaganda is used to control a totalitarian state. He offered insights that all of us must read.

The purpose of propaganda is to change people's perception of reality so that despite compelling counterevidence, people will not change their minds. The goal is to make people impervious to facts, scientific proof, and common sense. Of course, sometimes facts and scientific proof can be subject to interpretation. But often obvious arguments are set aside because people believe what they want to believe even in the face of mounting contrary evidence. Someone has said that the ultimate goal of propaganda is that we behave like a child with a finger in each ear, shouting, "I don't hear you!"

And when the radicals do hear a viewpoint that challenges their beliefs, they often "dox" the person who is saying it. They attempt to find some damaging personal information about the person and then put it on social media. This conveniently "cancels" the need to deal with the issues that challenge their thinking. In other words, "I don't like the message, so I will just destroy the messenger." Their response is outrage rather than rational arguments.

Only the power of propaganda can account for movements that clamor for defunding the police and vilify law enforcement officers as a great threat to our society while, at the same time, excusing or even defending anarchists. All this is happening at a time when crime rates are spiking in our cities and people fear that they will have to defend themselves when the mob arrives at their door. The destruction of law and order is sold under the banner of progress. And, of course, the very noble goal of *justice*.

Propaganda is used by every political party of whatever stripe. You and I may resort to propaganda when we attempt to sell an idea or seek to defend ourselves. When God condemned Adam for eating the fruit of the forbidden tree, Adam blamed Eve for his actions.

What he said was not exactly false, but it was not the whole story. He used language in a futile attempt to change the reality of what happened. *Spin.*

In the garden, the serpent enticed Adam and Eve with fruit that looked good in order to give them something bad. The devil appealed to their desires rather than their minds; he knew appetites can be more powerful than reason. Like a trapper who offers meat but conceals a deadly trap underneath, so propaganda lures us into believing we are getting one thing but in reality, we are getting another. Behind the trap is the trapper, and behind the lie is the liar.

In this chapter we will look at how a radical agenda is crafted to deceive people. We will see how the bizarre has to be normalized in the guise of bringing freedom, and reality has to be denied to persuade people to accept an alternate "truth."

As Christians, we need to become better at recognizing propaganda and identifying its most egregious uses in our culture, the media, and social networks. We should do our best to understand how we are being manipulated unawares, and how we might also be manipulating others. And we should be willing to change our minds if the evidence warrants it.

How Propaganda Works

Edward Bernays, in his book *Propaganda*, defends the use of propaganda and the need for the "intelligent manipulation" of the masses. He explains, "Those who manipulate this unseen mechanism of society constitute an invisible government which is the true ruling power of our country."[2]

Bernays writes that "we are governed, our minds molded, our tastes formed, our ideas suggested, largely by men we have never heard of...It is they who pull the wires which control the public mind, who harness old social forces and contrive new ways to bind and guide the world."[3]

Look more closely at his description: Propaganda is "an unseen mechanism," "an invisible government," it includes "new ways to bind and guide" us. It controls what we think *without us knowing that we are being controlled.*

Propaganda takes many different forms. Sometimes it hides the truth; sometimes it uses half-truths; sometimes it distorts the truth by the selective use of facts or history, or it uses one-sided assertions. Almost always it seeks to present its argument by appealing to a higher goal, such as "the common good" or "it's a matter of rights" or "justice." It claims the high moral ground and is sold as a noble cause.

Appealing to a Higher Goal

As an example, let us consider how a tobacco company convinced women that they should smoke and do so in public. Until about 1926, it was considered improper for women to smoke publicly. George Washington Hill's American Tobacco Company (which included the brand Lucky Strike) hired Edward Bernays to change this unwanted impediment to their business. If they could convince women to smoke openly, they might almost double their business.

Bernays, who combined his philosophies of propaganda with psychology (his uncle was Sigmund Freud), came up with an ingenious idea: Remind women that they are oppressed, and call cigarettes their "torches of freedom."

In 1929, they gathered a group of women who marched in New York's Easter Sunday parade while smoking, proudly displaying their "torches of freedom." For women, smoking publicly now became a symbol of nonconformity, of independence and strength. It was a sign of rebellion against male dominance.

Nothing, of course, was said about the negative effects of smoking, its addictive power, and its connections with lung disease (to be fair, back in those days, these effects were not widely known). But when smoking became a symbol of equality and liberation for women, Lucky Strike found a new and lucrative market. And the rest is history.

From now on, advertising would be based not only on *need*, but *desire*. In this way, people would be turned into consumers and keep buying what they didn't need. New cars would be sold to men as symbols of masculinity or sexuality; women would be willing to buy very uncomfortable clothes and wear them proudly if only to be in style. And because the styles were constantly changing, they would almost continually be buying what they didn't need in order to remain fashionable. In advertising, hidden desires are constantly exploited to make us want what we don't need.

Translate this into our moral climate. Any cause can appear legitimate if it is tied to some noble idea. Even evil, if packaged correctly, can appear to be good, and good can be packaged as evil. Isaiah wrote, "Woe to those who call evil good and good evil, who put darkness for light and light for darkness, who put bitter for sweet and sweet for bitter!" (5:20).

Radical secularists strategize on how to call that which is evil good, but even then their task is not yet finished. They must not only call evil good, but they must also call good evil. Only then are they able to sell their agenda. This is done not by rational argument but by appealing to human desire. When Edmond White, coauthor of *The Joy of Gay Sex*, proposed that "gay men should wear their sexually transmitted diseases like red badges of courage in a war against a sex-negative society,"[4] he gave an example of how even the most sordid and self-destructive behavior can be sold as empowerment. Sell something as liberation, and you will probably succeed. Control the language, and you control the debate.

Saul Alinsky, the Marxist radical, told his followers how to mask their real agenda. Speaking of the current political structure, he said, "They have the guns and therefore we are for peace and for reformation through the ballot. When we have the guns then it will be through the bullet."[5]

Note the deception: For now, let us be in favor of peace and reformation until we are in power. Then we'll abandon the *ballot box* in favor of the *bullet.*

Preach noble goals. Hide your end game.

Using Slogans to Mask Evil

Slogans are often used to mask sinister evil.

An extreme example of this was when Hitler starved children—he called it "putting them on a low-calorie diet." The extermination of Jews was called "cleansing the land." Euthanasia was referred to as "the best of modern therapy." Children deemed unsuitable for society were put to death in "children's specialty centers." Hitler's cronies did not publicly proclaim they were going to kill people. Even when they made plans to exterminate millions, the Nazi leaders spoke in abstract slogans such as "the final solution." Sanitized terms were used to camouflage unspeakable crimes. Evil was described in clinical terms.

Radical Muslims call the horrors of shariah law a new form of liberation, and the cruelty of conquering armies is said to bring peace. Christians sold into slavery are innocuously categorized as a protected people. Chasing Christians out of their homes is called justifiable resettlement, and torture for believing in the deity of Christ is honorable for the sake of Allah.

James Lindsay, in a lecture titled "The Truth About Critical Methods," says of those who propound social justice that *the label on the box does not match the contents inside.* The label might say

"Social Justice," but when you open the box, you find something different. You discover that it is about deconstructing everything in society and seeking to overthrow the existing order; it is about a grab for power.[6]

During the race riots of 2020, the slogan "No justice, no peace" was used to justify violence, theft, and mayhem. The cause was believed to be righteous, so in the words of one radical, "If this country doesn't give us what we want, then we will burn down this system...I just want Black liberation and Black sovereignty—by any means necessary."[7]

Slogans are actively used by those who are pro-abortion to advance their cause. Those who oppose abortion are described as being "at war with women." Pro-abortion advocates are "protecting women's health" and sponsor the "Reproductive Health Act," which will legally protect a woman's "right to make her own health-care decisions" right up to the point of the infant's birth.

"Reproductive health care" or "reproductive justice" or "terminating a pregnancy"—all of these are code for killing preborn infants. Politicians speak of being in favor of "a woman's right to choose...," but they seldom complete the sentence. Somehow to say they are in favor of a woman's right to choose to kill her preborn infant is too honest, too clear—and too *chilling*.

When the government in Australia chose to legalize abortion, it did so by simply saying that it would no longer be a legal issue, but a health issue. Officials were simply implementing what they said was reproductive justice. Yet no justice was given to the unborn because they are powerless; they are unable to vote. Preborn infants are viewed as expendable if they are going to interfere with the lifestyle of the child's mother and father. In today's throwaway culture, whatever stands in the way of a person's sexual freedom and personal convenience must be discarded, and with the help of slogans, this can be done *justly*. If a late-term baby still manages to survive an abortion attempt and be born, it will be given "comfort care" as it is left to starve to death. Hitler would have put it more delicately: "We will just put the baby on a low-calorie diet."

More about the man who mastered propaganda.

Hitler, Propaganda, and the Power of Hate

Please understand that I am *not* calling the radical secularists Nazis (too often, *Nazi* is a label given to anyone with whom we have a disagreement). But I do want to refer to Hitler's view of propaganda because homosexual activists admit that their ideas of how to use propaganda were borrowed from him. For example, Eric Pollard, the founder of ACT-UP (a militant homosexual group), writes that lying was a tactic used by homosexual activists, and he references Hitler's book *Mein Kampf* as a model that provided strategies for the group.[8] Hitler himself said, "By clever and persevering use of propaganda even heaven can be represented as hell to the people, and conversely the most wretched life as paradise."[9]

Yes, there are ways that heaven can be represented as hell and hell as heaven. "The German people must be misled if the support of the masses is required," Hitler said.[10]

Let's pause and discuss Hitler's strategic use of propaganda in Germany. All the studies I have read indicate that the people of Nazi Germany were ordinary citizens capable of sympathy and a willingness to help their neighbors. They appeared to be no different than the people who live in the flyover parts of the United States. There was only one way for Hitler to mobilize these people to join his cause. *Hate* would do what reason could not. And *fear* would make certain that everyone fell in lockstep.

"Hate," Hitler said, was "more enduring than aversion [dislike]."[11]

He said he used emotion (hatred) to rile up the masses, while reason was reserved for just a few. Hitler knew that propaganda was important for preparing people for something much more drastic—namely, a revolution that would send them down a different path. "The most striking success of a revolution" he wrote, "will always have been achieved when the new philosophy of life as far as possible has been taught to all men, *and, if necessary, later forced upon them.*"[12] Yes, what begins as the sharing of information is eventually forced upon people. And those who objected were either thrown into prison, killed, or shamed into silence.

Targeting an enemy (the Jews) would unify the Germans, who then turned to Hitler as their economic and political "savior." So Germans were given reasons to hate the Jews, to hate democracy, and to hate anyone who disagreed with them. Stories of Jewish influence were used selectively and put in the worst light possible. Jews were described as treasonous, vermin, and subhuman. It was said that their betrayal caused Germany to lose World War I. Furthermore, Hitler falsely accused them of plotting to take over Germany economically.

Once the Jews were seen as a hated enemy, genocide could be sold both as necessary and desirable. Hate could do what reason could not. "He who spoke the words of Jesus," said Robert Waite, "hated all mankind."[13] If hate did not keep people in line, fear would. Losing your job, being dismissed from school, or being sent to prison was reserved for people who dared to think and speak for themselves.

In brief, Nazism created a parallel universe that identified enemy targets—namely Communism and the Jews—who were seen as the real reasons for Germany's woes. Science was then recruited to show that the Jews were subhuman. Driven by slogans and symbolism, the Nazi agenda moved forward. All was done for a noble goal, "for the good of the people." Hitler knew that people would set aside reason in favor of an irrational national pride, the culmination of which eventually brought about World War II.

How powerful is propaganda? William Shirer, who lived in Germany as a correspondent, wrote this in his classic *The Rise and the Fall of the Third Reich*:

> I myself was to experience how easily one is taken in by a lying and censored press and radio in a totalitarian state. Though unlike most Germans I had daily access to foreign newspapers, especially those of London, Paris and Zurich, which arrived the day after publication, and though I listened regularly to the BBC and other foreign broadcasts, my job necessitated the spending of many hours a day in combing the German press, checking the German radio, conferring with Nazi officials and going to party meetings. It was surprising and sometimes consternating to find that notwithstanding the opportunities I had to learn the facts and despite one's inherent distrust of what one learned from Nazi sources, a steady diet over the years of falsifications and distortions made a certain impression on one's mind and often misled it...I would meet with the most outlandish assertions from seemingly educated and intelligent persons. It was obvious that they were parroting some piece of nonsense they had heard on the radio or read in the newspapers. Sometimes one was tempted to say as much, but...one realized how useless it was even to try to make contact with a mind which had become warped and for whom the facts of life had become what Hitler and Goebbels, with their cynical disregard for truth, said they were.[14]

Notice—"one realized how useless it was to try to make contact with a mind which had become warped and for whom the facts of life had become what Hitler and Goebbels, with their cynical disregard for truth, said they were."

Creating a Cultural Stream

William Sargant, in his 1957 book *Battle for the Mind: A Physiology of Conversion and Brain-Washing*, wrote that people have "temporarily impaired judgment" and have "herd instinct" seen most clearly in "wartime, severe epidemics, and in all similar periods of common danger, which increase anxiety and individual mass suggestibility."[15]

Sargant was right. He correctly identified a pandemic as one of the times when people will display "temporarily impaired judgment." During the COVID-19 crisis, people were willing to give their private health information to unknown "contact tracers" so they could be informed whether they had been in close proximity to someone who tested positive for the virus. The plan is that eventually this information would be so accurate authorities would know which seat you sat in during a movie and who was around you. Of course, for now, officials are assuring us of our privacy, but this is the way that mass surveillance begins. The Chinese have surveillance that is far more detailed with information on what you believe, where you go, and who your friends are. And participation is mandatory.

As of this writing, there is no cure for COVID-19, so we must wait and see what happens when a vaccine is found. Will it be mandated, and our personal information stored in a massive database? We will have to wait and see.

According to an article titled "ID2020 Launches Technical Certificate Mark," there is an organization that brings together the various tech companies along with economists who insist that every human being receive a "digital certificate" as a legal document that would ensure that each person is properly identified. This certificate would record all your pertinent information, including your education, your profession, your wealth or lack of it. It is said this would bring about the socialist vision of the rich helping the poor and the excluded being welcomed into the world community. A digital chip would be used to keep track of all of your financial transactions and show that you are in compliance with the new economic order. And of course, we can be quite sure that such a chip would document proof that you have had your COVID-19 vaccine.

And what else? Let me quote: "With the application processes developed for the Certification Mark we will have enough data points and input to take a pretty good snapshot. And if we ever learn about (or suspect) non-compliance or foul play, we reserve the right to revoke the certification."[16] In other words, comply or else. And you can't argue with a computer. Will fear compel us to sign up despite the obvious threat of menacing surveillance?

We also saw a "herd instinct" become evident during the COVID-19 pandemic when health professionals changed their minds about the relative value of human life over racial demonstrations. For months, health professionals warned that we should self-quarantine and that if we went outside without a mask and practicing social distancing, we were putting other people's lives in danger. We were, in effect, potentially guilty of murder.

But once the riots began, ideology triumphed over public health. Health professionals came up with a different message. A June 5, 2020 CNN article was titled "Over 1,000 health professionals sign a letter saying, Don't shut down protests using coronavirus concerns as an excuse."[17]

Some political leaders who lectured us for months about social distancing joined the protests and publicly bowed the knee in the presence of radicals without wearing masks and practicing social distancing. They were virtue signaling that they were on board with the protests, which were more important than people's safety from a destructive virus.

A population in panic mode
is easily led. Or rather, misled.

Hitler knew that a mass movement could create impaired judgment and herd instinct. And he knew that doubters who were unconvinced would find themselves to be a minority in the midst of a zealous majority. Such a mass movement would cause doubters to succumb to what he called "the magic influence of what we designate as 'mass suggestion.'"[18] And the few voices that dare to speak out against this "magic influence" of mass suggestion are either dismissed or, more ominously, reviled. Or forever silenced.

A population in panic mode is easily led. Or rather, misled.

The Power of Collective Demonization

China, Russia, Germany, and many other countries have experienced cultural streams fueled by propaganda that enflamed both hate and fear.

Izabella Tabarovsky, who immigrated to the United States from Russia and understands Marxism all too well, wrote, "Collective demonizations of prominent cultural figures were an integral part of the Soviet culture of denunciation that pervaded every workplace and apartment building." She goes on to speak about all who mouthed the made-up charges against writers and intellectuals whom the Soviet state chose to demonize: "Some of the greatest names in Soviet culture became targets of collective condemnations." Whether people agreed with the state or not, what they said had to line up with the party dictums or they would be subject to shame, humiliation, or worse.

Tabarovsky then gives an example of this collective demonization taking place here in the United States. She referenced the fiasco at *The New York Times* when opinion editor James Bennett had to resign for allowing an article to be published that was written by a sitting conservative senator, Tom Cotton.[19] Tabarovsky commented about this incident, saying, "When…the price of nonconformity is being publicly humiliated, expelled from the community of 'people of goodwill' (another Soviet cliché) and cut off from sources of income, the powers that be need to work less hard to enforce the rules."[20]

Diversity of opinion is demonized. James Bennett had to go.

Hitler and his ilk perfected collective demonization against the Jews and any other perceived enemies. This tapped into the depths of people's hatred and instilled fear into the hearts of those who didn't join his revolution. All this happened in an atmosphere of euphoric nationalism. One woman who lived through that time said to me, "You Americans will never understand the euphoria Hitler created. People prayed to him." People went to the Nazi rallies in Nuremberg as skeptics and returned saying, "Our father, Adolf, who art in Nuremberg, the Third Reich come."

No doubt Freud was wrong about many things, but he was right when he said human beings do not always make their decisions based on reason, but on *desire*; he who stirs up the most passions wins. A desperate people will cling to delusional promises. And you had best get on board.

Perhaps the most enduring lesson of Nazi Germany is that when propaganda is used to target an enemy and offer false promises, ordinary people can become a part of an evil cultural movement that sets reason aside in favor of irrational hopes and hidden desires. Hate and fear will do wonders.

Just ask Dietrich Bonhoeffer or Martin Niemöller how much it costs to withstand a cultural revolution among a people who are willing to abandon reason in order to avoid collective demonization. Propaganda can do what reason cannot.

And today, social media is used to vilify anyone who steps out of line.

Propaganda and the Sexual Revolution

As mentioned, the radicals admit to taking a page out of Hitler's playbook.

Following Hitler, the radical left believes that hate is more powerful than mere dislike. They don't say, "You disagree with me and I think you are wrong," but rather, "You disagree with me and you are evil." Thanks to social media, everyone is outraged about something or someone. Everyone has a grievance that needs resolution. As George Orwell is credited with saying, "The further a society drifts from the truth, the more it will hate those who speak it."

In 1987, homosexual activists Marshall Kirk and Hunter Madsen published an article titled, "The Overhauling of Straight America," and in 1989, they came out with the book *After the Ball*. A summary of their strategy is given in the excellent book *The Homosexual Agenda* by Alan Sears and Craig Osten. Here are some of the details of how they planned to change people's attitudes about homosexuality.

Lying was essential to their stated agenda to "overhaul straight America." They wrote that homosexuals must always be portrayed in positive light, saying, "It makes no difference that the ads [portraying homosexuals as icons of normality] are lies, not to us…nor to bigots."[21]

Desensitization was critical to change the opinion of Americans. Homosexuals should talk about gays and gayness as loudly and as often as possible. Kirk and Madsen wrote, "…almost any behavior begins to look normal if you are exposed to enough of it at close quarters and among your acquaintances."[22]

Intimidation and victimhood were essential. Homosexuals were to be portrayed as victims, not aggressive challengers, a strategy designed to play to most Americans' desire for fairness and a willingness to stand up for those who are oppressed. Kirk and Madsen continued, "A media campaign that casts gays as society's victims and encourages straights to be their protectors must make it easier for those who respond to assert that and explain their new perspectives."[23]

Next came the vilification of those who disagreed with them. Kirk and Madsen wrote, "We intend to make the anti-gays look so nasty that average Americans will want to disassociate themselves from such types."[24]

Here is one of the oldest schemes of propaganda: The radicals ignore what those who disagree with them are actually saying, finding it easier to simply dismiss them as "haters." The radicals themselves may be very hateful, but their hate is justified because they are *fighting* hate. Anyone who disagrees with them has no valid arguments; they just have a bigoted psychological condition that is hateful.

Once a cultural stream of propaganda
is created, no matter how irrational,
we all fear to speak against it.

Once a cultural stream of propaganda is created, no matter how irrational, we all fear to speak against it. Those who dare to disagree are shamed into silence.

Sell It as a Civil Right

Most Americans probably would not agree with the normalization of homosexual relationships unless it was sold as a noble cause. The advocates had to find a way to say they were taking the high moral ground; of course, the answer was to link the cause of same-sex marriage to civil rights. By reminding people of the great struggles of black Americans for equal rights, they joined one cause to the other.

Today, it's transgenderism that is being sold as a civil right. In the excellent book *When Harry Became Sally*, which exposes the agenda of the transgender movement, Ryan T. Anderson writes, "But political and cultural elites have tried to shut down the discussion before it starts by imposing a politically correct orthodoxy on the nation, an ideology in which 'gender identity' is both a subjective matter and a category meriting civil rights protection."[25] Civil rights protection is required; the right for a man to identify as a woman or vice versa is equated with black Americans' fight for freedom. Thus, the fight for "marriage equality."

This is a serious example of false equivalency. Pastor Bill Owen of Memphis, a black pastor who marched with Dr. Martin Luther King Jr. and knew the suffering that resulted from segregation, deeply resents this identification. In his book *A Dream Derailed*, he writes,

> It is a disgrace and a lie to say that blacks marched so that gays would have the right to marry today...I marched during the civil rights movement with many people who were as shocked as I was to hear gay and transgender rights

> being equated with civil rights for blacks. Not one person
> I have spoken to from back in the days of the civil rights
> marches has agreed with this comparison...What do the
> struggles of black Americans to be treated as humans have
> to do with men who claim to be women invading the dig-
> nity and privacy of women and girls in public spaces?[26]

Homosexuals and transgender persons have an important ally on their side—the media, which provides a platform for their propaganda. Sitcoms, movies, and documentaries are calculated to make the practice of homosexuality and transgenderism seem normal. With this barrage of media hype, we are either forced to accept their behavior as normal or we become weary of the battle and withdraw from the cultural debate.

Thus, the radical homosexuals, suavely cooperating with a willing media, keep pushing onto society as much as it will tolerate. Yes, history has shown it's true that "almost any behavior begins to look normal if you are exposed to enough of it at close quarters and among your acquaintances."[27] Sell it as equality, justice, civil rights, and love. The propaganda of today becomes the "truth" of tomorrow.

In Eden, the devil sold slavery to Adam and Eve, but called it independence; he sold them wisdom, but it turned out to be mental darkness; he put forth a beautiful vision of who they could become, but his offer was sweetly poisoned. He promised them fulfillment and gave them guilt. He appealed to their pride and gave them despair and an empty life. He promised like a god but paid them like the devil he was.

Sell It as Love and Compassion

Sell progressive Christianity as love, and you will attract many followers.

Eric Hoffer says that "propaganda does not deceive people; it merely helps them to deceive themselves."[28] People often do not perceive reality as it is but how they want it to be. By appealing to a false understanding of love, this enables people to call light darkness and darkness light. This detachment from reality under the banner of love enables people to normalize the bizarre and the unnatural.

"We need more love, not less!"

That's what the popular one-time preacher Rob Bell said in his defense of same-sex marriage. His book *Love Wins* is his story of how he came to abandon historic Christianity in favor of what he alleges is a more loving, tolerant, and accepting God. When love wins, homosexuals will have the right to marry one other, and hell will be redefined as "the terrible evil that comes from secrets hidden deep within our hearts."[29] When love wins, the gates of heaven are opened to a much wider audience than just those who believe in Christ. What a glorious day for all of us when love wins!

No wonder the leftists' agenda is proceeding at such a rapid pace. Once you say that your views are based on the high moral ground of love, everyone who doesn't agree with you must be filled with hate and irrational bigotry.

When Bishop Michael Curry preached his homily at Prince Harry and Meghan Markle's wedding in Windsor Castle, he said, "Where true love is found, God himself is there."[30] But for him, this "true love" includes immoral same-sex relationships. He speaks for many who appeal to love to justify what God condemns.

People don't realize that love can be sinful; it can be evil. When Adam and Eve disobeyed God in the Garden of Eden, they did not stop loving. Rather, they just stopped loving God, turning to love other things. They became lovers of themselves. "For people will be lovers of self, lovers of money, proud, arrogant, abusive, disobedient to their parents, ungrateful, unholy" (2 Timothy 3:2). And, as a commentary on our culture, they became "lovers of pleasure rather than lovers of God" (3:4).

We cannot take the word *love* and stretch it to justify sinful desires just because they are agreeable to us. "If you love me," said Jesus, "you will keep my commandments" (John 14:15). The progressives among us want to find beauty in the delusion that the pleasures of the flesh, divorced from God's design, can bring wholeness. But in moments of honesty, many admit that immoral relationships, no matter how deceitfully justified, lead to shame, self-loathing, deep pain, and regret.

Love and sympathy can be misused to override our better judgment. Parents have been known to abandon their biblical view of same-sex marriage when they discover that they have a child who claims to be gay. During the age of the judges, "everyone did what was right in his own eyes" (Judges 21:25). Their morality was based on love, compassion, justice, and fairness as they perceived it. The moral results were catastrophic.

This leads me to quote an observation that has been attributed to Winston Churchill: "The desire to believe something is much more persuasive than rational argument."

Gaslighting in Our Modern Culture

Gaslighting is a form of manipulation that "attempts to sow seeds of doubt in the target. It is used to make you question your memory, your perception, and your own sanity." In summary, *Psychology Today* defines it as "a tactic in which a person or entity, in order to gain more power, makes a victim question their reality."[31] The term originated in the systematic manipulation of a wife by her husband in the 1938 stage play *Gaslight* (subsequently adapted into a movie).

The purpose of gaslighting is to destabilize you, to make you question your judgment. A person who gaslights gives the impression that he or she knows more than you do. In other words, the messages sent are intended to distort the normal, the rational, and even scientific evidence that you intuitively thought you knew was true. As a result, decades of observation and research are discarded in favor of the modern ideological/cultural orthodoxy.

For example, I saw an ad that featured a teenage boy saying he was "having his period," so he was asking a store clerk for feminine products. Coca-Cola ran a Sprite ad in Argentina that celebrated mothers who helped their children to cross-dress.[32] Remember what Kirk and Madsen said: "Any behavior begins to look normal if you are exposed to enough of it at close quarters."[33]

The ACLU sent out this tweet on November 19, 2019:

> There's no one way to be a man.
> Men who get their periods are men.
> Men who get pregnant and give birth are men.
> Trans and non-binary men belong.
> #InternationalMensDay[34]

How many delusions do they expect us to believe?

The gaslighters know they are most effective when they can speak nonsense with authority. Debbie Mirza describes gaslighters this way:

> [They] will throw strong statements at you that make absolutely no sense and have no basis in reality, but they speak in such a strong and convincing way it makes you consider things that are so obviously false. Their accusations of you are almost as ludicrous as them saying you alone are responsible for the lack of affordable health care or the ice caps melting, and you take a moment to wonder if they are right. You do this because you have

been manipulated for a very long time. You have been brainwashed, and that takes time to unravel.[35]

Absurdity is no longer an argument against a point of view. If you are progressive, you have to detach from reality and self-righteously embrace the bizarre. This is the world of alternate facts, and the price one has to pay to see evil as good and good as evil.

No wonder George Orwell said that "to see what is in front of one's nose needs a constant struggle."[36] Today we are not allowed to see the obvious. We are to be good citizens carried along by a herd mentality; we are expected to accept a reality that is bent to suit an ideology.

Using Language to Destroy Gender

Zachary Evans writes,

> Merriam-Webster has updated its dictionary with an additional definition of "they," reflecting the word's increased usage as a pronoun that refers to those who conceive of themselves as neither male nor female, the company announced Monday on Twitter. The word "they" now has four definitions…[37]

The intention, of course is to use language to destroy gender; these types of changes are intended to deconstruct deeply held biblical truths about creation as well as science. Propaganda, remember, is able to take heaven and make it look like hell and make hell look like heaven.

Peggy Noonan wrote an excellent article about how pronouns are being manipulated to fit with the transgender cultural stream. She begins by pointing out that Robespierre, one of the leaders of the French Revolution, was a sociopath who used violence to accomplish his bloody ends. Violence was a source of the leaders' collective energy. Robespierre saw the French Revolution as an opportunity for the moral instruction of the nation. So he politicized reality by renaming it.

Then Noonan mentions The Inclusive Communications Task Force at Colorado State University, which has produced a speech guide. Don't call people "American," it directs: "This erases other cultures." Don't say a person is mad or a lunatic, call him "surprising/wild" or "sad." "Eskimo," "freshman" and "illegal alien" are out. "You guys" should be replaced by "all/folks." Don't say "male" or "female"; say "man," "woman" or "gender non-binary."

As Noonan points out, there is a special aspect of "self-infatuation, of arrogance, in telling people they must reorder the common language to suit your ideological preferences. There is something mad in thinking you should control the names of things. Or perhaps I mean surprising/wild." Ultimately, all of this is done with a tone of, "I am your moral teacher. Because you are incapable of sensitivity, I will help you, dumb farmer. I will start with the language you speak."

Noonan also addresses the insistence that everyone use gender-neutral pronouns. Businesses and schools are forced to grapple with properly using Zie, Sie, Zim, Em, Zir, Hir, Eirself, etc. It is also recommended that people use "their" and "they" because those terms are gender-neutral—even if such usage renders a sentence grammatically incorrect.

As a result, people are being urged to keep up with the ever-changing expectations of the cultural progressives and memorize what is appropriate or inappropriate—depending on the latest determinations of groups that perceive themselves as beleaguered.[38]

Changing Language to Lower the Crime Rate

Have you wondered why, when widespread rioting, looting, destruction, and arson occurs, progressive politicians ask the police to not intervene? These so-called progressives—the radical left—believe that if you are nice to criminals, they will be nice to you.

San Francisco has one of the highest crime rates of the 20 most populous cities in America,[39] and the thought police have found a way to reduce the crime: call it by a different name. The idea is that if we stop calling offenders criminals, they will behave much better.

The city is pushing for new language throughout the criminal justice system. In August 2019, a *San Francisco Chronicle* headline read, "SF Board of Supervisors sanitizes language of criminal justice system." And the headline on an article posted on Law Enforcement Today's website read: "San Francisco: No more 'convicted felons.' They're 'justice-involved' persons now."[40]

The thought police are alive and creative. From now on, a convicted felon will be referred to as "formerly incarcerated person" or "justice-involved person." Ex-cons are just "returning residents." Drug addicts and substance abusers simply have "a history of substance use" (not abuse). A parolee is a "person under supervision"; a delinquent is now "a person impacted by the justice system." Finally, a thief might be referred to as "a returning resident who was involved in the justice system who is currently under supervision with a history of substance abuse."

Why?

The goal is noble: No criminal is to be stigmatized. "We don't want people to be forever labeled for things that they have done," said the supervisor, Matt Haney. "We want them ultimately to become contributing citizens, and referring to them as felons is like a scarlet letter…"[41]

The idea is for criminals to feel better about themselves, and the hope is that if language decriminalizes those who break the law, they can no longer be labeled a criminal. The hope is that they will begin to see themselves in a better light and become productive citizens.

The naiveté of such reasoning staggers the imagination. One very serious consequence of playing such linguistic games is that it puts the man who rapes a woman on the same moral level as the innocent woman whose life he destroyed. Both end up being people who are "involved with the justice system."

There is another devastating consequence: This decriminalization language implies that the reason there are criminals is because of society. In other words, people do evil because of outside influences; there is no evil within them. In the past, the language we have employed has rightly identified individuals as being responsible for their actions. But the new terminology places the blame on the person who labels an offender a criminal or a felon.

The radical left is earnestly seeking to win the cultural debates by "sanitizing" the language we use, but this makes honest dialogue difficult, if not impossible. Their newly adopted terms force everyone to accommodate their way of thinking—and in this way, they achieve their goals in the culture wars.

The Response of the Church

Will we bow before the cultural streams fed by the propaganda of our media-driven, racially charged, and politically correct culture? Will the pressure be too great for us to resist?

Military leaders say that if France would have invaded Hitler's Germany in 1939, the Nazi insurgence would have been defeated. But the French military was in no mood to defend their country. A popular saying at the time was, "It is better to kneel speaking German than be killed speaking French."

We know what happened. A year later, Germany invaded France, and yes, many in France knelt before their German captors. They accepted their humiliation, but many were killed despite their submission to the Nazis. Looking back, I'm sure that many wished they had died speaking French rather than kneeling speaking German.

Will we bow when our reputations, vocations, and well-being are at risk? When it costs us vilification, fines, and even possible imprisonment? We must answer that question as individuals and corporately as a church.

We have to identify the lies in our racially overcharged, outraged, and sexually driven culture. Can we identify the wolves among the sheep and discern the false from the true even within the church? Ask yourself: Am I being manipulated to accept an unbiblical point of view? Are my opinions based on facts and truth, or are my beliefs based on emotion and a misunderstanding of compassion? Am I afraid to stand for truth?

At the same time, we must renew our commitment to integrity in our personal lives and ministries. German theologian Helmut Thielicke, it is said, told the story of riding his bicycle through Germany as a college student. One morning, after skipping breakfast, he rode past a shop with this sign on display: "Hot Rolls for Sale." He parked his bicycle, his hunger already generating saliva in his mouth. But to his dismay, he realized he had walked into a print shop. There were no hot rolls—the sign was put in the shop window to show the kind of lettering the shop was able to do.

Deceptive advertising.

Our churches may advertise the gospel, but once inside, you might find an extension of the culture around us. You might hear positive messages about the virtues of love and inclusion, or about our essential goodness and how to be a better person. You might see bright lights and upbeat music; you might see movie clips and well-timed announcements. But what you might not hear is a word from God. You might hear a lot about grace but nothing about sin; you might hear how to get blessed by God but nary a word about how to withstand the cultural pressures that are destroying our children and silencing our witness.

Truth and love must
always be kept together.

People come to church seeking hot rolls, but sometimes they find only the crumbs of a well-packaged service. They leave with unanswered questions and their hearts just as empty as when they entered. They are given opinions rather than convictions, platitudes rather than truth. They are given no clear path forward.

Paul wrote, "We refuse to practice cunning or to tamper with God's word, but by the open statement of the truth we would commend ourselves to everyone's conscience in the sight of God" (2 Corinthians 4:2). Truth and love must always be kept together.

We must distinguish truth from error, half-truths from lies. Each of us must ask ourselves what we are doing to advance the truth not just in our churches, but among our friends in the culture who are being misled. We must not only know the truth but ask, "Am I willing to speak it and act on it?"

Space limitations won't allow me to do so, but I could write an entire chapter on these words found in Proverbs: "Buy truth, and do not sell it" (Proverbs 23:23).

Having found the truth, would we sell it if the price were right?

A Prayer All of Us Must Pray

Father, in an age of rage, in an age of exaggeration and deception, help us not to turn to the right or the left. Teach us when to speak and when to remain silent. Grant us a firm place to stand and to speak and not be ashamed to remind this culture that Jesus said, "I am the way, and the truth, and the life. No one comes to the Father except through me" (John 14:6).

Let us affirm with Paul, "We have renounced disgraceful, underhanded ways. We refuse to practice cunning or to tamper with God's word, but by the open statement of the truth we would commend ourselves to everyone's conscience in the sight of God" (2 Corinthians 4:2).

Forgive us for flowing along with our culture's ideological streams that lead to a life of defeat, emptiness, and loss. Forgive us when our lives do not live up to the truth we profess. Grant us the courage of Nathan, who spoke the truth to David, and the courage of Jeremiah, who spoke the truth to the king and was rewarded by being thrown into a pit. We lack such courage. But help us to know that we love people best when we speak the truth to them. For it is the truth that sets people free.

Let us remember that we are accountable to Jesus Christ our Lord.

We pray this in Jesus' name, amen.

CHAPTER 6

Sexualize the Children

Parents—and I include most Christian parents—no longer raise their children. Rather, culture does—most significantly, through the Internet. Like one mother said to me, "I didn't know that when I gave my thirteen-year-old daughter a cellphone, I might as well have given her her first shot of heroin." As a nation, we have submitted our minds to electronic devices that now shape our thinking and provide endless entertainment.

In 2004, Pew Research polls showed that 60 percent of Americans were opposed to same-sex marriage. Today those numbers have flipped, with only 40 percent of Americans opposed. Why the change? Pulitzer Prize-winning *New York Times* columnist Thomas Friedman observed that Apple's iPhone was released in 2004. And that's not all. Social media apps Facebook and Twitter were rolled out. Google bought YouTube and launched their Android operating system. Amazon released their Kindle e-reader. And there were now more than one billion people accessing the Internet. Thus, technology facilitated cultural change more quickly than anyone could have imagined.[1]

The cellphone in a teenager's hand is doing more to shape their worldview than one hour of Sunday school or the admonitions of parents. We are failing to pass our faith on to the next generation because they are captives to the culture, social media, their peers, and the indoctrination by the public schools. Parents clothe their children, feed them, and send them to school, but the hearts of their kids are being stolen and molded by a world that many of us don't understand.

Parents are bewildered when their children come home from school saying they believe they are not the gender they were "assigned" at birth. Recently, a teenage girl told her parents she wanted her breasts removed because she thinks she's a boy; another girl told her parents she was a "fuzzy" cat. According to today's culture, you are whatever you feel you are. Some children go by a different gender at school than they do at home. A Christian teacher texted me and asked how to navigate his principal's orders that when parents come for their parent-teacher's conference, the parents should *not* be told that their biologically male son Bert is identifying as a girl named Berta when at school.

And if you think this is not happening in Christian families, you are living in a bubble that is becoming increasingly smaller every day. More and more children are coming home and telling their parents that they are gay or transgender.

Perhaps nowhere do we see the work of Satan in America as clearly as we do in the sexualization of children—destroying their identity, confusing their gender, and creating unresolved guilt and self-hatred. Jesus warned, "Whoever receives one such child in my name receives me, but whoever causes one of these little ones who believe in me to sin, it would be better for him to have a great millstone fastened around his neck and to be drowned in the depth of the sea" (Matthew 18:5-6).

This chapter, perhaps more than any other in this book, touches the heart of Jesus.

The Corrupting Influence of Our Public Schools

Peter Hitchens, in his book *The Rage Against God*, writes that "the youth movements of Nazi Germany and Communist Russia were startlingly similar. Any ideological or revolutionary state must always alienate the young from their pre-revolutionary parents if it hopes to survive into future generations."[2] Hitchens should know because as a correspondent in Moscow, he saw firsthand how Communism operated. As for Nazi Germany, Hitler was right: "He alone, who owns the youth, gains the future."[3]

And through laws and coercion, the education of America's youth is being taken out of the hands of parents and placed in the hands of secular educators. As MSNBC host Melissa Harris-Perry said, "We have to break through our private idea that kids belong to their parents or kids belong to their families, and recognize that kids belong to whole communities."[4] And in order for children to belong to "whole communities" it's necessary that they be indoctrinated with certain core beliefs about the world in general and sexuality in particular.

Using education to change the worldview of children has always been the goal of cultural Marxism. American Communist party leader William Z. Foster, in his book *Toward Soviet America*, lays out socialism's agenda. He speaks confidently about the coming "American Soviet government."

Among the elementary measures the American Soviet government will adopt to further the cultural revolution are the following: the schools, colleges, and universities will be coordinated and grouped under the National Department of Education...The studies will be revolutionized, being cleansed of religious, patriotic and other features of the bourgeois ideology."[5]

Note carefully: The National Department of Education, not the parents, will set the agenda and determine what is being taught. Through the clever use of curricula, it will cleanse our schools of religious and patriotic influence. And the best way to do that is through sex-education classes. The sensitive issue of sexuality and gender can be the gateway to the glories of the "equality" of all who reside in the state. As we have said before, it will all be sold under the banner of a noble cause.

Without the consent of the parents, the *Comprehensive Sexuality Education* curriculum is being introduced in many schools. This curriculum was created by Planned Parenthood and the Sexual Information and Education Council of the United States (SEICUS), which was founded by a devout follower of Alfred Kinsey (a pedophile who believed that children can be sexual from birth).

The emphasis is on how to have sexual pleasure either with partners or alone. Lisa Hudson describes what is taught: "Students as young as four or five are taught that parts of their bodies feel good when touched...this is called masturbation and that they should always masturbate in private...By the second grade, they learn that the same act can be performed with a partner."[6] In brief, all forms of sex, as long as it is consensual, is normal and to be enjoyed.

Boys are taught how to wear condoms and girls are taught how to put condoms on plastic replicas of male genitalia. They are given graphic images of various forms of characters experiencing sexual pleasure. Through all this, parental authority is consistently undermined.

What is not taught is what we already know: This kind of education stimulates the desires of children, leading to various expressions of sexuality that end up destroying and defiling their souls. "The Effect of Early Sexual Activity on Mental Health" is a 2018 report that evaluated 28 studies of peer-reviewed medical literature from 1966 to the present. Researchers found that "early sexual debut increased levels of depression, suicidal ideation, aggressive behavior, psychological distress, anxiety, stress, loneliness, poor well-being, regret and guilt. It also increased negative social behavior such as substance abuse and risky sexual behavior."[7]

The goal of the secularists is clear: attack any form of decency, sacredness, or normal sexual relations. Confuse the children by awakening sexual desires reserved for adults, and utterly destroy any concept of the traditional family. Encourage children to have multiple sexual experiences. And in the process, reap the consequences: more abortions, more antireligious bigotry, and most importantly, more broken homes. The more children are born out of wedlock, the more susceptible they are to being shaped according to Marxist principles.

Sell the new curriculum as "seeking respect for all forms of sexuality." Sell it as "inclusion and not exclusion" and "compassion not bullying." Sell it as "human flourishing," not sexual oppression. Sell it as "coming to maturity in sexual matters." Above all, *sell* it!

And call all those who oppose these measures bigots, haters, and right-wing religious fanatics.

In Martin Luther's day, schools were under the control of a Christian culture, but even back then, Luther feared for the children. "I am much afraid that the universities will prove to be the great gates of hell, unless they diligently labour in explaining the Holy Scriptures, and engraving them in the hearts of youth."[8]

Coming to a High School Near You

Here is something we should know.

> Planned Parenthood is pioneering a new model of reproductive health services for Los Angeles County teens by opening 50 clinics at area high schools…
>
> The program…will offer a full range of birth control options, testing and treatment for sexually transmitted infections, and pregnancy counseling, but not abortion, for an estimated 75,000 teens. The program will also train hundreds of teens to be "peer advocates" to help provide information about safe sex and relationships…
>
> Students will be able to walk into the clinics or make appointments and will be allowed to leave class for them. Information about the appointments will be in protected medical files not accessible to school officials. Under California law, minors can consent to certain medical services, such as receiving birth control or mental health counseling, and health care providers are not allowed to inform a parent without the minor's permission.[9]

Here we see the strategy of the radical left: Create a problem, then create an agency to respond to it. Once again, an arsonist is being sent to douse the flames of the very fire he started; the leftists have the "answer" to the very problem they created.

Consider the scenario: first, you introduce young children to all forms of deviant sexuality, encourage them to experiment with their sexual desires, and the result will be a guaranteed increase in teen pregnancies and sexually transmitted diseases. Then you install a clinic next to the school and announce that it is a strategy for combating the area's alarming rise in sexually transmitted diseases in young people.

Then you call the clinics "Well-Being Centers" because they will do more than provide simple medical services. As Barbara Ferrer, the director of the Los Angeles County Department of Public

Health, said, "We want to support their general well-being, the ups and downs of being a teen."[10]

What begins in California will spread across the nation.

Christian Colleges Submit to LGBTQ Values

And what about issues of sexuality in Christian colleges?

In an article titled "Christian Higher Ed Can't Win," David P. Gushee, who at one time held to the traditional view of sexuality, argues that evangelicals cannot win the LGBTQ debate on their Christian campuses. They must adapt culture's views of sexuality and accommodate the spirit of the times. The article says that schools will have an "eruption" of LGBTQ policies and find themselves in the national headlines. LGBTQ students are "unwilling to accept some straight guy declaring to them that they can't be both Christian and gay; they won't tolerate second-class status on campus."[11] Gushee says that students—even Christian students—arrive on campus having been exposed to tolerance, inclusion, and full acceptance of LGBTQ students.

No matter what the school's doctrinal and lifestyle statement says, the argument is that LGBTQ rights are a core value in our culture and the schools cannot (or will not) withstand the pressure. The bottom line: Christian colleges and seminaries are going to have to compromise the historic Christian understanding of sexuality and gender or be hopelessly left behind. They will lose their voice and credibility. They will be on "the wrong side of history."

There is already a call for legislation to deny funding to all schools that receive financial loans if they don't accept the full spectrum of LGBTQ rights.[12] As a result, many Christian colleges are bowing to the pressure by allowing campus support groups for LGBTQ students, and communicating to students that the school is a safe place for them to wrestle with their sexuality. The next logical step is for the schools to hire sympathetic staff who want to stand up for the rights of the same-sex and transgender students. But this will not be enough. Once a school's administration has started down this road, there is no stopping until the full spectrum of the LGBTQ agenda is dutifully embraced.

The same kind of pressure is brought to bear on Christian ministries, Christian businesses, and even churches. The Equality Act (H.R. 5) passed the US House of Representatives on May 20, 2019:

> The sweeping legislation would amend the Civil Rights Act of 1964 to include sexual orientation and gender identity as protected characteristics…Under the guise of anti-discrimination protections, the bill redefines sex to include gender identity, undermines religious freedom, gives males who identify as females the right to women's spaces, and sets a dangerous political precedent for the medicalization of gender-confused youth.[13]

There is no place to hide. Will our families, churches, and schools remain faithful? Or will we, as did the church in ancient Sardis (Revelation 3:1-6), comfortably embrace pagan sexuality?

The Larger Culture Goes Woke

A transgender doll!

The sexual revolution continues to accelerate, taking everything in its wake. Given its disdain for biology, science, and decency, it intends to destroy the very concept of masculinity and femininity in a child's earliest ages. Social justice requires it.

In the *Time* article "It Can Be a Boy, a Girl, Neither or Both," Eliana Dockterman writes about this transformation to gender-neutral dolls. She says, "Mattel, the manufacturer of Barbie dolls, is hoping to break taboos and appeal to a generation that demands social justice in brands." Describing the new doll, she writes, "Carefully manicured features betray no obvious gender: the lips are not too full, the eyelashes not too long and fluttery, the jaw not too wide. There are no Barbie-like breasts or broad, Ken-like shoulders."

The article continues, "The population of young people who identify as gender-nonbinary is growing…[one survey indicates] that 27% of California teens identify as gender-nonconforming."[14]

There is no doubt that the transgender revolution is a fad; it is yet another way teenagers seek their sense of independence, and it appeals to a young person's natural desire to rebel against the status quo. One mother said to me that her daughter says, "If you're not trans, you're weird."

Welcome a Drag Queen to Your Library

How do you corrupt children? As we've seen earlier in this book, you normalize the bizarre.

In public libraries across America, drag queens are hosting story hours for children. In this phenomenon that has been sweeping the nation, grown men dressed in lurid outfits and wearing excessive makeup read books promoting the LGBTQ agenda to children as young as three years old.

Progress in the wrong direction is not something to celebrate—especially when it goes against the natural order of creation or even the established facts of science.

These presentations are used to indoctrinate young children into accepting transgenderism, encourage them to dress as the opposite sex, and promote other deviant behaviors and belief systems. Dylan Pontiff, aka Santana Pilar Andrews when in drag, uses his stage name at both the adult clubs where he performs sexual acts and at the Lafayette Public Library when he's with young children.

In his own words, he reveals his intentions: "I'm here to let you know that this event is something that's going to be very beautiful and for the children and the people that supported are going to realize that this is going to be the grooming of the next generation."[15]

Grooming, of course, is a word used to describe the effort to desensitize children to the sexual abuse of adults. This is the culture in which we find ourselves. Parents who object are called bigots.

Progress in the Wrong Direction

Back in 1958, Justice Earl Warren spoke of the "evolving standards of decency."[16] The implication is that when it comes to morality, including sexual matters, change is progress. But progress in the wrong direction is not something to celebrate—especially when it goes against the natural order of creation or even the established facts of science. Who would have ever imagined that to be truly "woke" one would have to believe that men give birth to babies or have periods, or that it is fair for women to be required to compete in sports with biological males who identify as females? Today, to be a radical secularist is to accept chaos, irrationality, and absurdity.

Michael Brown has correctly written, "The great enemy of the radical transgender movement is science. Biological realities can be stubborn, and no amount of human tampering can change those realities."[17] Realities or not, the radicals hold to their agenda no matter how irrational it is.

What Next?

In November 2019, I was one of the speakers at the Truth for a New Generation conference in Cincinnati, Ohio. Another speaker was Anne Paulk, a former lesbian who has since left the lifestyle, married, and has children. In her talk, she said, "When God was not in my life, I had no reason to say no to anything." She's right. Without God, there is no reason for anyone to say no to the most perverse, previously unimaginable sexual relationships.

After same-sex marriage was legalized by the US Supreme Court in 2015, transgenderism has swept through the country, seemingly arising from nowhere. It was the next domino to fall—and the moral slide continues.

The new growing trend is the "throuple," a threesome relationship. This relationship can be any combination of three people. But if three isn't enough, polyamory may be your thing—that is, multiple relationships simultaneously with significant others in an open or "poly" marriage. After all, traditional marriage just isn't keeping up with the times. As Janie B. Cheaney states in *World* magazine, "Shifting norms [to same-sex and/or poly marriages] have washed out the stigma of nontraditional domestic arrangements."[18]

Beyond that, there are calls for pedophilia to be seen as a legitimate and healthy kind of relationship. Back in 2002, Judith Levine wrote a book titled *Harmful to Minors: The Perils of Protecting Children from Sex*, which promotes the idea that "consensual" sex with young children is not harmful to them. Author Sharon Lamb wrote a review of the book in which she stated, "We must look at the issue of consent from a psychological perspective, not just a legal one; and that not everyone who has been abused ends up traumatized for life."[19]

We may find it hard to believe that pedophilia could ever be legalized, but the groundwork is already in place for that to happen. The propaganda is already out there in the sex-education messaging, the normalizing of deviant behaviors, and the use of the banner of civil rights as a blanket to protect such behaviors. "K–12 classrooms are becoming labs in which kids are being programmed to serve such [political] agendas," Stella Morabito says. "In arguments to push social acceptance of adult sex with prepubescent children you will find nearly an exact parallel to all of the arguments for all manner of 'progressive' causes, including, of course, LGBT preferences."[20] Expect laws protecting "consensual" adult-child sexual relationships to be the next domino to fall.

As far back as 2003, Tammy Bruce, who had been an advocate of the leftist agenda but has since become a critic of the movement, said that the reason the radicals seek to sexualize children is that it guarantees control of future generations. She writes, "It also promises sex-addicted future consumers on which the porn industry relies. By destroying those lives, they strike the final blow to family, faith, tradition, decency and judgment."[21]

What next?

The next logical step is to ban anyone who dares to offer help to those who, of their own initiative, desire to leave the homosexual or transgender lifestyle. If you read through the comments in response to articles about helping those who desire to change, and you'll see scores of people accusing Christians of cruelty and bigotry, being harmful to anyone seeking counsel for dealing with the very real struggles that result from transgender or same-sex relationships.

When it becomes illegal to help homosexuals and transgenders who desire to pursue biblical sexuality, we can expect that the illegality of gospel "ideology" won't be far behind. According to culture, the problem isn't one of sexual deviancy, but of Christianity and the Bible. That being the case, what's to keep the government from branding Christianity as a dangerous psychological neurosis that harms people? In fact, C.S. Lewis already predicted, in 1949, "When this particular neurosis becomes inconvenient to government, what is to hinder government from proceeding to 'cure' it?"[22]

Indeed. Without God, there is no reason to say no to anything.

The Demonic Nature of What's Happening in the Transgender Phenomenon

When it comes to the transgender movement, parental rights are being rejected, and to the despair of parents whose child might be diagnosed with one or more disorders, such children are often persuaded by peers and public-school authorities that they are transgender. Parents are criticized for not being "affirming" and too rigid in traditional norms.

"Parents are told that that puberty blockers and cross-sex hormones may be the only way to prevent their children from committing suicide."[23] And yet studies of gender dysphoria show that 80 to 95 percent of those who at some point identify as transgender will end up identifying with their bodily sex.[24] As some have said, biology is not bigotry.

In New Jersey, the Child Abuse and Neglect and Missing Children webpage suggests that staff might be encouraged to report parents who disagree with the assessment that their child is transitioning.[25] Parents are also afraid to speak out for fear of being attacked by the LGBTQ mob. Meanwhile, in Oregon, children can make their own decisions not only about their preferred sexual identity, but can get state-subsidized sex-change operations without parental consent.[26]

Just ask Jay Keck, who lives near Chicago, about the undermining of parental rights. His 14-year-old daughter became convinced she was a boy, and the staff at her school endorsed her delusion, in opposition to her parents. Their teenage daughter had shown no inclination toward gender dysphoria, but she declared herself to be a boy after hanging out with another girl who professed to be a boy. The school accepted a name change without notifying the parents; when the parents discovered this and insisted that she be called by her legal name, their wishes were ignored.[27]

> The National Education Association has partnered with the Human Rights Campaign and other groups to produce materials advocating automatic affirmation of identities, name changes and pronouns regardless of parents' concerns. In 18 states and the District of Columbia, including my home state of Illinois, there are "conversion therapy" bans, which prevent therapists from questioning a child's gender identity.[28]

Children in our schools are, in effect, being recruited to declare themselves as transgender.

Consider this scenario: A teenage boy decides he is actually a girl and is given the hormone therapy to make the transition, even going on to have body-altering surgery that can cost as much as $140,000.[29] This "girl" grows up and is now a "woman." Suppose a man (perhaps your son) falls in love with this "woman" who has the DNA of a man. Is your son attracted to a man or a woman? If they get married, they will not be able to have children together. And who will pay for the rising cost of those hormones that artificially keep this biological male looking like a woman?

Is this progress?

My word to parents: Be very wary of public schools. Regrettably, the radicals have captured the media, the progressive politicians, and the elites that write the curricula. We should not throw our children into a culture that is anti-Christian, despises natural law, and rejects science and civility. We should not put our children at the mercy of those who try to normalize the bizarre and are "grooming" our children, making them susceptible to adult sexual abuse.

We are here to shine a
light into this dark culture.

Every Christian parent has to pray and search for the best education options for their children. I remember Tony Evans saying that when his children came home from school, he and his wife would discuss what they had learned and "deprogram" them from any wrong ideas they were taught. Meanwhile, homeschooling is becoming more accessible because of the networks and curricula that have been developed. Faith-based schools are also an option, with some offering financial help for those who can't afford the tuition.

We must heed the warning of those who speak the truth and are not intimidated by cultural thinking. Let's hear this from Will Malone, MD: "You can't be born in the wrong body—it's our minds that need treatment, not our sex. The mental health services will look back at this episode [in American history] as another dark chapter in the treatment of people with psychological difficulties."[30]

We are here to shine a light into this dark culture.

Where Is the Church?

If we aren't protecting our children, why do we call ourselves Christ followers? Jesus was not neutral when it came to children. To all those who would cause one of these little ones to sin, He had strong words, "Whoever receives one such child in my name receives me, but whoever causes one of these little ones who believe in me to sin, it would be better for him to have a great millstone fastened around his neck and to be drowned in the depth of the sea" (Matthew 18:5-6).

I love the title of the book *Raising Lambs Among Wolves*, which was written by my late friend Mark Bubeck. Although the book has been revised and reprinted under a different title, I return to the words in the original title, derived from Jesus' use of the "lambs and wolves" imagery.

As for those children who think they are transgender, we must listen to what they say, hear their concerns, and provide a safe place where they feel free to express their feelings and desires. We must warn against body-altering surgery that is done in the name of being "authentic." There are a growing number of stories of those who have gone through these surgeries who discover that this didn't heal their dysphoria or bring about the sense of well-being they expected. Their suicide rate is as high as 41 percent.[31]

It is dangerous to place our lambs in public schools if they are being indoctrinated into pagan sexuality, the normalcy of deviant behavior, and the mockery of God's intention for men and women. I'm reminded of Jesus' words, "Let the little children come to me and do not hinder them, for to such belongs the kingdom of heaven" (Matthew 19:14). Then we read that He took them in His arms and blessed them.

I can't imagine Jesus then taking the children and passing them off to pagans waiting to teach them that you can have two mommies or two daddies or any combination thereof. I can't imagine Him giving the children to those who would encourage them to experiment with their sexuality and choose one of any number of "genders" they wish to be.

Back in the early 1970s, I planted a tree outside the home that was supplied for us by the church I was pastoring. I knew at the time that the trunk was a bit crooked, so after I dug a hole and put it in the ground, I straightened it out as best I could and wished it the best. Now, nearly 50 years later, I drive past that house every once in a while, noticing that the tree, now perhaps 30 feet tall, has a trunk that still retains its crookedness.

We must return to the creation account to remind ourselves that God created only two genders: male and female. Without a belief in God as Creator, there is little hope of making sense of our lives and the roles we are intended to have in marriage, the family, and of course, sexuality. To quote Michael Brown again, "We want to see people freed from their internal pain. We want to see them find resolution for the emotional torment they're experiencing...But no amount of compassion can change biological and chromosomal realities. That is why the transgender movement is starting to hit the wall. Science is against it."[32]

Godlessness and aberrant sexuality always go hand in hand:

> Although they knew God, they did not honor him as God or give thanks to him, but they became futile in their thinking, and their foolish hearts were darkened. Claiming to be wise, they became fools, and exchanged the glory of the immortal God for images resembling mortal man and birds and animals and creeping things. Therefore God gave them up in the lusts of their hearts to impurity, to the dishonoring of their bodies among themselves, because they exchanged the truth about God for a lie and worshiped and served the creature rather than the Creator (Romans 1:21-25).

Do we have the courage to stand against this assault on our children? Or will the bullies win the battle for the next generation? Seductive delusions are gaining currency in our media-driven, politically correct culture. We must be prepared for the radicals who will call us hateful names, all the while claiming that they have taken the moral high ground.

Let's wake up and realize that there are many people who struggle with their gender identity; they may be gay or trans or struggling with sexual issues. Heath Lambert of the Association of Certified Biblical Counselors says, "To love transgenders we must work through the complicated layers of sin and pain—a process that requires the relational context churches can provide. It will be the death knell if we say this is wrong, but then we can't help."[33] People have to lean into their pain and not seek a deceptive antidote for their internal dysphoria and suffering.

Our churches should count it a privilege to be welcoming of all people who struggle with their sexual identities, while recognizing that God does not affirm sexual relationships outside of the one-man, one-woman relationship in marriage. What do we say to someone who says, "I am a gay Christian," or "I am a trans Christian"? To this, Anne Paulk had a wise answer: "Satan calls you by your sinful name; God calls you a Christian who struggles with identity issues." Gender identity—the gender that you were born with—is fundamental to self-knowledge.

Only when we recognize the human heart's propensity to deception are we able to help others see their problems from a divine perspective. Remember, those who walk in darkness do not see things as they are, but rather, see things the way they want them to be. "The way of the wicked is like deep darkness; they do not know over what they stumble" (Proverbs 4:19).

In my opinion, the church is the last barrier against a total breakdown of sexual sanity in today's culture. And if we feel powerless against the media, the courts, and our politicians, let us remind ourselves who is the head of the church (see Ephesians 1:21-22).

To a world blinded by pain and searching to soothe the emptiness, Jesus makes this promise: "Come unto me, all ye that labour and are heavy laden, and I will give you rest. Take my yoke upon you, and learn of me; for I am meek and lowly in heart: and ye shall find rest unto your souls" (Matthew 11:28-29 KJV).

Jesus is in the trenches with us.

(Please note that after the prayer I've provided a list of helpful resources for parents.)

A Prayer All of Us Must Pray

Father, all of us have experienced the brokenness that sin always brings. Today our hearts are heavy for children born into one-parent families, as well as children who are abused, neglected, and who struggle with emptiness and confusion. Our hearts break for children who are reaching out, trying to find hope in the maze of moral and cultural lies that are widely accepted today.

We read in Your Word that even pagan children belong to You, and You accused the people of Israel of "slaughtering my children" to foreign gods (Ezekiel 16:21). All the children of the world belong to You; and Jesus exemplified His love to children by taking them into His arms and blessing them.

Forgive us; we repent of letting the culture raise our children because we didn't want to be thought of as bigoted, unloving, or out of touch with reality. We repent of giving our children to the foreign gods of so-called tolerance and unbridled sensuality. We confess that we have not exercised sufficient care to protect our families from the cultural lies that are broadcast through the technologies that have gained a foothold in all of our lives.

Father, give us the wisdom we need to take steps to prevent the secular agenda presented in schools from reshaping the core values of our children. We pray that that our children's hearts might not be drawn away by cultural pressures and expectations.

Let us be done with cowardice. Let us bow before Your Word, keeping in mind what Paul said to Timothy:

> *Evil people and impostors will go on from bad to worse, deceiving and being deceived. But as for you, continue in what you have learned and have firmly believed, knowing from whom you learned it and how from childhood you have been acquainted with the sacred writings, which are able to make you wise for salvation through faith in Christ Jesus (2 Timothy 3:13-15).*

God, have mercy. In Jesus' name, amen.

One of the best ways we can prepare ourselves is by making use of resources that address culture's overwhelming influences upon our children's lives. Three I can recommend here are *Keeping Your Kids on God's Side: 40 Conversations to Help Them Build a Lasting Faith* by Natasha Crain (Eugene, OR: Harvest House Publishers, 2016); *Mama Bear Apologetics: Empowering Your Kids to Challenge Cultural Lies* with general editor Hillary Morgan Ferrer (Eugene, OR: Harvest House Publishers, 2019); and *Irreversible Damage: The Transgender Craze Seducing Our Daughters* by Abigail Shrier (Washington, DC: Regnery Publishing, 2020).

In addition, here is a website dedicated to helping parents evaluate pop culture from a biblical point of view. It stays up to date on movies, podcasts, and websites and is a great resource: CounterCultureMom.com

CHAPTER 7

Capitalism Is the Disease; Socialism Is the Cure

P eople, not profits!" the protesters shout.

You might be surprised at the number of people advocating socialism who do not know how to define it. For them, it is summed up by one word: *free*. Socialism would provide *free* college, *free* healthcare, *free* retirement income, a guaranteed job, and a decent living. Allegedly, in a socialist world, no one would be left behind because the government would assure income equality. Why should those who are rich not share their wealth with the poor, the underprivileged, and racially disenfranchised?

You might wonder why a book that focuses on the church's role in our culture includes a chapter on socialism. After all, Christianity has proven it can survive under any economic and political system. The church began under the rule of the Caesars and survived very well. Under decades of Communist rule in Russia, the church has persevered even though it was hampered by severe persecution. The church in China continues to survive despite widespread crackdowns and horrid persecution. The church can survive under Communism and socialism, even of the worst kind.

My concern has to do with the deceptions of socialism and why, although it may appear to be an attractive system, it must of necessity perpetuate poverty, restrict freedom, and otherwise demoralize those who are under it. Socialism by its very nature encroaches on the freedom of the church and its ability to be generous with gospel ministries. The United States—for all of its faults—must be thanked for the more than $400 billion its citizens give each year to charitable causes, including missions and help for the poor.[1] You can't name a socialist country that comes anywhere near to America's generosity.

The United States is the most generous nation to give assistance to other countries when they experience a national tragedy. There is a reason our quality of life is the envy of the world. Yes, we have poverty in America, but it is a problem socialism is ill equipped to fix. As we will see, only a capitalistic economy can generate the wealth needed to bring more opportunities to a greater number of people. Our capitalist economy has been able to support gospel-driven ministries around the world that also provide medical care, food supplies, and much more.

What is socialism? In a nutshell, it is the spremacy of the state over the individual. Or if you want a one-word definition, it's *statism*. It's when the government takes ownership of the means of production and promises to redistribute wealth in what is claimed to be a fair-minded way. On the surface, this seems like an attractive solution to poverty and fiscal insecurity. We remember the Occupy Wall Street movement, whose slogan can be summed up, "Let Wall Street pay!" It seems like an option that is too good to pass up.

The COVID-19 pandemic has fueled the notion that the government *can* pay. Trillions of dollars were approved to bail out businesses and give checks to millions of newly unemployed workers. We have to ask: Is not this an example of big government taking over the economy for the benefit of our nation? We will look at this more closely later in this chapter.

For now, let us consider the philosophical view of Karl Marx, whose economic theories impact us even to this day. Then we will distinguish what he taught from the "democratic socialism" that is widely advocated by some politicians.

Yes, Marx Does, in Fact, Rule from the Grave

Karl Marx was born to Jewish parents in the Rhineland of Germany. When he was six years old, his father had the entire family baptized as Lutherans. While studying in Paris, Marx met Friedrich Engels in 1844, and four years later, they released their famous political document *The Communist Manifesto*.

Marx was concerned about the abuses he saw in England's industrial revolution. An abundance of cheap labor made it possible for the wealthy to pay low wages while maintaining poor working conditions. Women and children were being forced to work long hours and overcrowded slums were rampant. In Marx's view, these exploited workers (proletariat) needed to gain control of the means of production.

His philosophy was based on the beliefs that (1) matter is the final reality (materialism); there is no God nor a human soul that survives the death of the body; (2) economic forces propel history ever onward and upward; and (3) private property is the source of all evil.

Marx hated Christianity, which he saw as a source of oppression. To him, the God of the Bible was a cruel tyrant who kept people bound to injustice and social repression; he described religion as "the opium of the people." For economic equality to be established, loyalty to the church had to be replaced by loyalty to the state. The nuclear family, which he believed had been artificially constructed, had to be reordered, and oppressed mothers had to be freed. As Lenin has been quoted as saying, "We cannot be free if one half of the population is enslaved in the kitchen."[2]

Marx believed that mothers should work outside the home so that government-approved schools could raise the children who, in reality, belonged to the state. The family unit was no longer to be seen as an independent, economic unit of society; communal housing had to replace private housing. The goal was a classless society with no kings and servants, no owners and workers, no rich and poor, no wives and husbands shaping the worldview of their children.

The basic economic axiom of Marxism is that the poor are poor because the rich are rich. Capitalists are the oppressors; the poor are their victims. Because the rich will not share their wealth voluntarily, the only just course is to confiscate private property and let the state redistribute wealth and benefits. Through tight controls and the monitoring of the economy, equality and justice are able to prevail. "From each according to his ability, to each according to his needs."[3]

Capitalism, we are told, is based on *greed*; socialism is based on *need*!

What about laws? Marx viewed laws as a means of class oppression. To quote him, "Legislation, whether political or civil, never does more than proclaim, express in words, the will of economic relations."[4] From Marx's perspective, there are no fixed laws that transcend all cultures; they are invented by the rulers as a means of controlling the proletariat. To put it simply, laws exist only as a means for class exploitation.

Marx taught that after a revolution was complete, people would change from capitalistic law to Marxist law, which says there are no God-given rights, only those granted by the state. In fact, years later, when women in Marxist Russia were recruited to serve as prostitutes to act as spies, they were told, "Your body does not belong to you, it belongs to the state."

By the way, it was this Marxist notion of state-granted rights that, in 1973, was the basis for the US Supreme Court decision in the *Roe v. Wade* case to legalize abortion. The ruling, which gave a mother the right to kill her preborn infant, was based on the supposition that the state did not have a compelling interest in protecting the lives of the unborn. Nothing was said about the inherent God-given right of a preborn infant to live; rather, the privacy of the mother was the determining factor.

When state rights take the place of God-given rights, we can easily move from abortion to infanticide to euthanasia. China also bases its forced proabortion laws on the same assumption, and births are simply a matter of state planning, just like any other economic decision. Couples should not be allowed to have a baby just because they want to.

Because it is the state, and not God, that creates rights, it follows that one cannot logically criticize the state for human rights violations. After all, without the state there would be no human rights whatsoever. If the state says you have no right to criticize the state, so be it. The state gives rights and revokes them. Chesterton put it so well: "It is only by believing in God that we can ever criticize the Government. Once abolish the God, and the Government becomes the God...The truth is that Irreligion is the opium of the people."[5]

Although Marx's theories should be shunned because of their purely materialistic and anti-God foundation, we can still understand the attraction of Marxism. In places such as Latin America, liberation theology (cultural Marxism) is popular because the capitalist system is corrupt and the poor are exploited. A revolution that promises that the wealthy will be deprived of their riches and the poor given their fair share of the economic pie sounds fair and just. After all, the wealthy exploit the poor, the politicians accept bribes, the bureaucrats steal from the public treasury and enrich themselves at the expense of the powerless. A revolution in which the state would control this madness by insisting on a philosophy of equal distribution seems like a good thing. What's there to lose?

After visiting Russia in the mid-1980s (before the Berlin Wall came down in 1989), I gained a better understanding of why, initially, Marxism was so attractive to the Russian people. They had suffered terribly under the leadership of the Russian tsars, who had enslaved the people and treated them harshly, with deliberate disregard for their suffering and abject poverty. The people worked for these extravagant rulers whose wealth and pomp knew no bounds. Would it not make sense to have all that wealth and power confiscated and given to the state, which would distribute it with some degree of equality and fairness? In many minds, the Bolsheviks were fighting for the common man, taking the side of the oppressed people who were entitled to some measure of decent living conditions and security.

But alas, it was not to be. The promises evaporated in the top-heavy Communist bureaucracy. The state controlled the wages, determined which jobs were given to whom, and corruption multiplied. Increasing state power meant that churches were closed, freedom of religion was denied, and those who refused to play by the state rules were executed. Wages were equalized, but state-run businesses collapsed under the weight of inefficiency and disinterested workers. And the bureaucrats who promised liberation became thieves.

The multiplied millions of people killed by Communist regimes died in vain. The Marxist experience of government ownership, guaranteed wages, and the primacy of the state failed; it could only succeed behind barbed-wire fences, severe penalties for opposing state policies, and state-run censorship. And wherever Communism is tried again, it will fail. Fail it must.

But is capitalism any better? Capitalism is being assailed by many today in the United States and in other countries. Thirty-five years ago, Robert Nash described the attacks being leveled against capitalism:

> Capitalism is blamed for every evil in contemporary society including its greed, materialism and selfishness, the prevalence of fraudulent behavior, the debasement of society's tastes, the pollution of the environment, the alienation and despair within society, and the vast disparities of wealth. Even racism and sexism are treated as effects of capitalism.[6]

Capitalism, we are told, is not only the reason for financial inequality; it's also the root of all of America's sexism, xenophobia, and white supremacy. Some go so far as to say that America's capitalistic system has been a detriment to the whole world. Other countries have been reduced to poverty by American capitalism, which exploits other countries. They say that capitalism must be unmasked and exposed for the evil that it is. "The last capitalist we hang" Marxists have said, "will be the one who sold us the rope."

We are told there are reasons for the failure of the Marxist regime in Russia; cultural Marxism or socialism would fix these weaknesses. Cultural Marxism, remember, promotes the idea that the state can take over companies and wealth incrementally. This change could be installed democratically by the will of the people. Once they see the "value" of this form of government, they will want it.

Cultural Marxism or Democratic Socialism

Democratic socialism (cultural Marxism), promises to eliminate the excesses of the Marxist philosophy. It is Marxism Lite. This form of Marxist socialism, we are told, can be combined with democratic values. By electing the right candidates to office, Wall Street will become Main Street as the wealth is shared. Why not redistribute resources so everyone can enjoy the kind of privileges limited to the rich? I repeat the Marxist principle "From each according to his ability, to each according to his needs."[7]

Herbert Marcuse, the Marxist we met in previous chapters, claimed that "the traditional idea of revolution and the traditional strategy of revolution has ended. These ideas are old-fashioned... What we must undertake is a type of diffuse and dispersed disintegration of the system."[8] In other words, Marxism incrementally gains both strength and adherents by political and cultural control. Eventually this will result in a utopia of sorts.

The vision of cultural Marxism is an America free of greed, racism, and class structure. As David Horowitz explains, "In the radical view, once human beings have been freed from institutional oppressions, their natural goodness asserts itself and the traditional dilemmas of power no longer exist. It is a future in which 'social justice' prevails and there are no troubling questions about the dispensations of authority."[9] This end justifies every means to get there.

To repeat: Democratic socialism purports to honor individual freedom even though the state incrementally owns more and more of the means of production and therefore controls goods and services. It would begin by setting up a universal healthcare system that restricts medical options and sets wages and costs for procedures. It would provide free college and give increased subsidies to the poor. It is said to reduce the gap between the haves and the have nots, therefore making the lifestyles and living conditions of the citizens fairer. It would be democratic, but as we will see, it would eventually become a form of democratic totalitarianism.

Can democratic socialism deliver on its promises?

We will evaluate democratic socialism, but first, let me digress for a moment so we can talk about another Marxist-driven goal.

The Importance of Climate Change

Former Vice President Al Gore has long warned people about the dangers of "global warming." But because there is less evidence than previously claimed to prove that the planet has heated up, the terminology has been adjusted to "climate change," which is said to be an existential threat to our planet.

When the teenager Greta Thunberg stood before the United Nations assembly, she said, "We are in the beginning of a mass extinction, and all you can talk about is money and fairy tales of eternal economic growth. How dare you!"[10] Many people agreed with her, pushing a "We must do something now" agenda.

There are two reasons the radical secularists are so adamant about climate change. The first is because of the Marxist notion that capitalism is oppressive and exploits nature, making the world unlivable. Stephen Hicks explains, "And capitalism, since it is so good at producing wealth, must therefore be the environment's number one enemy."[11]

Secularists say that all of nature is equally sacred. "All species from bacteria to wood lice to aardvarks to humans are equal in moral value."[12] After all, evolution teaches that we have ascended up through the animal world; therefore, we are only a part of a continuum of life, which means that animal life is just as sacred as our own. This explains why the secularists, who are most bent on promoting abortion, are also refusing to allow a pipeline to be built—because it will disturb the habitat of insects and animals. Beetles and preborn babies are viewed as equals.

At Union Theological Seminary in New York City, students confessed to plants—yes, you read that right: They confessed to *plants*. They even tweeted about it. "Together, we held our grief, joy, regret, hope, guilt and sorrow in prayer; offering them to the beings who sustain us but whose gift we too often fail to honor." The seminary explained that this was part of a class called "Extractivism: A Ritual/Liturgical Response."[13]

As Christians, we most assuredly should be good stewards of the environment. God gave us the world of nature and animals not to exploit, but to use responsibly. We will give an account for our stewardship. Reducing the use of plastics, properly disposing of waste, and dozens of other environmentally conscientious actions should be on our agenda. Yet we should also distinguish the Creator from the creature.

And there is more to be said.

A second reason secularists want to invest trillions of dollars in addressing climate change is that it would give the government more control of the economy. This, in the eyes of cultural Marxists, is always a plus. Big government is always better than big business. And as America shares more of its wealth with other countries committed to climate change, this also provides a form of equality—the oppressor is returning resources to the oppressed. After all, the ills of the world are blamed on American global dominance. Take the phrase *white supremacy* and translate that concept into "American supremacy," and you will better understand the cultural Marxists' reasoning as to why we should all hate "rich" America.

America owes the world.

A Case Study of Democratic Socialism

Might democratic socialism be an answer to poverty and the racial disparities in our culture? One of the biggest arguments in favor of democratic socialism is that it brings wage and price controls; it's not subject to the "competitive bidding" that capitalism inspires. The government can make value judgments and subsidize various goods even if they are not selling and otherwise would disappear in a capitalistic economy. Government control would bring stability to wages and not allow the wealthy (the top 1 percent) to have more than the other 99 percent combined. Equality would necessitate that there should be a minimum wage at the bottom of the income scale and a maximum wage at the top.

But there are reasons that socialism, even of the democratic variety, cannot keep its promises for very long. Though well intended, if followed through for a length of time, it will fail. Socialism builds a ladder to a place that does not exist. *It talks about distributing wealth, but it has no way to create it!*

Sweden is often upheld as an example of democratic socialism done right. But it's actually an example of the failed policies of socialism. The historian of ideas, Johan Norberg, has pointed out that by the early 1980s, Sweden was a country made wealthy by capitalism, limited government, and low taxes. It enjoyed a high standard of living. With wealth to spare, the country decided to experiment with socialism, increasing the size of government and distributing free goods and services paid for by higher taxes. Wage and price controls were intended to provide income equality for all citizens.

As a result, businesses began leaving Sweden because the country was no longer hospitable to innovative growth and competition. Its standard of living began to decline and the money accumulated by capitalist policies began to dry up. By the 1990s, Sweden found it necessary to make changes to avoid economic ruin. The government encouraged private property ownership, lowered taxes, cut regulations, and even partially privatized social security. With open bidding in the public sector, the economy began to recover. Today, Sweden's economy is largely market-driven.[14]

Venezuela is another country that used its wealth gained by capitalism to transition to socialism. This oil-rich country elected a socialist leader in their regular election cycle. There was no need for a political revolution; a democratic country-wide election installed a socialist who held out the promise of widespread wealth and equality. The people thought the promises of socialism were too good to pass up. (This story is told in the May 25, 2019 issue of *World* magazine.[15])

In 1999, Hugo Chávez campaigned on the slogan "Esperanza y Cambio" ("Hope and Change"). He told the masses that it was unfair that businesses were wealthy and the common people were poor. If he were elected, he would put people in charge who would run the state better than the capitalists, thus allowing everyone to share in the profits.

At the time Chávez was elected, Venezuela was prospering. The country had a growing middle class and economic stability. True to his promise, Chávez slowly transformed Venezuela into a socialist country. Step by step, his government took control of the means of production. The government took over FertiNitro, a producer of nitrogen fertilizer, as well as huge tracts of land owned by British companies. Many other businesses were nationalized, with Chávez sometimes paying off the companies and at other times just taking them.

At first this nation had full employment, guaranteed salaries, and national healthcare. Ecstatic socialists around the world lauded the changes; they considered this an example of how democratic socialism could work. British Labor Party leader Jeremy Corbyn said that former Venezuelan President Hugo Chávez "showed us there is a different, and better way of doing things. It's called socialism, it's called social justice."[16] Hollywood elites visited Venezuela to tout the great success progressive socialism supposedly could bring.

Yet now, as I write, Venezuela's economy has collapsed and

people are scrounging for food. Adults can afford protein-rich food only twice a month; malnutrition and starvation are everywhere. Criminals break into houses searching for food. If you criticize the regime, you will be persecuted or killed. Those who can obtain passports or visas are leaving, willing to depart their homes and relatives so they can make a living once again.

What went wrong in this oil-rich country?

Socialism is deceptive because it works for a while. But it cannot work indefinitely. The late Margaret Thatcher is reported to have observed, "The problem with socialism is that sooner or later you run out of other people's money." Olasky writes:

> Neither Chávez nor his successor, Nicolás Maduro, ran out of money: When they ran short, they printed more. The economic death spiral began: Huge deficits, print money, inflation, price controls, shortages, protests, more authoritarianism, more crime, more shortages, more refugees.[17]

Venezuela did not default economically. Rather, the government printed more money, creating inflation of more than two million percent. Once a country embraces socialism, there is no easy way back. There is, after all, no end to money...just print more. But as Germany learned after World War I, printing more money to pay a nation's debt can only be a temporary answer before economic disaster. A German friend gave me a 1937 German bill for two million marks; I have laminated it and keep it as a reminder of what happens when a government prints money to pay its debts.

Of course Chávez personally became very wealthy, as did members of his family. After he died of cancer in 2013, his daughter, Maria Gabriela, had a net worth of $4.2 billion. His successor, Nicolás Maduro, has become wealthy as well. Greed and corruption are widespread. The elite who control the economy are doing well in the midst of a country that is starving, scrounging, and dying.

I quote Olasky one more time:

> [A Venezuelan] wonders why many young Americans, according to polls, see socialism as the "most compassionate system." He has seen how "socialism operates under the assumption that an insulated leader and his legion of bureaucrats are the best judges of what people are worth. Socialism…crushes ambition in pursuit of a uniform, unfulfilling and arbitrary definition of "equality." And it does all of this in the name of "the greater good."[18]

The citizens of Venezuela thought they were electing a system of government that would root out corruption, but they elected one that expanded corruption and ruined the economy. And when an economy begins to collapse, the government has to resort to desperate measures to maintain control over people. It will restrict freedom of speech, freedom of travel, and even freedom of religion. Desperate people act out of desperation; and desperate bureaucrats do the same. To cover their mistakes, they rule with an iron fist. The Venezuelan people loved socialism until they began to starve.

In Hemingway's novel *The Sun Also Rises*, Bill asked Mike how he went bankrupt. Mike replied, "Two ways. Gradually and then suddenly."[19]

In a socialist economy, bankruptcy happens *gradually* and then *suddenly*.

COVID-19 Bailouts and the Push for Socialism

The world changed when the COVID-19 pandemic, which started in Wuhan, China, quickly erupted around the globe. What began as a disease in one region of Asia soon spread exponentially to every part of the world, including the United States. In response, large numbers of businesses were shut down (except those deemed essential), sports events were cancelled, and "stay at home" orders came from mayors, governors, and the US president himself. Our cities became ghost towns. Fear caused us to surrender our constitutional right to assemble so we could comply with our politicians' edicts that all church services be cancelled. Although many of us went along with these orders, we should never forget the words of Benjamin Franklin: "Those who would give up essential Liberty, to purchase a little temporary Safety, deserve neither Liberty nor Safety."[20]

Stepping Toward Socialism

The economic effects of the shutdowns were catastrophic. After much political posturing, Congress passed an initial $2.2 trillion bailout package to maintain economic stability and give hope even as millions filed unemployment claims. Never before has any government created this much money to keep an economy afloat. Of course, the $2.2 trillion was a first step in a series of other similar measures. Millions of desperate people were now working (or *not* working!) for the government. Thus big government, which seemed to many of us to be a threat to capitalism, now appeared to be the right move.

These bailouts, at least as far as we can tell, were needed. However, they were not just a step toward socialism but a lurch toward it. Some have argued that the economic intervention is merely temporary; that when the virus runs its course, the economy will rebound quickly. They also add that because the government hasn't taken over the healthcare system, implemented wage and price controls, or assumed ownership of businesses, capitalism is still the order of the day. But as one commentator put it, the economy cannot be turned off and on like a light switch.[21]

Contributing editor Gary Abernathy of *The Washington Post* wrote an article on March 25, 2020, suggesting that indeed this response of our government to COVID-19 will bring about the incremental socialism many have advocated.

Abernathy writes:

> Our march toward socialism began incrementally decades ago. But our response to the coronavirus will lead to its permanent implementation after elected officials of both parties shuttered businesses, ordered citizens not to go to work and made clear that there would be more draconian measures to come. The delicate balance between freedom and risk was less than an afterthought as our economy was gutted in a matter of days.

He continues:

> We have crossed the Rubicon. When historians record the moment that the U.S. economy transitioned from free-market capitalism to democratic socialism, they will point to this week. Watching it all unfold has been like witnessing a plane crash in slow motion. When the smoke clears, what's left will be a feeble relic of the United States we once knew.

Abernathy ends, "We are all socialists now."[22]

Thankfully, he is wrong. We are not all socialists now. At least not yet. But we have taken many steps in that direction, and rest assured, there will be increased pressure for the government to continue implementing draconian measures and pursue socialist policies. Expect politicians to promise more free services in their bids for more votes.

The Making of Fiat Money

Where did the US Federal Reserve get the $2.2 trillion to compensate workers and businesses that were shut down in the face of the COVID-19 pandemic? The money was simply created by *fiat*; the word comes from a Latin term that means "let it be done." As the word implies, the money was simply created out of thin air by the Federal Reserve's decree that it exist. It was created digitally without anything to back it up except our faith in our government. The Fed prints very little actual money; printed money is only a fraction of the total money the government owns. These trillions of dollars exist only digitally.

The ability of the Federal Reserve to create billions or even trillions of dollars by fiat reminds us that money itself has no real value; its value is always based on trust. Even gold itself has no special value, except that throughout the centuries, people have assigned value to it. The Knights of Malta stamped *Non Aes, sed Fides* ("Not the metal, but trust") on their coins. I believe calls for the government to create more money for more bailouts and programs will continue to escalate in the days ahead.

The greater Caesar's *role,*
the greater Caesar's *control.*

Modern Monetary Theory (MMT) is the name given to a relatively new idea for an economic plan by which the government never runs out of money. Stephanie Kelton, an advisor on the Bernie Sanders 2016 presidential campaign team, said, "The federal government cannot run out of dollars...The federal government—as the issuer of the U.S. dollar—can create all the money that is needed to guarantee health care for all of its people."[23] So money can appear like magic, and socialism can thrive.

At the time of this writing, the full effects of the COVID-19 crisis have not yet been determined. Perhaps we will be able to reverse these steps toward government bailouts and government control. But with every step the United States takes in the direction of socialism, there will be more calls for the equal distribution of wealth. More politicians will promise free money to get elected, and more regulations will follow. Once a government goes down that path, it is almost impossible to reverse course.

As Mayer Amschel Rothschild has been quoted as saying, "Permit me to issue and control the money of a nation, and I care not who makes its laws!"[24]

Yes, the greater Caesar's *role*, the greater Caesar's *control*.

Stay tuned.

Does the Bible Teach Socialism?

Once in a while, I meet someone who thinks that socialism is found in the Bible. Indeed, Hugo Chávez made this claim while campaigning in Venezuela. The argument is that the early church in Jerusalem was socialist in nature: "No one said that any of the things that belonged to him was his own, but they had everything in common" (Acts 4:32). It's also pointed out that Ananias and Sapphira were struck down because they held back wealth for themselves. The fact that Jesus preached compassion toward the poor is upheld as support for socialism, which is said to be more compassionate than capitalism because it distributes wealth.

Not so fast.

The story of the early church cannot possibly apply to governmental policy. First, the believers' commitment to have "everything in common" was voluntary. No one—including Ananias and Sapphira—was obligated to participate. Peter made this very clear when he visited the couple and traced their sin to the deception of saying they had given all the money to the apostles when they had given only part of it. He clarified that the land and the money received for it was theirs to give or to keep. Peter said, "While it remained unsold, did it not remain your own? And after it was sold, was it not at your disposal?" (Acts 5:4). In other words, the land was theirs, and they were free to sell it and keep the money or keep ownership of the property. *Deception* was their only sin.

The Bible repeatedly affirms the right to private property even in the Ten Commandments, where we read, "You shall not steal" (Exodus 20:15). Whether the theft comes from another individual or the state, stealing is still stealing.

The Bible does not put forth an economic plan for the nations of the world. But there are reasons that capitalism has its roots in the Protestant Reformation, which proposed the idea that it is good if a man seeks to gain wealth through making products that people want—as long as it is done with honesty and integrity. This approach developed into what is known as "the Protestant work ethic," which says hard work, discipline, and frugality are biblical. God gave Adam work to do in the Garden of Eden, expecting him to tend it with care and integrity. Ecclesiastes 2:24 reads, "There is nothing better for a person than that he should eat and drink and find enjoyment in his toil. This also, I saw, is from the hand of God."

All things, including the most mundane, should be done to the glory of God, and it is not wrong to expect rewards for our labor. To amass wealth has its dangers, as the Bible affirms, but by no means is it unbiblical to be rich.

All forms of socialism require the forced redistribution of wealth from those who possess it to those who do not. No one gives any-thing; the state takes and the state gives away. But socialism can-not work indefinitely, for it "rewards malingering and laziness by detaching work from prosperity. But the apostle Paul says, 'If any-one is not willing to work, let him not eat.'"[25]

And there is more.

Economic Theory and Human Nature

Is it true that capitalism is based on *greed* and socialism is based on *need*?

Actually, the opposite is true.

Think this through: Capitalism only works when capitalists cre-ate businesses that meet people's needs. Capitalism is dependent on producing products that people will actually want and buy; con-sumers are voting in favor of capitalism with their dollars. There-fore, it is democratic: If you have no consumers, then there are no profits. The power is in the hands of the consumer.

Contrast that with socialism, which places the power in the hands of the government elites. Products are created without con-cern for meeting people's needs. The government determines what people should have and how much they should pay for it. And those in charge of redistributing the wealth can give themselves extra "bonuses" for their hard work. In socialism, corruption can be conveniently legislated by the state bureaucrats.

A case in point: When my wife and I visited Russia in the 1980s, our interpreter told us of a factory that made shoes no one could wear. The contour of the shoe was wrong and because no one bought them, the shoes were piled high in the warehouse as the factory con-tinued its production. The workers didn't care that they were mak-ing a product that no one wanted because they were continuing to receive their guaranteed wages from the government. The needs of the people were ignored.

A Romanian friend of mine told me that he worked in a foundry where the workers were required to produce a certain amount of iron products. Much of what they produced was unusable because of bad equipment and shoddy craftsmanship, but everyone got paid the same: the slackers, the latecomers, and the somewhat hard workers all got their guaranteed wages.

Whether it is cars, refrigerators, or public housing, the stories we heard were the same. Nothing worked efficiently, nothing was made with the customer in mind. The workers did not have to produce anything the people wanted or needed. Or anything that could even be used.

We even noticed this in stores. In capitalist countries, store clerks are anxious to please their customers, knowing that they are dependent on meeting the needs of their clientele. In a Communist/socialist state, the clerks can be dismissive or even rude. They couldn't care less whether you bought their goods because they don't share in the profits; they get paid the same regardless.

No one wakes up in the morning excited to work for the state. In socialism, indifference, laziness, and lack of ingenuity are all rewarded through guaranteed wages. Whether the work is done well or poorly, efficiently, or with indifference, all share their poverty equally. Over and over we heard, "We pretend to work, and they pretend to pay us."

In the 1950s, Gerald L.K. Smith warned, "You cannot legislate the poor into freedom by legislating the wealthy out of freedom. What one person receives without working for, another must work for without receiving. The government cannot give to anybody anything that the government does not first take from somebody else."[26] Because the government takes and then gives, it must have tight controls. The more centralized the economy, the more it must rule with an iron fist. And rule with an iron fist, it does. I repeat: *Socialism always speaks about distributing wealth, never about creating it.*

No wonder people in Russia could only survive if they formed a shadow economy built on bartering outside of the designated channels. When we were in Russia, we heard one story after another of how the people survived. They paid a repairman with a bag of potatoes and swapped a table for a bed. They traded a day's work in a field for a pair of used shoes. Their ingenuity knew no bounds. We were told that virtually everyone had to have access to vegetables in the fields because they couldn't survive on their wages and pensions.

Which economic system is more compassionate? The one that, of necessity, has to meet the needs of its customers? Or the one that can operate without any thought for benefitting people?

Imagine that our economy was a pie; socialists want to cut the various pieces and distribute them evenly. But after the pie is distributed, there are no other pies to distribute. Only the government can bake another "pie," and because there is no personal profit in baking pies, everything stagnates. Or think of socialism as a caste system: If you're at the back of the line, you stay there. There can be no real path forward. No corporation like Boeing could ever have developed under a socialistic system.

In capitalism, if a company fails, its workers suffer. Now imagine a government of bureaucrats running the entire country according to their sense of equality. When they fail, as they will, the entire country collapses. Whether it's Russia, China, Cuba, or Hitler's National Socialist Germany, the story is always the same: When the state owns the means of production, it needs strict wage and price controls; it needs to restrict the freedom of the people. When hospitals are overcrowded and there's a shortage of doctors who are willing to work for state-limited wages, services have to be cut back. Healthcare has to be rationed, and older people are seen as dispensable.

What Karl Marx did not foresee was the rise of trade unions that have played a role in helping workers get better benefits and wages. The disparities between the haves and the have nots that Marx saw in England have been addressed to a significant extent. No system of economics is perfect; all have flaws, all need correction. Because of our fallenness as humans, we are only capable of seeking that which is best, not that which is perfect.

Greed and Corruption

Socialism cannot function indefinitely because it has a fatal flaw. It neither understands nor appreciates a biblical view of human nature, which puts an end to the utopian dreams of a socialist or Marxist state. It is an economic theory that is deceptive and must fail because it cannot meet the basic needs of its population.

What form of economics is most corrupt? Socialism or capitalism? Of course, both forms are capable of fostering greed and corruption, a sad but true commentary on the human heart. But both reason and history assure us that socialism, by its very nature, gives more opportunity for greed and corruption. In socialism, you are taught early on that if you want to better your lifestyle, you cannot do so by working harder, but by gaming the system. Your job is to find ways to cheat the system to get what is "free."

As Israel discovered when it began to run its kibbutzim on socialist principles, people began to misuse the system because food and services were "free." They left their lights and heat on longer than necessary because they didn't have to pay market price for electricity. Pets ate at the dining room table because the food was "free." As one of the kibbutzim pioneers said, "It became a paradise for parasites."[27]

A paradise for parasites!

What makes anyone think that if only the means of production were in the hands of the government, greed would disappear?
Yes, we as humans harbor self-interest, and greed lies deep in every
human heart. But under socialism, greed is institutionalized because
of the competition among the populace to get what is "free." Greed
runs amok both among the rulers who distribute the wealth and
among the poor people who try to survive on their guaranteed
income. Yes, you must find creative ways to bypass the government
programs to survive.

Of course, capitalism is far from perfect. Greed, corruption, and
vicious competition often abound. And yes, the elites pay themselves large salaries and seek to undercut their competitors. Wall
Street is abuzz with loan sharks and cutthroat investors constantly
monitoring their profits. But at least there are strict rules that make
prosecution possible.

Socialism rewards laziness, stifles competition, and restricts individual liberties. Under socialism, the corruption remains largely
unchecked because it is more difficult to discover and uproot; it is
next to impossible to prosecute. The bureaucrats who dictate where
the money goes are the ones who make the laws and reward themselves. No wonder even the poor under capitalism fare much better
than most of the poor in socialist countries.

Venezuelan Daniel Milán notes that "to make a truly socialist
country you'd need a bunch of zombies and robots, because real
human beings were not meant for socialism."[28] Socialism submerges
the individual in an ocean of bureaucracy and tightfisted regulations.

Marx's utopian dream was that if the proletariat took control,
a classless society would eventually emerge. This defies human
experience and even a cursory understanding of a biblical view of
humanity. Marx believed that capitalists exploited the poor and

manipulated the economic system to suit their own ends, and with incredible naiveté, he thought that human nature would suddenly become selfless and caring once a suitable economic environment was provided. He believed that under the right conditions, humans would spontaneously act lawfully, and eventually both the state and the law would wither away. Marx's delusions are still believed today.

In the book *Divided by Faith: Evangelical Religion and the Problem of Race in America*, which is frequently recommended by evangelicals but based on sociology and not the Bible, the authors write, "Progressives view humans as essentially good, provided they are released from social arrangements that prevent people from living happily, productively, and equally—for example, racism, inequality, and lack of educational opportunity."[29] Marx would have agreed. His error was to believe that people's difficulties are merely the product of external social conditions. As John Warwick Montgomery points out,

> Man himself created the conditions of exploitation—and therefore what kind of logic justifies the belief that by removing those conditions man will suddenly be rendered incapable of recapitulating them? The root difficulty lies not with the "economy" (or with any other impersonal factor); it lies in the heart of man himself.[30]

Nevertheless, some people will always be enamored with state control. After the fall of the Berlin Wall, a Russian newspaper featured a cartoon picturing a fork in the road. One path was labeled "freedom," the other "sausage." As we might guess, the path to freedom had few takers; the path to sausage was crowded with footprints.

Progress down a wrong path leads to disaster. These words of Winston Churchill quoted in an earlier chapter are worth repeating:

"The inherent vice of capitalism is the unequal sharing of blessings. The inherent virtue of Socialism is the equal sharing of miseries."[31]

There is plenty of room for disagreement, but surely we all believe that government has an important role in keeping its citizens safe (which includes border control), enforcing laws that keep citizens from harming each other, creating laws that will ensure that appropriate standards are met when goods are produced, and establishing laws that prevent corruption. But when it comes to company ownership, determining wages and prices, and figuring out who gets what, private businesses with a vested interest in their survival as well as building a loyal consumer base will get the job done much better.

To summarize: The more the state owns, the more it controls its citizens. The more it controls its citizens, the more it limits their freedoms. In the end, those who control the economic system are the ones who benefit from it. As George Orwell put it in *Animal Farm*, "All animals are equal, but some animals are more equal than others."[32] Someone once made an observation to the effect that people were born with a yearning for the kind of freedom that socialism must deny its citizens.

A final warning from an unknown source is quite apropos with regard to socialism: "Mice die in mousetraps because they do not understand why the cheese is free."

The Response of the Church

As Christians, we must ask: What does the above discussion about monetary policy teach us about what money *really* is? Millions of Christians are surviving under socialist regimes run by corrupt bureaucrats. And capitalist countries have their share of greed and corruption along with the poor living among the rich. Does all this really matter?

It matters for several reasons.

Capitalism has given many Christians in the West the opportunity to make more money than they need. This wealth has fueled countless missionary projects around the world. Think of any mission work in so-called Third World countries, and you'll discover they are operated by funds supplied by the West. When mission agencies need help, they don't look for supporters in socialist countries because they know the Christians there are fortunate if they have enough money merely to survive. Only a capitalist economy can lift the living standards of ordinary people above subsistence levels.

And yet even in poverty, Christians can show generosity. During the COVID-19 pandemic, I connected with some Christians in a socialist country who didn't have government bailouts or wage guarantees. Yet with barely enough for themselves, they were collecting money to feed the poor and to give help wherever they could. Generosity is not just a matter of money—it is a matter of heart.

The Good Samaritan did not look to a state-run program to take care of the wounded man along the road to Jericho. Nor did he look to the self-righteous religious leaders who thought only about themselves. Jesus tells us the Samaritan "set him on his own animal and brought him to an inn and took care of him. And the next day he took out two denarii and gave them to the innkeeper, saying, 'Take care of him, and whatever more you spend, I will repay you when I come back'" (Luke 10:34-35). This was voluntary, sacrificial giving.

Let me share my burden.

We need to rethink what money really is and ponder more deeply what Jesus taught about how we use our funds. Why did Jesus repeatedly warn about dependence on money? And what did He mean when He spoke about true riches? Why is money so deceitful?

Money makes the same promises God does. In effect, money

says, "I will be with you in sickness and in health; I will be there when your friends fail you. I will be there when others are starving and there are long lines at food banks. I promise you security, health, and pleasure." Wave big money in the faces of most people and they'll lie, cheat, and otherwise throw out their basic principles to get it. You may have heard some variation of this slogan: "Get it honestly if you can; get it deceitfully if you must, but *get it.*"

Yet money cannot keep its promises. I read a true account about two gold miners who were caught in a terrible blizzard in northern Canada and were not able to leave in time to escape the coming winter. Months later, they were found starved to death in their hut surrounded by pieces of gold. Money has no inherent value unless it's transmuted into some other form of wealth: food, clothing, or if we are wise, we will invest in eternal riches.

The passage of Scripture about money that lodges most deeply in my heart is what Jesus taught in Luke 16:9 in the context of a parable. He said to use your wealth "so that when it fails [friends] may receive you into the eternal dwellings" (Luke 16:9). In other words, take the money you have and transmute it into a form that will survive inflation, deflation, a change of political regimes, and your own certain death. This, Jesus said, is "true riches" (verse 11).

Eventually, all human currencies will become worthless. In his book *The Day the Dollar Dies*, Willard Cantelon tells a story I will never forget. He speaks about a Bible school that was going to be built in Berlin after WWII. Amid the rubble, Christians were coming together to train German young people for Christian living and ministry.

A German mother, wanting to assist the Bible school, brought her gift of 10,000 marks for the building program. She held her money with pride and tenderness as if it were a part of her very life. And in a literal sense it was just that—she had worked hard to earn the money and guarded it all through the war. She beamed with pride as she offered her contribution.

Yet Cantelon had to tell her a sad fact. He writes, "How could I tell her she had held this money too long? Why did it fall to my lot to shock this sensitive soul with the news that her money was virtually worthless? Why had she not read the morning paper or heard the announcement that the new government at Bonn had canceled this currency?

"Madam" I said slowly, "I'm awful sorry but I cannot accept your money…" As gently as I could, I said, "It has been canceled."[33] One month earlier, that money could have been used to purchase materials; it could have fed workers and helped prospective students. But a month later, the money had become worthless.

> Our love and sacrifice should be an attractive alternative to the false hopes of utopian dreams.

All believers—and I am especially thinking of those who have benefited from capitalism—will someday stand before the judgment seat of Christ with worthless money left in their banks and retirement funds. When the Lord comes, "the heavens will pass away with a roar, and the heavenly bodies will be burned up and dissolved, and the earth and the works that are done on it will be exposed" (2 Peter 3:10). Everything will be cancelled. Of that we can be certain.

As Francis Schaeffer is said to have put it, we must have "capitalism with compassion." Yes, too often capitalism exploits the poor and appeals to the greed of the human heart. But we must do all we can to make money with the intention of giving it away, using it so that there will be people who will meet us in "the eternal dwellings."

Our love and sacrifice should be an attractive alternative to the false hopes of utopian dreams. And even where Karl Marx still rules, the church is called to be the church.

To whom much is given, much is required (see Luke 12:48).

A Prayer All of Us Must Pray

Father, so often we say that You own everything we have. And intellectually, we know You do, but please help us to act on this. May we transfer our funds from our ownership to Yours; may we genuinely acknowledge that You are Lord and seek Your guidance on how to best use what we have so that it may reap eternal good. Let the words "lay up for yourselves treasures in heaven" (Matthew 6:20) be our motivation, our motto, and our glad mandate.

Let us remember that stinginess is a denial of the Christ who generously and freely gave Himself for us. May our treasures in heaven be many and our treasures on earth be few.

Let this prayer not be just a matter of words, but deeds.

In Jesus' name, amen.

CHAPTER 8

Join with Radical
Islam to Destroy America

We will use the freedoms of the Constitution to destroy the Constitution!"

Those were the words on a sign carried by a Muslim demonstrator near Detroit, Michigan. *Use our freedoms to destroy our freedoms!*

Why would two ideologies—one radically secular and one radically and oppressively religious—find common ground in the United States? And why are these two groups joining hands in their attacks on basic Judeo-Christian values? Radical Islamists and radical secularists are fighting side by side, brought together by a common enemy.

To begin, I need to emphasize that the majority of Muslims who live in America have come to accept Western values and have no interest in attacking America's religious history or economic system. They benefit from the West's freedom and opportunities, and they hope that they will continue to do so. Most of us are acquainted with a Westernized version of Islam that does not reflect the true nature of this religion.

Yet there are radical Islamists who have a burning passion to implement shariah law in the United States and see their flag fly over the White House. These leaders are by no means the majority, but they have disproportionate control and influence. They have the ability to stir up others—oftentimes by deceptive means—and enlist them in their fight against America.

The cofounder of CAIR (Counsel on American-Islamic Relations) said, "Islam isn't in America to be equal to any other faith, but to become dominant. The Koran should be the highest authority in America, and Islam the only accepted religion on Earth."[1]

In a raid in 2004, the FBI discovered a secret document that revealed the Muslim Brotherhood's plans to overtake America, called The Project. I will not review it point by point, but I will give a summary written by an antiterrorist consultant, Patrick Poole.

He describes it this way:

> [The Project] represents a flexible, multi-phased, long-term approach to the "cultural invasion" of the West. Calling for the utilization of various tactics, ranging from immigration, infiltration, surveillance, propaganda, protest, deception, political legitimacy and terrorism, The Project has served for more than two decades as the Muslim Brotherhood "master plan."[2]

The Muslim Brotherhood's plans teach us that "the intrusion of Islam will erupt in multiple locations using multiple means."[3] Our danger is that we brush aside this strategy as the ranting of a few radicals, just as Germany initially dismissed the ravings of Adolf Hitler.

As early as the 1950s, Islamists began to realize they had an ally in the radical left. Sayyid Qutb, who was the leading theoretician of the Muslim Brotherhood, wrote the seminal text, *Social Justice in Islam*. His agenda was to impose Islamic law throughout the world to liberate humanity and bring about purification and redemption. His view of social justice found common ground with that of the radical left, and this is one reason the latter are anxious to please the Islamists and support rights for Muslims that it denies to Christians.

At the time of this writing in 2020, don't be surprised that we have not had any terror attacks recently in the United States. The radical Islamists know that terrorism can work against their strategy; it is best if they maintain their "stealth jihad," insisting on what they see as their rights. Andrew McCarthy, a former chief assistant US Attorney in New York, has emphasized that our real threat is not terrorism but Islamism. He writes, "Leftists and Islamists are well aware that their designs for society—which for both involve drastic transformation—are anathema to most Americans. They have to advance their cause in stealth."[4]

In the United States, the Muslim Brotherhood has dozens of front organizations through which they operate. Such organizations are the troops on the ground, so to speak, that implement the "Grand Jihad," as they call it. The hope of the Brotherhood is that people in the West will be so focused on terrorism that they'll turn a blind eye to the inner transformation of America happening away from the headlines.

To again quote McCarthy, who has been decorated with the Justice Department's highest honors, "Policymakers won't come to grips [with the nature of the enemy]. Focused myopically on only one of the jihadist's means, violence, they mistakenly assume that ending the violence would perforce end Islamism's threat to our way of life."[5] He warns it is "national suicide for a free, self-determining people to pretend that our problems are limited to Muslim terrorists."[6] So the threat of terrorism is but a foil for a more insidious campaign of deception and infiltration.

Both radical Islamists and radical secularists believe in utopia— Muslims believe in a religious utopia, the radical left believes in a secular one. But both groups believe that their vision cannot be fulfilled until Christian influence and capitalism are destroyed. After that, the secularists and the Islamists will have to part ways, for they have two very different visions for America. For now, however, they find themselves side by side as cultural warriors. As someone has said, the radical left sees Islam as a "battering ram" that can help de-Christianize America.

Even Pilate and Herod set aside their differences and became friends to kill their common enemy, Jesus (Luke 23:12). As they say in battle, "The enemy of my enemy is my friend."

The Opportunity of 9/11

If we can pinpoint a time when the radical left joined Islamists to undermine America, it would be after the horrible terrorist attacks of September 11, 2001, when almost 3,000 Americans were killed. The time afterward was one of renewed patriotism among US citizens, but also of critical introspection.

The radical left eagerly accepted the Islamic narrative that this act of terrorism was America's fault. The terrorists did what oppressed people do—they attacked their enemies. When American flags were being flown in schools, office buildings, and lawns in a show of unity, the left began its assault on the flag, on patriotism, and on America in general.

After a rant about how hateful America was, influential novelist Barbara Kingsolver wrote an op-ed piece on September 25 (just 14 days after the terror attack) in which she was critical of US leaders who wanted to track down and punish the perpetrators.

She asked, "Who are we calling terrorists here?"

To continue:

> Patriotism threatens free speech with death. It is infuriated by thoughtful hesitation, constructive criticism of our leaders, and pleas for peace. It despises people of foreign birth who've spent years learning our culture and contributing their talents to our economy.

Then she ended with an assault on the flag, saying that "the American flag stands for intimidation, censorship, violence, bigotry, sexism, homophobia, and shoving the Constitution through a paper shredder."[7]

And so, in the minds of the left, the common enemy was America, not radical Islam. Never mind that Islam allows men to have multiple wives and seeks global supremacy, and that the laws of Saudi Arabia insist that those who convert from Islam to another religion should be executed. The left's willingness to defend a fundamentalist theocracy that believes in stoning homosexuals, religious supremacism, and the oppression of women (if not violence against them) is surprising. But a common enemy makes them join hands in the fight. The left defends radical Muslims, arguing that they have a good reason to hate us.

The influential philosopher Noam Chomsky says that whatever evil has been committed against America pales in comparison to the evils that America has committed against others. As David Horowitz writes, "For 40 years Noam Chomsky has turned out book after book, pamphlet after pamphlet and speech after speech with one message, and one message alone: America is the Great Satan; it is the fount of evil in the world."[8]

So, in the minds of both radical Islamists and radical leftists, a nation conceived in liberty and where all people are said to be created equal is really the Great Satan built on slavery and dedicated to conquest. It has been said that for centuries America has been responsible for the oppression, poverty, and injustice within its borders and around the world—and the blame continues through today.

There are those who say the United States' war on terror is nothing more than an American ploy to mask the nation's own dark side. The terror attacks on 9/11 only highlighted the fact that America is evil, and the chickens had finally come home to roost. Even America's right to defend itself was held up to ridicule. In summary, the war on terror was invented to serve as a scapegoat for everything that is wrong with American society.

We even saw this hesitancy of the media to call out the Muslim terrorists on the eighteenth anniversary of the 9/11 terror attacks. *The New York Times* tweeted (and later deleted), "Airplanes took aim and brought down the World Trade Center."[9] The *Times* didn't identify who was flying the planes; it did all it could to distance itself from blaming people—specifically al-Qaeda Muslim terrorists who committed the ghastly attacks.

Yes, two planes flew into the Twin Towers. But the planes did not fly themselves. The point of much of the discussion on talk shows was on how America also kills people with its bombs in its war against the Taliban. This is, of course a false equivalency, but it's what is used to give cover to those who blame America for what happened.

David Horowitz writes, "According to every reputable survey, hundreds of millions of Muslims supported those attacks, and tens of thousands of 'infidels' had already died at the hands of Islamic terrorists. Yet President Obama denied that Islam had anything to do with these facts."[10]

Professor Nicholas De Genova, at a Colombia University teach-in, said, "Peace is not patriotic. Peace is subversive, because peace anticipates a very different world than the one in which we live—a world where the U.S. would have no place."[11]

Peace is "a world where the U.S. would have no place."

The cultural Marxists believe the naïve notion that people do evil only because they are oppressed. Remove the oppression, and they will be peaceful and accommodating. Dennis Prager, who has talked with large numbers of people across a wide spectrum of America, says this about the left: "They really believe that people who strap bombs to their bodies to blow up families...plant bombs at a nightclub...slit stewardesses' throats and ram airplanes filled with innocent Americans into office buildings do so because they lack sufficient incomes."[12]

Or, as the cultural Marxists would add, because of what America has done to them. In other words, the terrorists are not to blame. It's America who made them terrorists.

The left believes that if the United States were to cease its alleged oppression, the reason for the Islamists' radicalization would be removed. They would no longer fly their planes into skyscrapers and kill thousands of people if the United States had the right foreign policy. *Oppression*—specifically American oppression—is at fault. Thus, the left believes that if capitalism were uprooted and a socialist state were to emerge, radical Islam would no longer have to be radical.

This attitude fits nicely with the Muslim claim of victimhood that goes back to the time of Muhammad. Their "victimhood" has always been said to be greater than the evil they inflict on others. During the Danish cartoon controversy, "mob attacks and assassinations...claimed the lives of over 200 people utterly uninvolved with the 'blasphemous' drawings."[13] Yet the violent actions were said to be justified because Islam had been insulted. The blame for the deaths was laid at the doorstep of the cartoonist who "inflicted" this suffering on Islam. The riots taught the world a lesson: "Don't criticize us or we will come after you and it will all be your fault."

The Unity of Mosque and State

In the United States, the separation of church and state is an article of faith among the radical left. But the phrase "separation of church and state" does not appear in the US Constitution. Instead, it is mentioned in a letter written by Thomas Jefferson to assure a church that the government should not interfere with the free exercise of religion. This fact evidently has no bearing on the left's agenda to stamp out all Christian influence in our public schools.

In the minds of the secularists, however, there is no such thing as the separation of mosque and state. Following 9/11, Islamists were permitted—even encouraged—to evangelize for their religion. The American Civil Liberties Union did not object, nor did the Freedom from Religion Foundation. Although the left had made sure that schools would be scrubbed clean of any Christian influence, it welcomed the teachings and proselytizing of Islam, the very religion that inspired the 9/11 attacks. Leftists do not care about whether religion is actively promoted in our schools as long as it is a religion that seeks to destroy Western values. Christianity, not Islam, is the villain.

In 2018, two mothers of students at Chatham Middle School in New Jersey filed a federal lawsuit against the school for showing two videos intending to proselytize students to Islam. One was called *Intro to Islam,* and the other *5 Pillars.* These mothers appealed directly to the school but were rebuffed. When they continued to pursue the matter, they were attacked on social media as bigots and Islamophobics—hateful, ignorant, intolerant, and racist. The

Thomas More Law Center filed suit against the school because the videos gave a distorted picture of Islam's history and what it teaches.[14]

Students in many schools have had to endure similar indoctrination attempts. In 2015, students at Spring Hill Middle School in Tennessee were required to write, "There is no god but Allah; and Muhammed is his prophet," which is a statement used by those who convert into Islam.[15] Students in some schools have been told to memorize parts of the Qur'an, shout, "Allahu Akbar!," and to fast over lunch in honor of Ramadan. Schools in Maryland, Michigan, and Arizona are allowing Muslim students to pray during school hours.

In 2008, The American Textbook Council, an independent national research organization, issued a report finding that ten of the most widely used middle school and high school social studies textbooks "present an incomplete and confected [falsely constructed] view of Islam that misrepresents its foundations and challenges to international security."[16] The bottom line is that these textbooks whitewash the history and teaching of Islam and denigrate Western history and values.

The Council also noted,

> While seventh-grade textbooks describe Islam in glowing language, they portray Christianity in harsh light. Students encounter a startling contrast. Islam is featured as a model of interfaith tolerance; Christians wage wars of aggression and kill Jews. Islam provides models of harmony and civilization. Anti-Semitism, the Inquisition and wars of religion bespot the Christian record.[17]

Not surprisingly, in these textbooks, America is blamed for the world's woes.

There's one statement from The American Textbook Council

report that should be read carefully. It says that the Council on Islamic Education now enjoys "virtually unchecked power over publishers" and is an "agent of contemporary censorship," informing publishers that it may "decline requests for reviewing published materials, unless a substantial and substantive revision is planned by the publisher."[18] The taboo about teaching religion in schools—so zealously promoted by the ACLU and our courts—is conveniently set aside in deference to Muslim demands.

Today, the tax dollars of American citizens are being used to build prayer rooms for Muslims in some public schools and ensure that halal foods (prepared according to standards set by Islamic law) are served in cafeterias. And organizations such as The Institute on Religion and Civic Values (formerly known as The Council on Islamic Education) provide federally funded materials to teach Islam in public schools. Videos are available that present a sanitized version of Islam and teach how the Qur'an can be used in daily life.

If those on the left were genuinely concerned about the integrity of the First Amendment (as they interpret it), the same alleged wall that separates church and state would also separate mosque and state. Instead, the left celebrates not just teaching about Islam but actively *proselytizing* for Islam in the public schools.

Why? The left despises Christianity. Fundamentalist Islam has declared war on "infidel" cultures like America's with its Judeo-Christian respect for individual liberty and constitutional restraints on the power of government.

And why are feminists silent when it comes to Islam's abhorrent treatment of women? Feminists are verbally paralyzed—on the one hand they disagree with how women are treated in Islam, but on the other they choose to give Islam a pass. The leftist progressives are silent even though homosexuals are executed in Muslim countries. The leftists do not want to be critical of a religion that is helping them destroy the foundations of Western civilization. To quote David Horowitz, "On their hatred of Christianity and contempt for the Constitution, both the left and political Islam agree."[19]

And there is more.

The Muslim Doctrine of Immigration

"Diversity makes us stronger!"

You may have heard that statement uttered by people who are advocating some cause or other. But let's examine what it actually says. Is it really true that the less we have in common, the stronger we will be? When God brought confusion at the tower of Babel by causing people to speak different languages, their "diversity" did not make them stronger. Rather, their diversity scattered them and made them weaker. A nation is held together by people who share common core values and a common language. We could wish that all those we welcome to live in the United States would be held together with a common commitment to the Constitution and its core values.

Immigration is integral to Islam's goals of Islamizing America. As mentioned earlier, many Muslims have integrated and have accepted Western values such as the freedom of religion—they respect this freedom as a core value. But there are some who take the Qur'an and the Hadith (the sayings of Muhammad) literally and are committed to the supremacy of Islam in America.

Both the Qur'an and the Hadith contain commands urging Muslims to immigrate. For example: "I charge you with five of what Allah has charged me with: To assemble, to listen, to obey, to immigrate and to wage Jihad for the sake of Allah" (Hadith 17344). Historically, Muhammad left Mecca in the seventh century and traveled with a small band of followers to Medina to strengthen his forces so that he could return to capture Mecca at a later time. This became known as the *Hijrah* (migration). This model of migration is not for the purpose of assimilating into a new host nation, but for colonizing and transforming host countries.

Let us remember the first major point of the Muslim Brotherhood plan to destroy America: "To expand the Muslim presence by birth rate, immigration and a refusal to assimilate."[20] This strategy transformed Indonesia from a Buddhist and Hindu country to the largest Muslim-dominated country in the world. As Europe has discovered, open borders for refugees may be viewed as a compassionate response to a catastrophic humanitarian crisis, but it has long-term risks and consequences.

The radical hope of Islamists is that through Muslim immigration and population growth in the West, shariah law will eventually replace US laws.

The Deception of Political Correctness

"We don't discriminate!"

These words are the rallying cry of leftists who claim to be tolerant. Of course, the reality is that everyone discriminates. Employers discriminate among potential employees; people discriminate as to which church, mosque, or temple they attend (or none of the above). And we all discriminate when we decide who our friends will be and who we take out for dinner over the weekend. Every day and in every way we make choices about people, and each choice is, in some sense, discrimination.

Political correctness divorced from common sense has discouraged people from taking care to wisely discriminate against harmful and dangerous ideologies and influences. The fear of being on the wrong side of discrimination issues drives some people to buckle and make foolish decisions. One of our great faults as a nation is that we don't know how to properly discriminate; so the fear that we could be accused of discrimination makes even our security services bow to the winds of political correctness.

Political correctness divorced from common sense has discouraged people from taking care to wisely discriminate against harmful and dangerous ideologies and influences.

Because our national security agencies have become paralyzed by multiculturalism and obsessions with diversity, investigations into the extent of the jihad agenda have been hindered. No one wants to appear anti-Muslim, and this has led to serious lapses in national security. In the security report *Shariah: The Threat to America* (abridged version), the authors conclude, "Multiculturalism, political correctness, misguided notions of tolerance and sheer willful blindness have combined to create an atmosphere of confusion and denial in America about the current threat confronting the nation."[21] They concur that the breaches in our security systems are nothing short of criminal.

Islamophobia is a word invented by a Muslim to shame anyone who is critical of Islam, even if the criticism is factually accurate. The same political correctness used to weaken—if not destroy—capitalism is the same political correctness that allows Islam to flourish. Our culture is trading wisdom for mindless acceptance and courage for cowardice.

Thankfully, God has raised up the church for such a time as this.

The Response of the Church

We who are Christians must reach out with a welcoming hand to the Muslims who live among us. We dare not let fear cause us to turn away from the Muslims in our communities. Eric Metaxas says, "If you are fear-based, you are not worshipping Jesus."

We must not see Muslims as our enemies, but rather, as people who have been misled by a religion that keeps them in spiritual and cultural bondage. We should become as familiar with their religion as possible. Martin Luther insisted that the Qur'an be translated into German because he believed that this was the best way to make sure that the Germans would not convert to Islam. Anyone who reads the Qur'an, he contended, would immediately recognize that this book is not from God. We have to be as "wise as serpents and innocent as doves" (Matthew 10:16). The church must equip believers to engage followers of Islam, fully understanding their history, beliefs, and goals.

However, as I stated in my book *The Church in Babylon*, I must warn against the growing trend for churches to have "interfaith dialogues with Muslims." From the Muslim point of view, the goal of interfaith dialogue is stated by Seyyid Qutb: "The chasm between Islam and jahiliyyah [the society of unbelievers] is great and a bridge is not to be built across so that people on the two sides may mix with each other, *but only so that people of Jahiliyyah [the society of unbelievers] may come over to Islam.*"[22] From a Muslim perspective, interfaith dialogue doubletalk is acceptable and even necessary. The goal is to present an inviting but false narrative of Islam, making it palatable and acceptable to Western audiences and casually committed Christians.

I took the time to read *Interfaith Dialogue: A Guide for Muslims* by Muhammad Shafiq and Mohammed Abu-Nimer so that I might better understand the Muslim motivation in interfaith dialogue.

This book, written by Muslims and for Muslims, speaks in very neutral tones, many of which would be acceptable to Christians. They talk about fairness, politeness, careful listening, and the need for coexistence.[23]

However, the goal of the book is to teach Muslims how to present their faith in a way that would make it acceptable to non-Muslims. In brief, it was written to present a sanitized version of Islam by reinterpreting its sacred texts and history. Several times the book says that Muslims must use interfaith dialogue to remove the "misconceptions" that exist about Islam.

Read this carefully: "Each dialogue partner has the right to define his or her own religion and beliefs [so that] the rest can only describe what it looks like to them from the outside."[24] And again: "These seminars should address both Christian and Muslim's beliefs and provide a comparative view of each, without attempting to judge between the two."[25]

The bottom line: Muslim participants in interfaith dialogue want an uncontested platform where they can present a version of Islam without undesirable references from the Qur'an or Islam's aggressive and bloody history. Each participant should take the other's words at face value and not criticize what the other is saying. In other words, a critical analysis of the respective religions is discouraged. No wonder Muslims are eager for "interfaith dialogue"—it gives them an opportunity to deceptively spread their faith among gullible American audiences.

A better means of introducing Muslims to the gospel is through building personal relationships with them. This means communicating the gospel by backing your words with deeds of kindness and genuine friendship, whether your Muslim acquaintances are open or not to the possibility of accepting Jesus as Savior. Despite the plans and actions of radical Islamists—whether carried out through covert infiltration or through blatant violence—God is always in control of what happens in this world.

Many of us actively pray for countries that are closed to the gospel and help support missionaries sent to Muslim nations. What if a part of God's answer to our prayers for the Muslim world is to bring Muslims to America so they can be introduced to genuine Christians and not the caricatures promoted in their home countries? Though Muslim immigration presents potential risks, it also presents wonderful opportunities. I could give many examples of churches and individual Christians who are reaching out to Islamic communities here in America, especially among refugees.

Our witness must be coupled with discernment. Frequently, American Christians are so willing to believe the best about others that they are often blind to those who would mislead them. In many quarters, Christians enter interfaith dialogue with Muslims. The rules of such engagement are clear: Christians are free to explain what they believe, and then the Muslim leader has an equal turn to explain what Islam believes. Because these dialogues are not given to cross-examination, the Muslim is free to present a version of Islam that is sanitized for an American audience. (Again, I have written more extensively about this in my book *The Church in Babylon*—see pages 215-221.)

And what happens if we should eventually lose our freedoms to radicals?

Sam Solomon was trained in shariah law and taught it for 15 years before he converted to Christianity. When he was visiting here in America, I attended a lecture he gave on what this nation would be like if Islamists were to have their way and shariah law prevailed. His presentation was well-researched and compelling—and frightening. Later that day we met in a dining room, and we talked.

I asked him a simple question: "In light of what you have shared, and considering the gains that radical Islam is making in America, what is my responsibility as the pastor of a church?" He pressed his index finger against my chest and said, "Your responsibility is to teach your people to be ready to die as martyrs for the faith!"

I had never thought of that as a part of my job description. But his words have never left me, and ever since, I have studied martyrdom both from the Bible and church history. There are millions of Christians who have been put to death for their faith, and they have died in numerous ways. Islam's favorite method of execution is to use a sword. God willing, I hope to eventually write a book on the subject of martyrdom.

Courage armed with
truth is our calling.

On one occasion after terrorists killed many Christians in Egypt, I am told that young Christians in Cairo marched down the streets with T-shirts emblazoned with the words, "Martyr by Request!" I'm not sure that we in America would have that kind of courage. Truth be told, we are often unwilling to give up any comforts, let alone our lives.

We probably will not be faced with martyrdom here in America, but we have to ask whether the church will be courageous enough to withstand the cultural and legal pressures that secularism is determined to impose upon us as Islam expands its influence and asserts its "rights," which so often conflict with our rights. Will political correctness and laws that prohibit the criticism of Islam (blasphemy laws) paralyze the church? Already, criticism of Islam—no matter how accurate and thoughtful—is taboo in the wider culture.

Huldrych Zwingli, a leader of the Reformation in Switzerland, is purported to have said, "For God's sake, do something courageous!" Courage armed with truth is our calling.

A Prayer All of Us Must Pray

Let us pray selected passages from Daniel's prayer in Daniel chapter 9.

> *To us, O LORD, belongs open shame, to our kings, to our princes, and to our fathers, because we have sinned against you. To the LORD our God belong mercy and forgiveness, for we have rebelled against him and have not obeyed the voice of the LORD our God by walking in his laws (verses 8-10).*
>
> *O my God, incline your ear and hear. Open your eyes and see our desolations [in our country and its churches]. For we do not present our pleas before you because of our righteousness, but because of your great mercy. O Lord, hear; O Lord, forgive. O Lord, pay attention and act. Delay not, for your own sake, O my God, because your city and your people are called by your name (verses 18-19).*

Father, we are Yours. Help us to represent You faithfully in a nation that has lost its way. Help us to love and honor You by our lives and witness. Help us to show grace and respect to all who differ from us and be courageous in sharing Your holy Word.

In Jesus' name, amen.

CHAPTER 9

Vilify! Vilify! Vilify!

"Pick the target, freeze it, personalize it, and polarize it."[1] That's what activist Saul Alinsky wrote in his book *Rules for Radicals*.

The radical secularists are not satisfied with "live and let live." Rather, they demand that we totally capitulate to their agenda. And they have discovered that vilifying those who disagree with them gets more results than reason and civility. Whether they know it or not, they are following the above-cited instructions from the Marxist Saul Alinsky.

When Alinsky speaks of polarizing the target, this is what he means: "Cut off the support network and isolate the target from sympathy. Go after people and not institutions; people hurt faster than institutions. (This is cruel but very effective. Direct, personalized criticism and ridicule works.)"[2]

Direct, personalized criticism and ridicule works!

Right from the outset, those who practiced Alinsky's methods would make use of three weapons: shame, ridicule, and intimidation. Going back to 1973, homosexual activists persuaded the American Psychiatric Association to remove homosexuality from its list of psychiatric illnesses and reclassify it as normal behavior.[3] This change was made not on account of scientific data but because radicals planned a systematic effort to disrupt the annual meetings of the APA. Three years earlier, activists grabbed the microphone in an APA meeting and said, "Psychiatry is the enemy incarnate. Psychiatry has waged a relentless war of extermination against us. You may take this as a declaration of war against you…We're rejecting you all as our owners."[4]

The result? A scientific society ignored empirical studies and yielded to the demands of a militant group. Through this one action, the gay movement let it be known that intimidation would replace research, science, civility, and dialogue. Bullying would overcome any obstacles in their path.

David Horowitz, in *Dark Agenda*, writes, "The left…has no conscience or restraint when it comes to destroying people who stand in its way. The war began with the removal of the religious presence from America's public schools. Since then, it has only grown more divisive and intense."[5] The radicals are viscerally intolerant of anyone who does not agree with their view of tolerance. They insist on nothing less than being celebrated by all members of society, including within our churches.

Arguments about natural law, questioning the wisdom of letting homosexuals adopt children, arguments in favor of the traditional family—none of these are up for discussion. Their argument is simply stated: Those who oppose any aspect of LGBTQ rights are bigots. And bigots deserve to be ostracized and, if possible, punished.

Slander and intimidation are more powerful than rational discussion.

Public Shaming

Proposition 8

When Proposition 8 (which defined marriage as between one man and one woman) was passed in 2008 by the voters of California, the LGBTQ lobby retaliated. Supporters were shamed by disclosing their names and addresses online, inviting harassment by the radicals.[6] Many supporters of the ban on gay marriage lost their jobs and businesses were boycotted. Employees were threatened and their homes and property vandalized. Some radical activists entered establishments to publicly shame those who had voted to support the amendment. Proponents were bullied into submission or at least into silence.

A full-page ad in *The New York Times* denounced the tactics of the LGBTQ community backlash as "a mob veto" and encouraged them to stop the violence against the supporters of Proposition 8. Yet six years later, the ongoing effects of this backlash became evident when the cofounder and newly appointed CEO of Mozilla (the firm behind the Firefox web browser), Brendan Eich, was pressured to resign because he had donated $1,000 to support the California amendment.[7] No matter that his record showed that he had never discriminated against gays in his business positions—he was denounced as hateful and bigoted. Even after Eich was fired, the LGBTQ community has continued to release lists of people and businesses so that activists could punish those who had supported the "one man one woman" amendment.

This has caused some churches who refuse to accept same-sex marriage to no longer publish the names of their pastoral staff or elders online; they might be bullied, targeted, and harassed. The philosophy of the LGBTQ community can be stated this way: If you don't support us, we not only disagree with your views, you are evil and deserve to be shouted down.

Chick-fil-A opened a restaurant in Reading, England, and was warmly accepted by the populace; people were waiting in long lines to get a taste of their special chicken. Years earlier, the CEO, Dan T. Cathy, told an interviewer, "We are very much supportive of the family—the biblical definition of the family unit…We know that it might not be popular with everyone, but thank the Lord, we live in a country where we can share our values and operate on biblical principles."[8]

That, and the fact Chick-fil-A supports social organizations that favor a biblical view of the family, was enough to attract the opposition of radicals, first here in the United States and then in England. After eight days of nonstop protests, Chick-fil-A closed their restaurant in England. They were driven out by hate, name calling, and nonstop harassment.

In the Marxist playbook, peaceful coexistence does not mean peace. It means to continue the struggle for utopia without resorting to war. In the radicals' minds, those who hold to traditional values and stand against the leftist onslaught are bigots who do not deserve a place at the table. The radicals believe their side must triumph and do so at the expense of reason, debate, and mutual respect. The revolution continues until the left wins, and then the totalitarianism will be full blown. Those who disagree with their agenda for moral reasons must bow or be shamed.

Our culture is being changed by coercion and force.

Private Schools

Private schools are under political, moral, and economic pressure to surrender their convictions to the ruthless sexual revolution. The *Orlando Sentinel* published an article that detailed an investigation which pointed out that 150 private schools that take scholarships (called vouchers) have moral standards that prohibit immoral behavior, including homosexuality.[9]

Now corporations that fund these vouchers are under pressure to discontinue their support. A bill has been filed that would prohibit private schools from establishing anti-LGBTQ policies. Those that continue to have such policies would not receive the vouchers that are so necessary for students to attend these schools. Already some corporations have reported that they will discontinue their support even though they have been receiving tax credits for contributing to these Florida schools.

Let's think about this: Parents choose these private schools because they want their children to be in an environment that does not condone LGBTQ lifestyles. But the LGBTQ community seeks to take such freedom away from parents and force them to bow to their agenda. The notion is that parents don't know what is best for their children; those who represent the sexual revolution are the true arbiters of morality: "Accept our morality, no matter how much you disagree with it, or else!"

I'm reminded of the words of George Orwell, who described totalitarian rule as "a boot stamping on a human face—forever."[10]

Shame! Shame! Shame!

Denunciation in the Public Square

Demonstrations that protest various groups or ideas are somewhat common and constitutional. What made the demonstration in Toronto different is the person who was targeted. Jonathon Van Maren describes an angry mob protesting outside of a library in Toronto:

> Hostility and molten fury bubbled just beneath the surface as hundreds of assembled men and women, wielding signs featuring slogans such as "No Free Speech for

Hate Speech" and launching into chants such as "Trans rights are human rights!" and "Take back TPL [Toronto Public Library]!" and "Shame! Shame!"[11]

What was the offending event? A meeting of conservatives opposed to the LGBTQ agenda? A prolife rally? A politician denouncing socialism?

No, the protests were targeted against the founder of *Feminist Current*, Meghan Murphy, who is proabortion and pro-gay rights but refuses to agree that men can become women. This offense got her banned from Twitter, and the demonstrators accused her of being a vicious and hateful bigot. She was compared to a white supremacist.

Jonathon Van Maren asks this question: "If this is how much they hate a pro-gay feminist, and these are the lengths they will go to in order to ruin her life, what will they do to us when they get the chance?" He concludes, "Their blitzkrieg has cut through our institutions at breathtaking speed—and we need to understand that they are just getting started."[12]

Vilification on Campus

Incoming Texas students were told that if they joined a conservative organization they would be "doxed"—that is, personal information about them would be publicly broadcast for the purpose of inciting people to harass them. Anything in their past that could be used against them would be. Why? Because conservatives are alleged to be racist, homophobic, and greedy capitalists.[13]

When Milo Yiannopoulos was scheduled to speak at Berkeley in February of 2017, the police were alerted but were determined not to deter the violence that was to come. The event ended up being cancelled when rioters beat and pepper-sprayed those who were about to attend and threw explosive devices at the campus police. Then the rioters spread to the streets to do further mayhem that went unchecked by the police.

Activists later justified the violence by saying that allowing Yiannopoulos to speak "could have endangered campus students…over their identities." Thus, a columnist claimed, these attacks "were not acts of violence. They were acts of self-defense."[14]

As Heather Mac Donald put it, "Civility is shrinking and civil peace may be in jeopardy. Masked anarchists use force to block conservatives from speaking in public forums."[15] Freedom of speech and civility will not be restored until the victimology culture is shown to be the fiction it is.

Mac Donald concludes, "College graduates have been told for years that the United States is systematically racist and unjust. The rioters' nauseating sense of entitlement to destroy other people's property and to sucker punch ideological foes is a natural extension of this profound delegitimization of the American polity."[16]

The America we once knew is gone.

Hitler's Brownshirts and Antifa's Black Masks

This is a headline from *The Jerusalem Post*: "The Looting—and Muting—of America."

That headline appeared with an op-ed piece on June 18, 2020. It began, "America, I'm worried about you." Then after a description of the riots that occurred after George Floyd's death, the author continued,

> Extreme as it may sound, when I saw the scenes of hundreds of store windows smashed and wild gangs of

hoodlums allowed to rob at will—as law enforcement
personnel stood immobile on the sidelines—I could not
help but think of the image of Kristallnacht, 1938.[17]

Kristallnacht refers to "the night of broken glass," an evening in
November 1938 when Nazis attacked Jewish people and property
throughout Germany. The pretext (there always has to be a pretext!)
was the shooting in Paris of the German diplomat Ernst vom Rath,
who was killed by a Jewish student. Violent reprisals were organized
by propaganda minister Joseph Goebbels, who specified that the
reprisals should appear spontaneous.

The Gestapo chief Heinrich Müller sent a telegram to all police
units letting them know what was going to happen, and said these
events "were not to be interfered with." Fire departments were told
to let fires burn. Mobs killed Jews and vandalized businesses as the
police and politicians watched.

We can imagine that some of the looters and arsonists in Germany back in 1938 might have been carrying signs that read "Justice for Ernst." Likewise, the anarchists who looted, burned, and
destroyed more than 500 buildings in Minneapolis in May of 2020
were also "seeking justice for George Floyd."

Kristallnacht indeed.

There is a new fascist movement in America called Antifa (anti-
fascist) that no doubt participated in the violent riots of 2020. It
promotes itself as being anti-Nazi by calling for a revolution against
what they allege is the totalitarian state. Their targets are conservatives and capitalists. At a rally, one Antifa speaker echoed the words
of murdered Nazi official Gregor Strasser:

> We are Socialists, enemies, mortal enemies of the present
> capitalist economic system with its exploitation of the
> economically weak, with its injustice in wages, with its

immoral evaluation of individuals according to wealth
and money instead of responsibility and achievement,
and we are determined under all circumstances to abolish this system![18]

How will this political movement accomplish their objective? By
using the same tactics as the Nazi SA—Hitler's Brownshirts—who
disrupted meetings, halted free speech, and caused mayhem. No
wonder one observer said that "they claim the unlimited right to
police Americans' freedom of speech, using violence and illegality to
destroy anyone left-wing activists consider 'racist' or 'oppressive.'"[19]
Perhaps the only difference is that Hitler's SA wore brown shirts and
Antifa wears black masks.

According to Soeren Kern, in "A Brief History of Antifa," "A
common tactic used by Antifa in the United States and Europe is
to employ extreme violence and destruction of public and private
property to goad the police into a reaction, which then 'proves' Antifa's claim that the government is 'fascist.'"[20] We certainly saw this
tactic in Portland, Oregon, and other cities during the riots of 2020.

Antifa pillages, breaks windows, sets cars on fire, and creates
mayhem all the while saying that they are combating hate. To break
down all structures of society and achieve their own revolution, it is
necessary to vilify the authority structures. Along with this goes the
vilification of the police. Ostensibly, the reason for their protests are
because white police officers shoot black people.

Incredibly, the Defund the Police movement has gained momen-
tum among politicians at a time when violent crime in our cities
is increasing. I must again ask the question I raised earlier in this
book: How did we get to the point where the police are said to be
the threat to America and not the anarchists? Certainly, police must
be held accountable for any egregious actions they commit, such as

the murder of George Floyd. We all seek justice when wrong has been done. But to defund entire police departments in response to the bad actions of a very few is insanity.

Remember what I said earlier in this book: Radicals know that when police forces are defunded and even abolished, it is not that no one will be in charge. *The radicals will be in charge.* They will be free to pillage and destroy, looting what is not theirs. They will go from destroying property to destroying people.

My point is not to start a debate about whether black people are treated unfairly; certainly there are examples of racial injustice by the police. My point is simply this: The police represent the last line of defense against anarchy. And if they are continually vilified, blamed, disrespected, and ultimately, defunded, crime will only increase. There are plenty of interviews with those who represent the police that speak of the decreasing morale of our police officers and their desire to no longer be proactive in preventing crime. I saw one police commissioner begging people to show respect to police officers. To defund the police means less money for more police officers and less money for training, the very thing that police need most.

Here in Chicago, two black police officers told me that they are diligent in investigating crimes, but the courts let criminals back out on the streets all too soon. With no need for even posting bond, we end up with "turnstile" justice. Whereas the police used to do crime prevention by breaking up gangs and such, they no longer do so lest they be accused of profiling or using excessive force. Just check on the rising crime rate here in Chicago, and you'll see where the vilification of the police has brought us. While I write this, Chicago is experiencing a murder rate of almost double the number of people who were killed a year ago—even though the mayor opposes defunding the police.

Back in 2014, a group of protesters walked through the streets of

New York City chanting, "What do we want? Dead cops. When do we want it? Now."[21] A week after this march, shortly before Christmas, two police officers were gunned down in Brooklyn.[22] We will never know if the protesters' chant created an atmosphere that precipitated the murders. But the social justice warriors had their wish fulfilled.

Gone is civility, reason, and a dependence on the ballot box. Enraged activists fight and pillage in order to push back on what they allege to be the hate of others. For me, the ability of people to deceive themselves in their attempts to justify violence is a constant source of astonishment.

The Search for Allies

The LGBTQ community now adds an *A* to their moniker. It is now LGBTQA, with the *A* standing for Allies in their "struggle." They do not allow any space for disagreement with their agenda. Parents, schools, and yes, churches are being forced to surrender to their dictates. And if you don't submit? If you don't let them shape the worldview of your child, they will squeeze you financially, corporately, and personally. Accept their morality or pay the consequences.

While we are to be kind and gracious, we are not called to become allies by bowing the knee to cultural pressure.

We gladly celebrate Black History Month, but now we are told we should celebrate Gay Pride Month. Incredibly, many well-meaning

Christians comply by flying the rainbow flag or wearing an "ally pin" to show that they observe Gay Pride Month. As Joe Carter says, "In doing so, they show that they will not incur the wrath that will be poured out on those who are not 'affirming.'"

Carter goes on to say,

> We are so troubled by the thought that LGBT-friendly advocates will fall away from the faith that we fail to see that they've already rejected the faith of historic, orthodox Christianity and replaced it with an idolatrous heresy—one that is as destructive and hateful as any that has come before. We do not love our neighbor when we tell them they can continue to engage in unrepentant rebellion against God...If we truly love our LGBT neighbors, we must speak the Word of God with boldness (Acts 4:31).[23]

Certainly we should reach out with love and compassion to those who struggle with same-sex attraction, but we should also abide by what Scripture says. While we are to be kind and gracious, we are not called to become allies by bowing the knee to cultural pressure.

We have to choose whom we will serve.

The Roots of Injustice

I've already quoted David Horowitz several times in this book because of his keen analyses of our culture. He is Jewish and an agnostic, but he defends Christian values with clarity and conviction. He not only exposes the radical left's agenda, but also tells of his own journey from being a radical himself to developing a conservative view of America and the world. His story is instructive.

Horowitz was brought into reality when he joined the Black

Panthers, who called themselves freedom fighters; they claimed they were on the side of justice and equality for all. But as he got to know them better, he realized that the Black Panther Party "was a criminal gang engaging in extortion, arson, drug racketeering, and several murders." "The Panthers," he says, "conducted these crimes while enjoying the support of the leaders and institutions of the American left." Horowitz continues, "The left defended the killers because they were voices of the oppressed and champions of the progressive cause."[24]

It dawned on Horowitz that the source of injustice was not in society but within the human heart. The so-called liberal progressives are themselves filled with their own prejudices, hatreds, and injustice. In his words, "Nor was injustice caused by oppressive races and genders, or solely by our political enemies. Injustice is the result of human selfishness, deceitfulness, malice, envy, greed, and lust. 'Society' is not the cause of injustice. Society is merely a reflection of who we are."[25]

The point made in this next statement is so clear and obvious that it should be read with care:

> The politically correct, who think it is their mission to save the world, cannot fix the problems that afflict us, because the problems are our creations. Theirs and ours. Because the self-appointed social redeemers seek too much power, and do not understand the source of evil and injustice, they will only make matters worse—as the romance with Communism has shown.[26]

Horowitz then quotes Alexander Solzhenitsyn: "The line separating good and evil passes not through states, nor between classes, nor between political parties either, but right through every human heart, and through all human hearts."[27]

Well said.

Because we as Christians know that the problems of sin and deception lie in every human heart, we stress the need for individual conversion. As the Bible asserts, human nature can be changed only by God. We believe in individual responsibility. While we agree that we are influenced by our lot in life, we do not believe that we should seek a scapegoat for every social problem that exists. Even Horowitz, who is Jewish and not a Christian, says that the doctrine of original sin is a correct diagnosis of the human condition.

This explains why those who protest hate are often the most hateful of all.

Coming Soon to a Church Near You

Overnight, your gospel-preaching church could change from being "a cool place to worship" to being branded as a church of bigotry and hate. That's what happened at The Crossing in Columbia, Missouri—and it could happen anywhere.

On Sunday, October 13, 2019, pastor Keith Simon preached a message on Genesis 1:27 as part of a new sermon series on Genesis. His topic was gender. The sermon was thoughtful, welcoming, and nonjudgmental. In an attempt to speak to the issue of gender confusion, the tone was one of respect and compassion. However, he did affirm the biblical teaching that God created only two genders: male and female. He ended by raising a series of questions, including:

- "Are we sure that erasing the concept of father and mother and substituting parent 1 and parent 2—are we sure that this is good for families?"

- "Are we sure that it is fair for sports to have biological males [who transitioned to female] compete with biological women?"

- "Are we sure that we should give hormones to boys entering puberty to prepare them for gender reassignment surgery?"

- "Are we sure that our internal feelings of who we are always define reality?"

Normally, such a sermon would not only be expected in an evangelical church but would be accepted as consistent with Scripture and biology. Nothing unusual so far.

But by Monday, a social media firestorm ensued and the surrounding community was thrown into a polarizing debate. The church had been a long-time sponsor of a local art gallery and a documentary film festival. Within days, an online petition was created and was quickly signed by 1,000 citizens who urged the art community and film festival to cut their ties to the church.[28] They obediently did so. Personal attacks followed, including calling the pastor the antichrist. People who had never entered the church and did not even hear the sermon weighed in, fueling the fire of outrage. The widespread coverage in local newspapers and television drew national attention.

The Crossing has always been actively involved for the good of their community. For example, in August 2019, the church raised $430,000 to pay off the medical debt of 42,000 patients in Missouri (a sponsor partnered with the church, so the sum total of forgiven loans was in the millions). The church supports multiple local organizations that assist those in financial need, and plans annual missions trips to partner with effective ministries in countries with great poverty. Started 20 years ago, the church now has an attendance of 4,000. No wonder the word on the street was that this was the place to worship. They were known for what they were *for* not what they were *against*.

But the church crossed a tripwire. The current culture rejects civil discourse, rational discussions, and honest evaluations of biological and scientific evidence despite the fact many doctors say that gender tampering can be harmful for children and, for that matter, adults. There has been a consistent push to uncritically accept the contemporary dictum that gender is fluid, that it is a state of mind, and that it is defined not by biology, but by desires and inclinations. Not only can a man become a woman and a woman become a man, but there are also other genders on the spectrum.

The growing number of heartbreaking stories shared by those who have had transgender surgery only to determine that their gender dysphoria had not been resolved are being ignored. The mere act of raising questions about the ongoing struggles of transgenders has resulted in the vilification of those who dare to ask them.

Social media has provided the fuel for hatred, false accusations, and perpetual outrage. A single spark can light a firestorm of criticism and unrestrained anger.

There are many who suffer silently, not intending to impose their ideology on others, but seeking hope and healing. We need to be there for them.

This is the reality that many churches will likely face in the coming years. As gender and sexual issues divide families, communities, and churches, some will begin to separate themselves from organized religion and reject Christianity as a whole. Congregations may thin out. It seems that the church is in the process of being pruned. While some will remain, others will walk away.

Within our churches are many people who struggle with their sexual identities who are *not* a part of the militant minority who demonize those who disagree with them. There are many who suffer silently, not intending to impose their ideology on others, but seeking hope and healing. We need to be there for them. For us to ignore this reality is to turn away those who are coming to the very place where they should experience hope and healing. The church should be a safe place where they can share their struggles, ask questions, and grow.

The atheist Voltaire said, "I always made one prayer to God, a very short one. Here it is: 'O Lord, make our enemies quite ridiculous!' God granted it."[29] But even he did not use intimidation, shame, and bullying. He let his ideas, flawed though they were, do the work for him. But then he did not live in an era of social media, an age of rage.

The Response of the Church

Bonhoeffer was right when he said that to be silent is to speak. As we learned in an earlier chapter, Black Lives Matter has taken this mantra captive, implying that those who remained silent and didn't get on board with them were siding with racism. They are right in saying that we should speak, but they are wrong with regard to what we should speak about. We should speak against the violence BLM has fostered, and we should speak against our nation's plunge into the moral anarchy described in this chapter.

In a word, we must remain strong, restrained, and compassionate. We should not only pray for protection from those who attack us, but also pray that we might not be afraid. When attacked, the people in the early church did not ask God to remove the persecution. Rather, they prayed that they would face it fearlessly: "Lord, look upon their threats and grant to your servants to continue to speak your word with all boldness" (Acts 4:29).

We should not pray for deliverance
from those who attack us, but pray
that we might not be afraid.

For years I have wrestled with the oft-repeated statement "We have to be known for what we are *for* and not what we are *against.*" Given the present political and moral climate, what you are *for* will evaporate in the minds of many once they hear that you are *against* same-sex marriage, gender fluidity, and collective guilt. It won't be long before other convictions elicit the same response. We already know that from culture's perspective, to be prolife means you hate women, and to believe that Jesus is the only way to God is religious bigotry.

Let me emphasize that we must not see those who oppose us as our enemies, but as people who need to be freed. At a time when those who shout the loudest win the argument, we must not lose our cool. How should we view people who have lost their way? We must see beyond their anger and pain and respect them as human beings trying to find healing for their inner conflicts. We need to view them as the Allies viewed France during WWII: not as enemies, but as people who need to be liberated.

When we are falsely accused, we should see ourselves as blessed, not oppressed. "Blessed are you when others revile you and persecute you and utter all kinds of evil against you falsely on my account. Rejoice and be glad, for your reward is great in heaven, for so they persecuted the prophets who were before you" (Matthew 5:11-12).

We should be a welcoming church without affirming same-sex relationships. For those who struggle with gender identity, we must remind them that if they lean into their pain, if they trust God for help, they will be able to find more healing than they would through body-altering surgery or attempting to live with the guilt and self-loathing that comes with unbiblical sexual relationships.

We need to be resolute but understanding, firm but also wise. We take our example from Jesus. "When he was reviled, he did not revile in return; when he suffered, he did not threaten, but continued entrusting himself to him who judges justly" (1 Peter 2:23).

We don't have to shout louder than others when we stand our ground. We just need to know that we are being faithful to our Commander and King. Like Martin Luther, we should be willing to say, "Here we stand, we cannot do otherwise."

A Prayer All of Us Must Pray

Father, help us to understand that we are to be agents of healing and hope in an angry world. Amid the rancor, give us words of peace and hope. We pray that You will help us to fulfill these words of instruction: "When reviled, we bless; when persecuted, we endure; when slandered, we entreat. We have become, and are still, like the scum of the world, the refuse of all things" (1 Corinthians 4:12-13).

Help us to remember that Jesus was obedient to Your calling. "For the joy that was set before him [He] endured the cross, despising the shame" (Hebrews 12:2). May we remember that eternity and not time holds the final verdict. We rejoice in the privilege of suffering shame for Your name.

In Jesus' name, amen.

CHAPTER 10

Wake Up! Strengthen What Remains!

Τhe above words were spoken by Jesus to a church He loved. How much of the culture should we embrace in order to redeem it? That's a question that has been endlessly discussed throughout the history of the church. There are some aspects of the culture we can embrace, but there is much that must be opposed. Our ability to discern what we can and cannot embrace is critical to the continuation of our witness as a church.

My concern is that we are submitting to culture's most enticing temptations and justifying this in the name of compassion, love, and cultural relevance. We are willingly being deceived. And too often, we are feeling self-righteously good about it.

Many years ago, my wife, Rebecca, and I toured the sites of the seven churches of Revelation chapters 2–3. Among the cities we visited was Sardis, the one to whom Jesus wrote a letter and warned, "You have the reputation of being alive, but you are dead. Wake up, and strengthen what remains and is about to die, for I have not found your works complete in the sight of my God" (Revelation 3:1-2).

Wake up! Strengthen what remains!

What concerned Jesus about this church that its leaders had failed to notice? The answer isn't explicitly stated in the letter, but it's not too difficult for us to figure out where the deception lay. This church that had a reputation of being alive was now dead because the people had submitted to the surrounding culture. *They no longer saw the world of sin as an enemy.*

When our tour group visited ancient Sardis, we discovered that right next to the ruins of a third-century church building were the ruins of temples dedicated to pagan sexuality. Even though these buildings dated to two or three centuries after New Testament times, still, the juxtaposition of these ruins are a commentary on the history of the church in Sardis.

The church evidently felt comfortable next to these sexually permissive temples. It succumbed to the temptations offered by the surrounding culture and failed to stand against them. Perhaps some of its members worshipped in both locations: after they went to the church, they walked a few steps away and visited the tolerant gods of the pagan idols. For them, the sexual permissiveness was too attractive to resist.

Thankfully, not everyone in the church succumbed to the temptations of the sensual culture. Jesus went on to say, "Yet you have still a few names in Sardis, people who have not soiled their garments, and they will walk with me in white, for they are worthy" (verse 4). Thankfully, at least a few had not smudged their garments with the rampant sensuality.

So-called progressive Christians believe that traditional Christianity has failed them for one reason or another. This includes those who have been hurt by the self-righteousness of members and leaders in more traditional churches. They argue that Christianity has to be remade if it's to survive. The argument is that historic Christianity is out of touch with our culture and the shifting values of our society.

Progressives believe that the evangelical church is toxic, filled with racial injustice, sexism, Islamophobia, and shaming judgmentalism. Their goal is to purge the church from these nocuous attitudes and ideas and cultivate a more compassionate, inclusive, and culturally relevant form of Christianity. Thus they surrender ground to culture under the banner of progress.

Thanks to technology and the media, we have access to a pagan culture that is much closer to us than it was to the Christians of the first century. Pagan temples can be accessed through our computers, cell phones, or tablets. And the temptations are even stronger because so many of our homes are in disarray, with children who are searching for love and affirmation with no regard as to where they find it.

Many tsunamis are coming against the church today. The pressure to compromise and redefine the gospel by finding "a middle way" might well prove to undermine "the faith that was once for all delivered to the saints" (Jude 3). As contemporary culture grows more intolerant of historic Christianity, the church is lured into accomodation and ends up being absorbed by the world. The lamp flickers, and then goes out.

Hearing the Voice of Jesus Today

I don't pretend to know everything that Jesus would say to the church today—you may have your own thoughts about that. Let me humbly suggest three matters I believe He would speak to us about. And He would speak with both compassion and firmness, just as He did to Sardis. He would speak with love as well, reminding us that He purchased us at a high cost.

Let us listen.

"Be resolved to be gospel-driven in your life and witness."

Jesus said, "I am the way, and the truth, and the life. No one comes to the Father except through me" (John 14:6). Then after His resurrection, He urged, "Go into all the world and proclaim the gospel" (Mark 16:15).

Recently, I spoke to a Christian leader who, for at least 30 years, has been involved in a mission organization known for its emphasis on evangelism in America and around the world. But the ministry is now under the leadership of more progressive Christians. He told me that at their last conference, "You would have thought that you were at a conference on social justice." Gone was the urgency of getting the gospel to as many people as possible. Missing were discussions on how to motivate churches and pastors not to lose sight of the larger vision that "the harvest is plentiful, but the laborers are few" (Matthew 9:37).

Many of today's Millennials, feeling as though they don't fit with evangelicalism's romance with conservative politics, have chosen to devote themselves to social justice. And sadly, many of them have abandoned the doctrine of personal repentance, opting instead for what they see as a more practical gospel: helping the poor and needy. In other words, the gospel of social justice. Some of these Millennials talk about *justice* but not *judgment*.

According to Barna Group, many Christian Millennials are unsure about the actual practice of evangelism. Almost half (47 percent) agree at least somewhat that it is wrong to share one's personal beliefs with others of a different faith in hopes that they will one day share the same faith. They also "somewhat agree" that if some-one disagrees with you, they're judging you. And, I might add that in the responses, the most oft-quoted verse of the Bible is Matthew 7:1—"judge not, that you not be judged."[1]

To believe that Christ is the only way to the Father is regarded as bigotry, and belief in hell is viewed as a regression to medieval notions of primitive and cruel judgmentalism. God is seen as so tolerant that He extends grace even to people who don't think they have sinned enough to need it. Jonathan Edwards' classic message "Sinners in the Hands of an Angry God" might today be reworded as "God in the Hands of Angry Sinners."

This is a tragic loss. If we lose our passion for making the gos-pel known, if we abandon the biblical teaching about heaven and hell and Christ as the only way, if we work to make life better in this world and ignore the reality of the life to come, we are sacrific-ing the eternal on the altar of the temporal. We are trading heaven for earth and eternity for time. We are forgetting that "it is a fearful thing to fall into the hands of the living God" and that "our God is a consuming fire" (Hebrews 10:31; 12:29).

We are commanded to live radically like Christ, committing our-selves to the needs of others: body, soul, and spirit. We must remind ourselves that God is calling together a multinational community, believers of every race and culture, but such unity can only be built on the gospel itself.

We must also realize that the gospel comes not only in words, but through authentic, caring Christians who are willing to sacri-fice their all for others. We must serve with a redemptive mindset, always seeking opportunities to build bridges that will lead peo-ple to eternal life. If we don't see the singular importance of the message of the gospel, we substitute a temporal body for an eter-nal soul.

Let us remember that the gospel
is not what we can do for Jesus,
but what Jesus has done for us.

We as evangelicals need to return to our biblical roots. We need to talk about heaven and warn against hell. We need gospel-driven social work that serves people because they are needy and, yes, of course we should continue to serve them whether they believe in Christ or not. But our heart's cry should be for them to believe the gospel and be saved. If compassion motivates us to help alleviate the suffering in this present world, how much more should compassion motivate us to share the good news to alleviate their suffering in the world to come.

It's easy for the gospel to get lost in a social justice-driven world. Let us remember that the gospel is not what we can do for Jesus, but what Jesus has done for us. We must tell this generation that *social justice, even at its best, is not the gospel*!

"There is salvation in no one else, for there is no other name under heaven given among men by which we must be saved" (Acts 4:12).

Let us resolve to share the gospel and live it out without shame, no matter what the cost.[2]

Jesus would have more to say:

"Be resolved that you will not bow to the culture's sexual revolution."

Hear Jesus' words, "Blessed are the pure in heart, for they shall see God" (Matthew 5:8).

Hear Him pray, "Sanctify them in the truth; your word is truth" (John 17:17).

Many passages in the New Testament speak to our temptation to exchange purity for the fulfillment of our passions. Paul wrote, "The time is coming when people will not endure sound teaching, but having itching ears they will accumulate for themselves teachers *to suit their own passions,* and will turn away from listening to the truth and wander off into myths" (2 Timothy 4:3-4, emphasis added).

People will gravitate to teachers who "suit their own passions"—teachers who base their instruction on human experience, who promise health and wealth, who will embrace a theology of desire under the guise of love. Doctrine is reinterpreted or even rejected to justify what the heart really wants. This is sold as progressive Christianity.

Let me introduce you to two influential progressive Christians who represent many in the movement, as well as their teachings, which give false assurances to a hurting world.

Rachel Held Evans, who died unexpectedly at the age of 37, espoused progressive Christianity. After her death, *The Atlantic* noted that she "was part of a vanguard of progressive-Christian women who fought to change the way Christianity is taught and perceived in the United States." Her legacy is "her unwillingness to cede ownership of Christianity to its traditional conservative-male stewards."[3] At the height of her influence, four million people followed her blogs and tweets.

Did Rachel have legitimate concerns about the evangelical church she left? Probably. I haven't read much of her work, but maybe all of us should have paid closer attention to her personal journey away from the evangelical church. Even so, she clearly misled tens of thousands with her views about sexuality. Before she died, she endorsed a book titled *Shameless*. The significance of Evans' endorsement will become clear in a moment.

Nadia Bolz-Weber, the author of *Shameless*, began a church in

Colorado that embraces all forms of sexuality as long as it takes place between consenting adults. The thesis of her book can be stated this way: The traditional "purity" teachings of the church have done great harm by shaming all those who step outside the boundaries of a one-man, one-woman relationship in marriage. Few, if any, abide by these teachings, and those who do follow the traditional purity route often discover that it doesn't necessarily lead to a happy marriage. Bolz-Weber herself divorced her husband of 18 years and now lives with her boyfriend in what she says is a "more fulfilling" relationship.

What does Bolz-Weber do about the Bible's teaching on sexuality? Her views are best exemplified in a story she tells of a woman named Cindy, who, while standing next to a fire, reached into her bag and pulled out her Bible—the same one she had studied in church as a teenager. "Slowly, without words, she tore out eight very specific pages from her Bible—namely, those that mentioned homosexuality—and burned them one by one. As she stood there watching the inferno, she felt as if the people of her childhood church, the youth workers and pastors and other adults, rose from the grave of her psyche and stood in judgment of her around the fire. She saw them, but she didn't care. She was allowing herself to be free."

Then Cindy proceeded to tear out the pages of Matthew, Mark, Luke, and John, and with her right hand, "she clutched the pages of the Gospels over her heart, and with her left she tossed in the rest to burn."[4] She felt safe with the stories of Jesus because He had never hurt her. Cindy accepted the stories of Jesus, but the rest of the Bible was thrown into the fire.

This story serves as a lesson for all of us. It appears as though the church in which Cindy grew up hurt her deeply. Was she hurt by the judgmentalism of others? Was she condemned without anyone taking the time to listen to her story and offer her grace? We don't know, but whatever the case, she represents the kind of person who should find hope and healing in our churches.

Apparently, the church failed her. But is the answer for her pain to burn the teachings of the Bible regarding sexuality? She reminds me of a pastor who told his congregation, "Jesus is a gift who comes in a package called the Bible. Once you take out the gift, the package can be thrown away. Since Jesus didn't condemn homosexuality, we are free to accept it." And the implication is that homosexual relationships can be affirmed without shame. Really?

Given the fact Bolz-Weber's book is titled *Shameless,* I found her interpretation of the source of shame to be most interesting. In essence, it's this: Before Adam and Eve gave in to the serpent, they were "naked but not ashamed." Then she writes, "Who told them they were naked? My money is on the snake. For some reason God allows us to live in a world where alternatives to God's voice exist, and those alternatives are where shame originates."[5]

Don't miss this. According to Bolz-Weber, shame entered Adam and Eve when they listened to the voice of the devil, not God. Her conclusion: All shame is evil and comes from Satan. I read her entire book and don't recall even once the suggestion that some people should feel shame because what they're doing is shameful. I could paraphrase her view by saying, "Let's return to Eden, where there was no shame, and deny the reality of the fall; let's assume that the shame that originated in the garden was illegitimate."

Are there any limits at all to expressions of sexuality? According to Bolz-Weber, as long as you don't involve minors or have a desire for animals, all sexual relationships among consenting adults should be accepted as holy and without shame. After all, God does not shame anyone.

The apostle Paul would strongly disagree. He taught that some people should indeed experience shame because they do shameful acts: "Take no part in the unfruitful works of darkness, but instead expose them. For it is shameful even to speak of the things that they do in secret" (Ephesians 5:11-12). In other words, people who do shameful things should be ashamed. Elsewhere, Paul spoke about those who "glory in their shame." They are tragically deceived and their "end is destruction" (Philippians 3:19).

There is, of course, such a thing as false shame over sins that have been already been forgiven by God. It's also heartbreaking that those who have been abused sometimes feel shame even though they had no or little responsibility for what happened. False shame exists almost everywhere. In any case, on the cross, Jesus bore our shame; He shamed shame (Hebrews 12:2).

Biblically, shame is taken away not by burning the teachings of the Bible about homosexuality, but by acknowledging the wonder of God's gracious forgiveness and cleansing given to all who repent of their immorality. God grants forgiveness and grace to all repentant sinners, but He doesn't heal the souls of unrepentant sinners. They are left to undertake the hopeless task of healing their own souls, and they attempt to do it by justifying what God has condemned. They do it by throwing pages from the Bible into the fire.

Back to Rachel Held Evans. This progressive Christian woman said of the book *Shameless*, "[It] is one of the most important, life-changing books I've ever read. Expertly-crafted and lovingly delivered, it serves as both a bomb and a balm—blowing up the lies religion teaches about sex and tenderly healing the wounds those messages have inflicted...It's Nadia Bolz-Weber's best book yet. And that's saying something."[6]

Rachel Held Evans spoke for many progressive Christians who prefer a doctrine of desire, a theology in keeping with fleshly appetites. By nature, all of us want to worship a God who agrees with us about everything. We long to be deceived especially about matters of sexuality.

Paul knew that we are prone to justify whatever our hearts desire to do. This proclivity to self-deception is why he often prefaced his teaching about sexuality by saying:

> Be not deceived... (1 Corinthians 6:9 KJV).

> Do not be deceived... (Galatians 6:7).

Let me quote another of Paul's ominous warnings: "You may be sure of this, that everyone who is sexually immoral or impure, or who is covetous (that is, an idolater), has no inheritance in the kingdom of Christ and God. *Let no one deceive you with empty words*, for because of these things the wrath of God comes upon the sons of disobedience" (Ephesians 5:5-6, emphasis added).

Let no one deceive you with empty words!

We are not dealing with trivial matters. Let me repeat Paul's words: "because of these things the wrath of God comes upon the sons of disobedience." Sinful relationships can never cure sexual brokenness; they can only perpetuate it. The guilt, self-loathing, and regrets all come due. The deception of books like *Shameless* is deserving of tears. Self-healing can never accomplish what God can. *People are free to choose their own sexual lifestyle, but they are not free to choose the consequences of their decision.*

We must return to the example of Jesus. He brought emotional and spiritual healing to the sexually broken not by justifying their lifestyle, but by compassionately offering forgiveness and restoration. With a prostitute standing in the presence of self-righteous Pharisees, speaking of her, He said, "'Therefore I tell you, her sins, which are many, are forgiven—for she loved much. But he who is forgiven little, loves little.' And he said to her, 'Your sins are forgiven...Your faith has saved you; go in peace'" (Luke 7:47-50).

To the woman caught in adultery who was brought to Jesus by men who were guilty of the same sin, Jesus, when He was left alone with her, asked, 'Woman, where are they? Has no one condemned you?' She said, 'No one, Lord.' And Jesus said, 'Neither do I condemn you; go, and from now on sin no more'" (John 8:10-11). Imagine what those words meant to this woman who had been shamed by others.

We dare not abandon the Bible's teaching about sexuality despite personal and cultural pressures.

Look at Jesus: No lowering of the standard; no rewriting the rules to make a woman feel better about herself. But rather, He offered grace in the face of a hypocritical, self-righteous community. He offered forgiveness and glad acceptance with the view that these women would live differently going forward. We see a transformation of lifestyle based on transformation of heart.

We dare not abandon the Bible's teaching about sexuality despite personal and cultural pressures. I agree it's not enough that we hold to biblical doctrine; we must hold it with love, compassion, and respect for all people, no matter who they are or what they've done. All of us need the body of Christ, for we are all in various stages of spiritual growth in our quest for holiness. We should not ask the sexually broken to deny their pain, but rather, to lean into their pain by dependence on God and, through repentance, receive the joyful knowledge that they are a son or daughter of God, anticipating a guilt-free future.

Someone has well said, "Truth without humility is judgmentalism; humility without truth is cowardice." May we be characterized by both humility and truth.

Here is another word Jesus might have for us:

"Be resolved to love Me passionately and suffer well for My name."

"If you love me, you will keep my commandments" (John 14:15).

Jesus warned that in the end times, "because lawlessness will be increased, the love of many will grow cold" (Matthew 24:12). That, I think, describes much of evangelical Christianity today. We are weak because our love for Christ is weak; our love of worldly values and pursuits is greater than our love for Christ.

John, who was most closely identified with Jesus, warned,

> Do not love the world or the things in the world. If anyone loves the world, the love of the Father is not in him. For all that is in the world—the desires of the flesh and the desires of the eyes and pride of life—is not from the Father but is from the world. And the world is passing away along with its desires, but whoever does the will of God abides forever (1 John 2:15-17).

In an excellent article titled "The Church Boy Who Never Grew Up" Daron Roberts writes of the lackadaisical attitude of some the men he has seen in his church:

> Nobody trusts him to stand on God's Word alone and to suffer for a conviction. He has no stomach to fight for Christ because his loyalty is not to Christ—it is to himself. He will stand for truth occasionally, but only when he decides the cost is not too great. Convictions

that would cost him are too much for his lust for man's approval to endure.[7]

There are many ways we can love the world and, in my opinion, in our present world, this false love is best represented by our obsession with technology.

During the COVID-19 crisis in 2020, we all learned how technology can be used for the benefit of the church and evangelism. Most churches—The Moody Church included—made their worship services available online, streaming their worship and preaching to thousands beyond their walls. Thankfully, in this way technology is being used for good. The gospel is going out even to countries that are officially opposed or hostile to Christianity.

But there is a dark side to technology. Our generation (not just the progressives) is being lured into a worldview that is antithetical to Christianity. A survey showed that most Christians follow no guidelines for what they watch on television, their smart phones, tablets, or computers. Most teenagers have seen dozens of R-rated movies, and pornography is everywhere. What was once called "biblical separation" is neither taught nor applied. Finding no way to withstand the addictions of our culture, we have simply accommodated them.

We now know that social media damages the health of children. From lack of sleep due to social media use, we are also seeing a rise in cyberbullying, hate speech, low self-esteem, anxiety, depression, and even self-harm.[8] Every kind of kinky, unnatural, and even violent sex is now considered normal. Many of our children have no firm convictions about what must be avoided and shunned, even condemned. A rigorous application of biblical teaching is supplanted by YouTube and Netflix.

As individuals, families, and churches, we must ask: What lines must we draw to keep ourselves from a world that crashes into our lives through technology? James asks us, "Do you not know that friendship with the world is enmity with God? Therefore whoever wishes to be a friend of the world makes himself an enemy of God" (James 4:4). Really? Could our friendship with the world make us God's enemy?

We must see our calling as more than just keeping ourselves undefiled by the world, but rather, developing a love for Christ that is greater than our love of sin.

We must not make the mistake that took place at Sardis. Unlike that church, we must see the world as our enemy, not our friend. And we must see our calling as more than just keeping ourselves undefiled by the world. Rather, we must *develop a love for Christ that is greater than our love of sin.*

Can gospel-preaching churches survive the cultural pressures of an intolerant, winner-take-all secularism? Or can we win over a culturally driven progressive Christianity? Yes, but the road ahead is fraught with many temptations, distractions, and distortions. There will always be a remnant, even as there was in Sardis. And as we shall see, the rewards of triumph are worth the cost.

A Final Word from Jesus to Us

We return to the words of Jesus to the church in Sardis:

> I know your works. You have the reputation of being alive, but you are dead. Wake up, and strengthen what

remains and is about to die, for I have not found your works complete in the sight of my God. Remember, then, what you received and heard. Keep it, and repent. If you will not wake up, I will come like a thief, and you will not know at what hour I will come against you. Yet you have still a few names in Sardis, people who have not soiled their garments, and they will walk with me in white, for they are worthy (Revelation 3:1-4).

Let's ponder these words:

> ...repent. If you will not wake up, I will come like a thief...

> Yet you have still a few names in Sardis, people who have not soiled their garments, and they will walk with me in white, for they are worthy.

Like those in the church in Sardis, we want to be known as a church with a reputation of being alive, but Jesus sees what no church consultant can. He applied the stethoscope and could not find a heartbeat. As always, Christianity is just not a matter of show, but a matter of *heart*.

Someone has well said that we cannot conquer Canaan with a wilderness heart. We cannot follow Christ into the world unless we gladly take up His cross. At the beginning of this book I quoted the poet Vasily Zhukovsky: "We all have crosses to bear and we are constantly trying on different ones for a good fit."[9]

The word of Jesus to Sardis was "Repent!" That's not something we do only when we are converted; we cannot survive without daily, deep, and sustained repentance. And we must be a church enamored with God, a church that is constantly giving Him praise and heart-worship. We must constantly look beyond ourselves to God's

Word, which sustains us. Repentance is more easily talked about than practiced!

And we must have the courage to both engage the culture and stand against it.

The rewards for doing this? "The one who conquers will be clothed thus in white garments, and I will never blot his name out of the book of life. I will confess his name before my Father and before his angels. He who has an ear, let him hear what the Spirit says to the churches" (Revelation 3:5-6).

We must have the courage
to both engage the culture
and stand against it.

Cities back then had books containing the names of their citizens. When someone died, their name was blotted out of the book. But the book that Jesus mentions is "the book of life," and no one whose name is there need fear being blotted out. The glories that await the faithful are beyond description.

Meanwhile, a challenge is before us.

I realize that parallels between our situation in the United States and Nazi Germany can be easily overdrawn. But there is this similarity: At some point, God separates the chaff from the wheat in His church. After Hitler announced that criticism of the Reich was a crime, most of the churches in Germany were either silent or supportive of him.

But Martin Niemöller, who would spend time in a concentration camp for his boldness, preached these words to his congregation:

We have all of us—the whole Church and the whole community—we've been thrown into the Tempter's sieve, and he is shaking and the wind is blowing, and it must now become manifest whether we are wheat or chaff!…[we] must see that the calm of meditative Christianity is at an end…

It is now springtime for the hopeful and expectant Christian Church—it is testing time, and God is giving Satan a free hand, so he may shake us up and so that it may be seen what manner of men we are!

Satan swings his sieve and Christianity is thrown hither and thither; and he who is not ready to suffer, he who called himself a Christian only because he thereby hoped to gain something good for his race and his nation is blown away like chaff by the wind of time.[10]

Blown away like chaff by the wind!

We fear suffering—not the flames that past martyrs endured, but the cultural flames of shame and ridicule. It has been aptly stated that a Christianity without courage is cultural atheism. Let us resolve as a church that we will not bow to intimidation. Jesus commanded us to rejoice when others speak evil of us and to be prepared for what we are facing when He said, "If the world hates you, know that it has hated me before it hated you…In the world you will have tribulation. But take heart; I have overcome the world" (John 15:18; 16:33).

As we persevere, let us always be ready to graciously give a defense to anyone who asks the reason for the hope within us (see 1 Peter 3:15).

I think I hear Him saying to us what He said to the church in Sardis:

"Strengthen what remains!"

A Prayer All of Us Must Pray

Father, give us renewed honesty as we ask You to search our hearts. Let us resolve to live fully for Your glory, suffering as need be to prove Your faithfulness in our lives. Let us not fall into the sin of self-righteousness; let us always temper truth with love and a listening ear. Let us not allow Satan a foothold in our lives, and may our sins be severely dealt with through repentance and accountability.

Let us be among the remnant that has not soiled their garments but will walk with You "in white." Until that day, let us be faithful for Your glory and bring as many as possible with us as we travel the narrow road.

And let us hold up our Savior so that the world may see Him as their great hope. Thank You for giving us this privilege.

We pray in Jesus' name, amen.

Notes

The Surprising Response of Jesus

1. Robert Payne, *Life and Death of Lenin* (New York: Simon & Schuster, 1964), 209.

Chapter 1—How We Got Here

1. William Blackstone, *Commentaries on the Laws of England*, vol. 1 (Oxford: Clarendon Press, 1765), 38.

2. Karl Marx and Friedrich Engels, *Marx and Engels on the Trade Unions*, ed. Kenneth Lapides (New York: International Publishers, 1987), 68-69.

3. "What We Believe," *Black Lives Matter*, https://blacklivesmatter.com/what-we-believe/.

4. Watch Black Lives Matter cofounder Patrisse Cullors' interview with Real News Network, where she revealed, "Myself and Alicia [Garza] in particular are trained organizers. We are trained Marxists. We are super-versed on, sort of, ideological theories." You can see the interview at https://therealnews.com/stories/pcullors0722blacklives.

5. David Horowitz, *Dark Agenda: The War to Destroy Christian America* (West Palm Beach, FL: Humanix Books, 2018), 77.

6. Margaret Sanger, *Women and the New Race* (New York: Brentano's, 1920), 5.

7. David J. Garrow, *Liberty and Sexuality: The Right to Privacy and the Making of* Roe vs. Wade (Berkeley: University of California Press, 1998), 390.

8. Lawrence H. Summers, "Remarks at NBER Conference on Diversifying the Science & Engineering Workforce," January 14, 2005, https://web.archive.org/web/20080130023006/http://www.president.harvard.edu/speeches/2005/nber.html.

9. Sam Dillon, "Harvard Chief Defends His Talk on Women," *The New York Times*, January 18, 2005, https://www.nytimes.com/2005/01/18/us/harvard-chief-defends-his-talk-on-women.html; Marcella Bombardieri, "Summers' Remarks on Women Draw Fire," *Boston Globe*, January 17, 2005, http://archive.boston.com/news/education/higher/articles/2005/01/17/summers_remarks_on_women_draw_fire/.

10. Robert P. Jones, *The End of White Christian America* (New York: Simon & Schuster, 2016), 112.

11. Jones, *The End of White Christian America*, 113.

12. Jones, *The End of White Christian America*, 133.

13. Erin Griffith, "Venture Capital Is Putting Its Money into Astrology," *The New York Times,* April 15, 2019, https://www.nytimes.com/2019/04/15/style/astrology-apps-venture-capital.html.

14. George Orwell, *The Collected Essays, Journalism & Letters of George Orwell, Volume 2: My Country Right or Left 1940–1943* (Boston: Nonpareil Books, 2000), 15.

15. This quote has been attributed to George Orwell, but its origin is unconfirmed and unknown.

Chapter 2—Rewrite the Past to Control the Future

1. George Orwell, *1984* (New York: Signet Classics, 1977), 34.

2. Sara E. Wilson, "Arthur M. Schlesinger, Jr., National Humanities Medal, 1998," *National Endowment for the Humanities,* https://www.neh.gov/about/awards/national-humanities-medals/arthur-m-schlesinger-jr.

3. Graham Piro, "High school may erase mural of George Washington: 'traumatizes students,'" *The College Fix,* May 2, 2019, https://www.thecollegefix.com/high-school-may-erase-george-washington-murals-traumatizes-students/.

4. James P. Sutton, "It's Curtains for a George Washington Mural in San Francisco. Or Paint, or Panels. Just Hide It!," *National Review,* June 20, 2019, https://www.nationalreview.com/2019/06/george-washington-mural-san-francisco-progressive-politics/.

5. Ian Schwartz, "CNN's Angela Rye: Washington, Jefferson Statues 'Need to Come Down,'" *RealClearPolitics,* August 18, 2017, https://www.realclearpolitics.com/video/2017/08/18/cnns_angela_rye_washington_jefferson_statues_need_to_come_down.html.

6. CBS News, "George Washington statue toppled by protesters in Portland, Oregon," June 19, 2020, https://www.cbsnews.com/news/protesters-portland-oregon-topple-george-washington-statue/.

7. CBS3 Staff, "Tomb of the Unknown Soldier of the American Revolution Vandalized in Philadelphia's Washington Square," *CBS Philly,* June 12, 2020, https://philadelphia.cbslocal.com/2020/06/12/tomb-of-the-unknown-soldier-of-the-american-revolution-vandalized-in-philadelphias-washington-square/.

8. Greg Norman, "Christopher Columbus statue is beheaded in Boston," *Fox News,* June 10, 2020, https://www.foxnews.com/us/christopher-columbus-statue-beheaded.

9. Daily Wire News, "Rioters Tear Down Statue of Francis Scott Key. He Wrote The Star-Spangled Banner," *The Daily Wire,* June 20, 2020, https://www.dailywire.com/news/watch-rioters-tear-down-statue-of-francis-scott-key-he-wrote-the-star-spangled-banner.

10. State Journal Staff, "So who was Hans Christian Heg? Here's why the Civil War hero had a statue," *Wisconsin State Journal,* June 25, 2020, https://madison.com/wsj/news/local/crime-and-courts/photos-so-who-was-hans-christian-heg-heres-why-the-civil-war-hero-had-a/collection_31313606-691a-52d2-a4fa-cbe4eca84f73.html.

11. Aila Slisco, "White Jesus Statues Should Be Torn Down, Activist Shaun King Says," *Newsweek,* June 22, 2020, https://www.newsweek.com/white-jesus-statues-should-torn-down-black-lives-matters-leader-says-1512674.

12. Cynthia Haven, "The president of forgetting," *The Book Haven,* Stanford University, December 4, 2014, https://bookhaven.stanford.edu/2014/12/the-president-of-forgetting/.

13. Robin West, *Progressive Constitutionalism: Reconstructing the Fourteenth Amendment* (Durham, NC: Duke University Press, 1994), 17-18.

14. Allan Bloom, *Closing of the American Mind* (New York: Simon & Schuster, 2008), 26, 56.

15. Howard Zinn, *A People's History of the United States: 1492-Present* (New York: Routledge, 2013), 59.

16. David Horowitz, *Unholy Alliance: Radical Islam and the American Left* (Washington, DC: Regnery Publishing, 2004), 105.

17. Nikole Hannah-Jones, "The 1619 Project," *The New York Times,* August 14, 2019, https://www.nytimes.com/interactive/2019/08/14/magazine/black-history-american-democracy.html.

18. Jordan Davidson, "In Racist Screed, NYT's 1619 Project Founder Calls 'White Race' 'Barbaric Devils,' 'Bloodsuckers,' Columbus 'No Different Than Hitler,'" *The Federalist,* June 25, 2020, https://thefederalist.com/2020/06/25/in-racist-screed-nyts-1619-project-founder-calls-white-race-barbaric-devils-bloodsuckers-no-different-than-hitler/. Also see the original Nikole [Nicole] Hannah-Jones article here: https://www.scribd.com/document/466921269/NYT-s-1619-Project-Founder-Calls-White-Race-Barbaric-Devils-Bloodsuckers-No-Different-Than-Hitler-x#from_embed.

19. Nima Elbagir, Raja Razek, Alex Platt, and Bryony Jones, "People for Sale," *CNN,* November 14, 2017, https://edition.cnn.com/2017/11/14/africa/libya-migrant-auctions/index.html.

20. Patrick J. Buchanan, *The Death of the West* (New York: Thomas Dunne Books, 2002), 58.

21. Victor Wang, "Student petition urges English department to diversify curriculum," *Yale Daily News,* May 26, 2016, https://yaledailynews.com/blog/2016/05/26/student-petition-urges-english-department-to-diversify-curriculum/.

22. "Pack the Union: A Proposal to Admit New States for the Purpose of Amending the Constitution to Ensure Equal Representation," *Harvard Law Review,* January 10, 2020, https://harvardlawreview.org/2020/01/pack-the-union-a-proposal-to-admit-new-states-for-the-purpose-of-amending-the-constitution-to-ensure-equal-representation/.

23. "Pack the Union: A Proposal to Admit New States for the Purpose of Amending the Constitution to Ensure Equal Representation."

24. Paul Kurtz, *Humanist Manifestos I and II* (Indiana: Prometheus Books, 1973), 16-17.

25. Kurtz, *Humanist Manifestos I and II*, 21.

26. Kurtz, *Humanist Manifestos I and II*, 21-22.

27. "About Humanism," American Humanist Association, https://web.archive.org/web/20111107221355/http://www.americanhumanist.org/who_we_are/about_humanism/Humanist_Manifesto_I.

28. Antonia Noori Farzan, "A Minnesota city voted to eliminate the Pledge of Allegiance. It didn't go over well," *The Washington Post,* June 28, 2019, https://www.washingtonpost.com/nation/2019/06/28/minnesota-city-voted-eliminate-pledge-allegiance-it-didnt-go-over-well/.

29. Glen Clark, "Muslims in Australia: Singing National Anthem Is 'Forced Assimilation!,'" *The Federalist Papers,* January 24, 2016, https://thefederalistpapers.org/us/muslims-in-australia-singing-national-anthem-is-forced-assimilation.

30. Edmund DeMarche, "Deadly weekend in Seattle, Chicago, Minneapolis as New York City reports uptick in shootings," *Fox News,* June 22, 2020, https://www.foxnews.com/us/deadly-weekend-in-seattle-chicago-minneapolis-as-new-york-city-reports-uptick-in-shootings.

31. "104 shot, 15 fatally, over Father's Day weekend in Chicago," Fox 32, June 21, 2020, https://www.fox32chicago.com/news/104-shot-15-fatally-over-fathers-day-weekend-in-chicago.

32. Tom Schuba, Sam Charles, and Matthew Hendrickson, "18 murders in 24 hours: Inside the most violent day in 60 years in Chicago," *Chicago Sun Times,* June 8, 2020, https://chicago.suntime .com/crime/2020/6/8/21281998/chicago-deadliest-day-violence-murder-history-police-crime.

33. Charles Francis Adams, *The Works of John Adams, Second President of the United States; With a Life of the Author Notes and Illustrations of his Grandson Charles Francis Adams, Vol. IX* (Boston: Little, Brown, 1854), 228-229 (emphasis added).

34. D.H. Lawrence, Wikiquote, https://en.wikiquote.org/wiki/D._H._Lawrence.

35. Caleb Parke, "Pastors vow to 'defend' houses of worship, 'not allow Christian heritage to be erased,'" *Fox News*, June 26, 2020, https://www.foxnews.com/us/jesus-statue-church-pastors -defend-protests.

36. Parke, "Pastors vow to 'defend' houses of worship, 'not allow Christian heritage to be erased.'"

37. Eric Mason, *Woke Church: An Urgent Call for Christians in America to Confront Racism and Injustice* (Chicago: Moody Publishers, 2018), 70.

38. "Church of Canada May Disappear by 2040, Says New Report," *CEP Online*, November 18, 2019, https://cep.anglican.ca/church-of-canada-may-disappear-by-2040-says-new-report/.

39. John Longhurst, "Church of Canada may disappear by 2040, says new report," *Religion News Service*, November 18, 2019, https://religionnews.com/2019/11/18/church-of-canada-may-disappear -by-2040-says-new-report/.

40. Samuel John Stone, "The Church's One Foundation," 1866.

41. Corrie ten Boom, *I Stand at the Door and Knock: Meditations by the Author of* The Hiding Place (Grand Rapids, MI: Zondervan, 2008), 95.

Chapter 3—Use Diversity to Divide and Destroy

1. Saul D. Alinsky, *Rules for Radicals: A Pragmatic Primer for Realistic Radicals* (New York: Vintage Books, 1989), ix.

2. David Horowitz, *Dark Agenda: The War to Destroy Christian America* (West Palm Beach, FL: Humanix Books, 2018), 84.

3. Alinsky, *Rules for Radicals*, 117.

4. For a better understanding of the goals of Black Lives Matter, I suggest going to their website to learn about their larger agenda: https://blacklivesmatter.com. Watch Black Lives Matter cofounder Patrisse Cullors' interview with Real News Network, where she revealed, "Myself and Alicia [Garza] in particular are trained organizers. We are trained Marxists. We are super-versed on, sort of, ideological theories." You can see the interview at https://therealnews.com/stories/pcullors0722black lives. And read black Christian and prolife speaker and author Ryan Bomberger's article "Top 10 Reasons I Won't Support the #BlackLivesMatter Movement," which is found here: https://town hall.com/columnists/ryanbomberger/2020/06/05/top-10-reasons-i-reject-the-blm-n2570105.

5. The Declaration of Independence, National Archives, https://www.archives.gov/founding-docs/ declaration.

6. Gettysburg Address, Wikipedia, https://en.wikipedia.org/wiki/Gettysburg_Address#Text_of_the _Gettysburg_Address.

7. Dave Nemetz, "Hallmark to Reinstate Ads Featuring Same-Sex Wedding, CEO Apologizes," *TV Line*, December 15, 2019, https://tvline.com/2019/12/15/hallmark-channel-reversed-reinstating-ads-same-sex-wedding-zola-controversy/.

8. H.R.5—Equality Act, Congress.gov, https://www.congress.gov/bill/116th-congress/house-bill/5/text.

9. Winston Churchill, House of Commons, October 22, 1945.

10. Patrick J. Buchanan, *Suicide of a Superpower* (New York: Thomas Dunne Books, 2011), 207.

11. Martin Luther King Jr., "Letter from a Birmingham Jail," April 16, 1963, Stanford University, The Martin Luther King Jr. Research and Education Institute, https://kinginstitute.stanford.edu/king-papers/documents/letter-birmingham-jail.

12. Neil Shenvi, "Intro to Critical Theory," https://shenviapologetics.com/intro-to-critical-theory/.

13. Heather Mac Donald, *The Diversity Delusion* (New York: St. Martin's Press, 2018), 64.

14. William S. Lind, "The Sourge of Cultural Marxism," *The American Conservative,* May/June 2018, 12, https://www.theamericanconservative.com/pdf/mayjune-2018/mobile/index.html#p=12.

15. David J. Garrow, *Liberty and Sexuality: The Right to Privacy and the Making of* Roe vs. Wade (Berkeley: University of California Press, 1998), 390.

16. Mac Donald, *The Diversity Delusion*, 63.

17. Robby Soave, "Think the Green New Deal Is Crazy? Blame Intersectionality," *Reason,* February 8, 2019, https://reason.com/2019/02/08/green-new-deal-intersectionality-ocasio/.

18. Rudy Gray, "SBC Resolution 9: Statement on Critical Race Theory & Intersectionality Point of Controversy and Disagreement," *The Courier,* June 27, 2019, https://baptistcourier.com/2019/06/sbc-resolution-9-statement-on-critical-race-theory-intersectionality-point-of-controversy-and-disagreement/.

19. Mac Donald, *The Diversity Delusion*, 65-66.

20. Mac Donald, *The Diversity Delusion*, 68.

21. See Southeastern Baptist Theological Seminary, *Social Justice, Critical Theory, and Christianity: Are They Compatible?*, Neil Shenvi, https://youtu.be/E33aunwGQQ4.

22. "SBC 2019: Resolutions Committee 'severely altered' resolution against identity politics," *Capstone Report*, June 13, 2019, https://capstonereport.com/2019/06/13/sbc-2019-resolutions-committee-severely-altered-resolution-against-identity-politics/32605/.

23. Gray, "SBC Resolution."

24. Shelby Steele, *White Guilt: How Blacks and Whites Together Destroyed the Promise of the Civil Rights Era* (New York: HarperCollins, 2006), cover.

25. Steele, *White Guilt*, 72-73.

26. Rev. Bill Owens, *A Dream Derailed: How the Left Hijacked Civil Rights to Create a Permanent Underclass* (Fulshear, TX: A New Dream Publishers, 2019), 42.

27. Robby Soave, "Seattle Public Schools Will Start Teaching That Math Is Oppressive," *Reason*, October 22, 2019, https://reason.com/2019/10/22/seattle-math-oppressive-cultural-woke/.

28. Soave, "Seattle Public Schools Will Start Teaching That Math Is Oppressive."

29. Seattle Public Schools, "K–12 Math Ethnic Studies Framework (20.08.2019)," https://www.k12. wa.us/sites/default/files/public/socialstudies/pubdocs/Math%20SDS%20ES%20Framework .pdf.

30. "Text of Obama's fatherhood speech," *Politico*, June 15, 2008, https://www.politico.com/ story/2008/06/text-of-obamas-fatherhood-speech-011094.

31. Theodore Dalrymple, *Life at the Bottom: The Worldview That Makes the Underclass* (Chicago: Ivan R. Dee, 2001), x.

32. Dalrymple, *Life At The Bottom*, xi–xii.

33. Tom Ascol, "Yes, the Social Justice Movement Is a Threat to Evangelicals," Founders Ministries, https://founders.org/2019/09/04/yes-the-social-justice-movement-is-a-threat-to-evangelicals/.

34. Martin Luther, *Letters of Spiritual Counsel*, ed. Theodore G. Tappert, Library of Christian Classics (London: SCM Press, 1955), 110.

Chapter 4—Freedom of Speech for Me, but Not for Thee

1. Craig R. McCoy, "Stan Wischnowski resigns as *The Philadelphia Inquirer*'s top editor," *The Philadelphia Inquirer*, June 6, 2020, https://www.inquirer.com/news/stan-wischnowski-resigns-phil adelphia-inquirer-20200606.html.

2. Inga Saffron, "Black Lives Matter. Do Buildings?," *MSN News*, https://www.msn.com/en-us/ news/us/black-lives-matter-do-buildings/ar-BB14TqMX.

3. Inga Saffron, "Damaging buildings disproportionately hurts the people protesters are trying to uplift," *The Philadelphia Inquirer*, June 1, 2020, https://www.inquirer.com/columnists/floyd -protest-center-city-philadelphia-lootings-52nd-street-walnut-chestnut-street-20200601.html.

4. Ryan Gaydos, "Drew Brees refuses to budge on stance about protesting during national anthem," *Fox News*, June 3, 2020, https://www.foxnews.com/sports/drew-brees-refuses-budge-stance-about -protesting-during-national-anthem.

5. Christopher Brito, "Drew Brees says he will 'never agree' with players kneeling during national anthem," *CBS News*, June 4, 2020, https://www.cbsnews.com/news/drew-brees-kneeling-national -anthem-protest-nfl/.

6. Nicholas Humphrey, "What Shall We Tell the Children?" Oxford Amnesty Lecture, 1997, http://www.humphrey.org.uk/papers/1998WhatShallWeTell.pdf.

7. The Bill of Rights, https://www.archives.gov/founding-docs/bill-of-rights-transcript.

8. As cited by Wikipedia, https://en.wikipedia.org/wiki/National_Socialist_Party_of_America _v._Village_of_Skokie.

9. Jacob Poushter, "40% of Millennials OK with limiting speech offensive to minorities," *Pew Research Center*, November 20, 2015, https://www.pewresearch.org/fact-tank/2015/11/20/40-of -millennials-ok-with-limiting-speech-offensive-to-minorities/.

10. Jeffrey A. Tucker, "Why Free Speech on Campus Is Under Attack: Blame Marcuse," *Foundation for Economic Education*, April 24, 2017, https://fee.org/articles/why-free-speech-on-campus -is-under-attack-blame-marcuse/.

11. Herbert Marcuse, *The Essential Marcuse: Selected Writings of Philosopher and Social Critic Herbert Marcuse* (Boston: Beacon Press, 2007), 34.

12. Marcuse, *The Essential Marcuse*, 45.

13. Jeffrey A. Tucker, "Why Free Speech on Campus Is Under Attack: Blame Marcuse," *Foundation for Economic Education,* April 24, 2017, https://fee.org/articles/why-free-speech-on-campus-is-under-attack-blame-marcuse/.

14. Tucker, "Why Free Speech on Campus Is Under Attack: Blame Marcuse" (emphasis added).

15. Tucker, "Why Free Speech on Campus Is Under Attack: Blame Marcuse."

16. Herbert Marcuse, *Repressive Tolerance*, https://www.marcuse.org/herbert/publications/1960s/1965-repressive-tolerance-fulltext.html.

17. Marcuse, *Repressive Tolerance*.

18. Marcuse, *Repressive Tolerance*.

19. Tucker, "Why Free Speech on Campus Is Under Attack: Blame Marcuse."

20. David Horowitz, *Dark Agenda: The War to Destroy Christian America* (West Palm Beach, FL: Humanix Books, 2018), 142.

21. Stanley Fish, *There's No Such Thing as Free Speech: And It's a Good Thing, Too* (New York: Oxford University Press, 1994), 68.

22. Stephen R.C. Hicks, *Explaining Postmodernism: Skepticism and Socialism from Rousseau to Foucault* (Loves Park, IL: Ockham's Razor Publishing, 2004), 238.

23. Hicks, *Explaining Postmodernism*, 231.

24. Hicks, *Explaining Postmodernism*, 237.

25. Hicks, *Explaining Postmodernism*, 237.

26. Tiffany Jenkins, "Barbarians at Yale: PC idiocy kills classic art history class," *New York Post*, January 27, 2020, https://nypost.com/2020/01/27/barbarians-at-yale-pc-idiocy-kills-classic-art-history-class/.

27. Heather Mac Donald, *The Diversity Delusion* (New York: St. Martin's Press, 2018), 3.

28. Mac Donald, *The Diversity Delusion*, 29.

29. Andrew Sullivan, "We All Live on Campus Now, *New York Magazine,* February 9, 2018, https://nymag.com/intelligencer/2018/02/we-all-live-on-campus-now.html.

30. For more information regarding blasphemy laws against Islam, see Paul Marshall and Nina Shea, *Silenced: How Apostasy and Blasphemy Codes Are Choking Freedom Worldwide* (New York: Oxford University Press, 2011), 173-226.

31. Salman Rushdie, "Defend the right to be offended," *Open Democracy,* February 7, 2005, https://www.opendemocracy.net/en/article_2331jsp/.

32. George Orwell, "The Freedom of the Press," Orwell's proposed preface to *Animal Farm.* Originally published in *The Times Literary Supplement* on September 15, 1972 as "How the essay came to be written."

33. Mac Donald, *The Diversity Delusion*, 19.

34. Art Moore, "Punishment includes Islam indoctrination," *WorldNetDaily*, October 31, 2002, https://www.wnd.com/2002/10/15738/.

35. Richard Wurmbrand, *Tortured for Christ: The 50th Anniversary Edition* (Colorado Springs: David C. Cook, 2017), 151-152.

36. The source of this account is a sermon by J.C. Ryle, "Not Corrupting the Word," which can be found in J.C. Ryle, *Is All Scripture Inspired?* (Edinburgh: The Banner of Truth Trust, 1999).

37. As cited in Charles Bridges, *An Exposition of the Book of Proverbs* (London: Seeley, Burnside, and Seeley, 1847), 126.

Chapter 5—Sell It as a Noble Cause

1. George Orwell, *1984* (New York: Signet Classics, 1977), 4.

2. Edward Bernays, *Propaganda* (Brooklyn, NY: Ig Publishing, 2005), 37.

3. Bernays, *Propaganda*, 37-38.

4. David Horowitz, *Dark Agenda: The War to Destroy Christian America* (West Palm Beach, FL: Humanix Books, 2018), 113.

5. Saul D. Alinsky, *Rules for Radicals: A Pragmatic Primer for Realistic Radicals* (New York: Vintage Books, 1989), 37.

6. James Lindsay, "The Truth About Critical Methods," *New Discourses*, March 19, 2020, https://www.youtube.com/watch?v=rSHL-rSMIro.

7. Meghan Roos, "BLM Leader: We'll 'Burn' the System Down If U.S. Won't Give Us What We Want," *Newsweek*, June 25, 2020, https://www.newsweek.com/blm-leader-well-burn-system-down-if-us-wont-give-us-what-we-want-1513422.

8. Eric Pollard, "Time to Give Up Fascist Tactics," *Washington Blade*, Letters to the Editor, January 31, 1992.

9. Adolf Hitler, *Mein Kampf*, trans. Ralph Manheim (New York: Mariner Books, 1999), 276.

10. Stefan Kanfer, "Architect of Evil," *Time*, June 24, 2001, http://content.time.com/time/magazine/article/0,9171,152486,00.html.

11. Hitler, *Mein Kampf*, 337.

12. Hitler, *Mein Kampf*, 583.

13. Robert George Leeson Waite, *The Psychopathic God: Adolf Hitler* (New York: Signet, 1978), 63.

14. William Shirer, *The Rise and Fall of the Third Reich* (New York: Simon & Schuster, 1988), 247-248.

15. William Sargant, *Battle for the Mind* (New York: Doubleday, 1957), 145.

16. ID2020, "ID2020 Launches Technical Certification Mark," January 24, 2019, https://medium.com/id2020/id2020-launches-technical-certification-mark-e6743d3f70fd.

17. Mallory Simon, "Over 1,000 health professionals sign a letter saying, Don't shut down protests using coronavirus concerns as an excuse," *CNN*, June 5, 2020, https://www.cnn.com/2020/06/05/health/health-care-open-letter-protests-coronavirus-trnd/index.html.

18. Hitler, *Mein Kampf*, 479.

19. Marc Tracy, "James Bennet Resigns as *New York Times* Opinion Editor," *The New York Times*, June 7, 2020, https://www.nytimes.com/2020/06/07/business/media/james-bennet-resigns-nytimes -op-ed.html.

20. Izabella Tabarovsky, "The American Soviet Mentality," *Tablet*, June 15, 2020, https://www.tablet mag.com/sections/news/articles/american-soviet-mentality.

21. Quoted in Alan Sears and Craig Osten, *The Homosexual Agenda: Exposing the Principal Threat to Religious Freedom Today* (Nashville, TN: Broadman & Holman Publishers, 2003), 27.

22. Marshall Kirk and Erastes Pill [Hunter Madsen], "The Overhauling of Straight America," http://library.gayhomeland.org/0018/EN/EN_Overhauling_Straight.htm.

23. Quoted in Sears and Osten, *The Homosexual Agenda*, 23.

24. Kirk and Pill, "The Overhauling of Straight America."

25. Ryan T. Anderson, *When Harry Became Sally: Responding to the Transgender Moment* (New York: Encounter Books, 2018), 9.

26. Rev. Bill Owens, *A Dream Derailed: How the Left Hijacked Civil Rights to Create a Permanent Underclass* (Fulshear, TX: A New Dream Publishers, 2019), 87.

27. Kirk and Pill, "The Overhauling of Straight America."

28. From *The Passionate State of Mind, and Other Aphorisms* (1955), 260; as cited in *The Columbia Dictionary of Quotations*, ed. Robert Andrews (New York: Columbia University Press, 1993), 741.

29. Rob Bell, *Love Wins* (New York: HarperCollins, 2012), Kindle location 1183-1189.

30. For the full transcript of Bishop Michael Curry's wedding address, see https://www.cnn .com/2018/05/19/europe/michael-curry-royal-wedding-sermon-full-text-intl/index.html.

31. Debbie Mirza, *The Covert Passive Aggressive Narcissist* (Monument, CO: Place Publishing, 2017), 74.

32. Dr. Susan Berry, "Sprite Argentina LGBT Ad Celebrates Mothers Binding Breasts, Dressing Gender-Confused Children," *Breitbart,* November 12, 2019, https://www.breitbart.com/politics/2019/11/12/ sprite-argentina-lgbt-ad-celebrates-mothers-binding-breasts-dressing-gender-confused-children/.

33. Kirk and Pill, "The Overhauling of Straight America."

34. ACLU, on Twitter, November 19, 2019, https://twitter.com/ACLU/status/119687741581081395 5?s=20.

35. Mirza, *The Covert Passive Aggressive Narcissist*, 85.

36. George Orwell, "In Front of Your Nose," *The Orwell Foundation,* https://www.orwellfoundation .com/the-orwell-foundation/orwell/essays-and-other-works/in-front-of-your-nose/.

37. Zachary Evans, "Merriam-Webster Adds Non-Binary Definition of 'They' to Dictionary," *National Review,* September 17, 2019, https://www.nationalreview.com/news/merriam-webster-adds-non -binary-definition-of-they-to-dictionary/.

38. Peggy Noonan, "What Were Robespierre's Pronouns?," *The Wall Street Journal*, July 25, 2019, https://www.wsj.com/articles/what-were-robespierres-pronouns-11564095088.

39. Megan Cassidy and Sarah Ravani, "The Scanner: San Francisco ranks No. 1 in US in property crime," *San Francisco Chronicle,* October 1, 2018, https://www.sfchronicle.com/crime/article/The -Scanner-San-Francisco-ranks-No-1-in-13267113.php.

40. Phil Matier, "SF Board of Supervisors sanitizes language of criminal justice system," *San Francisco Chronicle,* August 11, 2019, https://www.sfchronicle.com/bayarea/philmatier/article/SF-Board-of -Supervisors-sanitizes-language-of-14292255.php. LET Staff, "San Francisco: No more 'convicted felons.' They're 'justice-involved' persons now," *Law Enforcement Today,* August 22, 2019, https:// www.lawenforcementtoday.com/san-francisco-rebrands-criminal-justice-convicted-felon/.

41. LET Staff, "San Francisco: No more 'convicted felons.' They're 'justice-involved' persons now."

Chapter 6—Sexualize the Children

1. James Emery White, "Five Things We Now Know the Online World Is Doing to Us That Has Never Been Done to Us Before," *Church & Culture,* August 19, 2019, https://www.churchand culture.org/blog/2019/8/19/five-things-we-now-know.

2. Peter Hitchens, *The Rage Against God: How Atheism Led Me to Faith* (Grand Rapids, MI: Zonder- van, 2010), 139.

3. Adolf Hitler, from a speech given at the Reichsparteitag in 1935.

4. Alex Newman, "Rescuing Our Children," *New American*, February 4, 2019, 7.

5. Quoted in Newman, "Rescuing Our Children," 7.

6. Lisa Hudson, "The Disturbing Reality Behind 'Comprehensive Sexuality Education,'" *The National Pulse,* September 5, 2019, https://thenationalpulse.com/commentary/disturbing-reality -behind-comprehensive-sexuality-education/.

7. Hudson, "The Disturbing Reality Behind 'Comprehensive Sexuality Education.'" "The Effect of Early Sexual Activity on Mental Health" report is found at https://teleiosresearch.com/wp -content/uploads/2018/12/2018-08-29-Sex-review-FINAL.pdf.

8. J.H. Merle d'Aubigné, *History of the Reformation of the Sixteenth Century* (London: Religious Tract Society, 1856), 190.

9. Ariana Eunjung Cha, "Planned Parenthood to open reproductive health centers at 50 Los Angeles high schools," *The Washington Post,* December 11, 2019, https://www.washington post.com/health/2019/12/11/planned-parenthood-open-reproductive-health-centers-los-angeles -high-schools/.

10. Eunjung Cha, "Planned Parenthood to open reproductive health centers at 50 Los Angeles high schools."

11. David P. Gushee, "Christian higher ed can't win the LGBTQ debate unless it transforms," *Reli- gion News Service,* December 3, 2019, https://religionnews.com/2019/12/03/christian-higher -ed-cant-win-the-lgbtq-debate-unless-it-transforms/.

12. Tom Gjelten, "Christian Colleges Are Tangled In Their Own LGBT Policies," *NPR,* March 27, 2018, https://www.npr.org/2018/03/27/591140811/christian-colleges-are-tangled-in-their-own-lgbt -policies. See also https://www.npr.org/2018/03/27/597390654/christian-colleges-that-oppose -lgbt-rights-worried-about-losing-funding-under-ti.

13. Madeleine Kearns, "The Equality Act Is a Time Bomb," *National Review,* May 20, 2019, https://www.nationalreview.com/corner/the-equality-act-is-a-time-bomb/.

14. Eliana Dockterman, "It Can Be a Boy, a Girl, Neither or Both," *Time,* October 7, 2019, 40-47.

15. "Drag Queen Story Hour Host Makes Disgusting Admission About What He Wants to Do to the Kids," *Tea Party 247,* https://www.teaparty247.org/drag-queen-story-hour-host-makes-disgusting-admission-about-what-he-wants-to-do-to-the-kids/.

16. Dr. R. Albert Mohler Jr., "Evolving Standards of Decency? How Progressivism Reshapes Society," August 13, 2019, https://albertmohler.com/2019/08/13/briefing-8-13-19.

17. Michael Brown, "The Great Transgender 'Awokening,'" *The Stream,* July 12, 2019, https://stream.org/great-transgender-awokening/.

18. Janie B. Cheaney, "Picture a Triangle: Polyamory makes deviance the norm," *World,* February 15, 2020, 18.

19. Quote is found on the *Minnesota Press* website promoting *Harmful to Minors,* https://www.upress.umn.edu/book-division/books/harmful-to-minors.

20. Stella Morabito, "The Pedophile Project: Your 7-Year-Old Is Next on the Sexual Revolution's Hit Parade," *The Federalist,* February 21, 2019, https://thefederalist.com/2019/02/21/pedophile-project-7-year-old-next-sexual-revolutions-hit-parade/.

21. Tammy Bruce, *The Death of Right and Wrong* (Roseville, CA: Forum, 2003), 195.

22. C.S. Lewis, "The Humanitarian Theory of Punishment," *God in the Dock* (Grand Rapids, MI: William B. Eerdmans, 2014), 325.

23. Ryan T. Anderson, *When Harry Became Sally: Responding to the Transgender Moment* (New York: Encounter Books, 2018), 2.

24. Jesse Singal, "What's Missing from the Conversation About Transgender Kids," *The Cut,* July 25, 2016, https://www.thecut.com/2016/07/whats-missing-from-the-conversation-about-transgender-kids.html.

25. Jay Keck, "My daughter thinks she's transgender. Her public school undermined my efforts to help her," *USA Today,* August 12, 2019, https://www.usatoday.com/story/opinion/voices/2019/08/12/transgender-daughter-school-undermines-parents-column/1546527001/.

26. Dan Springer, "Oregon allowing 15-year-olds to get state-subsidized sex-change operations," *Fox News,* May 2, 2016, https://www.foxnews.com/politics/oregon-allowing-15-year-olds-to-get-state-subsidized-sex-change-operations.

27. Keck, "My daughter thinks she's transgender. Her public school undermined my efforts to help her."

28. Jonathon Van Maren, "Dad horrified as public school convinces daughter she's a 'boy'…and he can't stop it," *Life Site,* August 13, 2019, https://www.lifesitenews.com/blogs/dad-horrified-as-public-school-convinces-daughter-shes-a-boyand-he-cant-stop-it.

29. Alyssa Jackson, Special to CNN, "The high cost of being transgender," *CNN,* July 31, 2015, https://www.cnn.com/2015/07/31/health/transgender-costs-irpt/index.html.

30. arp2020, "Shame on Sprite," *American Renewal Project,* https://theamericanrenewalproject.org/2019/11/shame-on-sprite/.

31. Lawrence S. Mayer and Paul R. McHugh, *Sexuality and Gender*, *The New Atlantis*, Fall 2016, https://www.thenewatlantis.com/publications/executive-summary-sexuality-and-gender.

32. Michael Brown, "The Great Transgender 'Awokening,'" *The Stream*, July 12, 2019, https://stream.org/great-transgender-awokening/.

33. Jamie Dean, "Suffer the children," *World*, April 15, 2017, https://world.wng.org/2017/03/suffer_the_children.

Chapter 7—Capitalism Is the Disease; Socialism Is the Cure

1. "Fewer Americans are giving money to charity but total donations are at record levels anyway," The Conversation, July 3, 2018, https://theconversation.com/fewer-americans-are-giving-money-to-charity-but-total-donations-are-at-record-levels-anyway-98291.

2. As cited in Joseph K. Folsom, *The Family and Democratic Society* (London: Routledge, 1949), 198.

3. Karl Marx, *Critique of the Gotha Program*, http://libcom.org/library/critique-of-the-gotha-program-karl-marx.

4. Karl Marx, *The Poverty of Philosophy* (Moscow: Foreign Languages Publishing House, 1955), 93; Quoted in John W. Montgomery, "The Marxist Approach to Human Rights Analysis and Critique," *The Simon Greenleaf Law Review* (Santa Ana, CA: Simon Greenleaf School of Law, 1981), 39.

5. G.K. Chesterton, *The Collected Works of G.K. Chesterton, Vol. 20* (San Francisco: Ignatius Press, 2001), 57–58.

6. Ronald H. Nash, ed. *Liberation Theology* (Milford, MI: Mott Media, 1984), 50.

7. Karl Marx, *Critique of the Gotha Program*.

8. William S. Lind, ed., "Political Correctness: A Short History of an Ideology," Free Congress Foundation, November 2004, 10, http://archive.discoverthenetworks.org/viewSubCategory.asp?id=1332.

9. David Horowitz, *Unholy Alliance: Radical Islam and the American Left* (Washington, DC: Regnery Publishing, 2004), 47.

10. Greta Thunberg's address to the United Nation's Climate Action Summit 2019, https://www.npr.org/2019/09/23/763452863/transcript-greta-thunbergs-speech-at-the-u-n-climate-action-summit.

11. Stephen R.C. Hicks, *Explaining Postmodernism: Skepticism and Socialism from Rousseau to Foucault* (Loves Park, IL: Ockham's Razor Publishing, 2004), 155.

12. Hicks, *Explaining Postmodernism*, 156.

13. Veery Huleatt, "Progressive seminary students offered a confession to plants. How do we think about sins against nature?" *The Washington Post*, September 18, 2019, https://www.washingtonpost.com/religion/2019/09/18/progressive-seminary-students-offered-confession-plants-what-are-we-make-it/.

14. Frank Camp, "INTERVIEW (Part I): Swedish Author Johan Norberg on the Devastating Impact of Socialism, and What It Could Cost The U.S.," *The Daily Wire*, February 14, 2020, https://www.dailywire.com/news/interview-part-i-swedish-author-johan-norberg-on-the-devastating-impact-of-socialism-and-what-it-could-cost-the-u-s.

15. Marvin Olasky, "The view from 'Doralzuela,'" *World*, May 25, 2019, https://world.wng .org/2019/05/the_view_from_doralzuela.

16. "Rees-Mogg movement ridicules Corbyn's 'socialist inspiration' Venezuela as it crumbles," *Express*, July 31, 2017, https://www.express.co.uk/news/uk/835146/Jeremy-Corbyn-mocked -Jacob-Rees-Mogg-Moggmentum-Venezuela-socialism-video.

17. Olasky, "The view from 'Doralzuela.'"

18. Olasky, "The view from 'Doralzuela.'"

19. Ernest Hemingway, *The Sun Also Rises* (New York: Simon & Schuster, 2014), 109.

20. Benjamin Franklin, Pennsylvania Assembly: Reply to the Governor, November 11, 1755, https:// founders.archives.gov/documents/Franklin/01-06-02-0107.

21. Emily Stewart, "You can't turn the economy back on like a light switch," *Vox*, May 21, 2020, https://www.vox.com/2020/5/21/21263934/economy-reopening-stock-market-v-shape -recovery-jerome-powell.

22. Gary Abernathy, "The coronavirus shows Bernie Sanders won," *The Washington Post*, March 25, 2020, https://www.washingtonpost.com/opinions/2020/03/25/we-are-all-socialists-now/.

23. Marvin Olasky, "Money like magic," *World*, May 25, 2019, https://world.wng.org/2019/05/ money_like_magic.

24. No primary source is known for this statement, but is it frequently attributed to Mayer Amschel Rothschild.

25. D. James Kennedy Ministries, *Why Do You Believe That?* (Fort Lauderdale, FL: D. James Kennedy Ministries, 2019), 15.

26. Gerald L.K. Smith, Wikipedia, https://en.wikipedia.org/wiki/Gerald_L._K._Smith.

27. Camp, "INTERVIEW (Part I): Swedish Author Johan Norberg on the Devastating Impact of Socialism, and What It Could Cost The U.S."

28. Olasky, "The view from 'Doralzuela.'"

29. Michael O. Emerson and Christian Smith, *Divided by Faith: Evangelical Religion and the Problem of Race in America* (Oxford: Oxford University Press, 2001), 76.

30. Quoted in John Warwick Montgomery, *The Law Above the Law* (Minneapolis: Bethany House, 1975), 169.

31. Winston Churchill, House of Commons, October 22, 1945.

32. George Orwell, *Animal Farm* (Orlando, FL: Houghton Mifflin Harcourt, 2009), 192.

33. Willard Cantelon, *The Day the Dollar Dies* (Plainfield, NJ: Logos International, 1973), vi-vii.

Chapter 8—Join with Radical Islam to Destroy America

1. *Shariah: The Threat to America: Abridged* (Washington, DC: The Center for Security Policy, 2016), 40, https://www.centerforsecuritypolicy.org/2016/06/30/shariah-the-threat-to-america-abridged/.

2. Patrick Poole, "The Muslim Brotherhood 'Project,'" *Frontpage*, May 11, 2006.

3. William J. Boykin et al., *Shariah: The Threat to America: An Exercise in Competitive Analysis* (Washington, DC: The Center for Security Policy, 2010), 47.

4. Andrew C. McCarthy, *The Grand Jihad: How Islam and the Left Sabotage America* (New York: Encounter Books, 2012), 162.

5. McCarthy, *The Grand Jihad*, 51.

6. McCarthy, *The Grand Jihad*, 28.

7. David Horowitz, *Unholy Alliance: Radical Islam and the American Left* (Washington, DC: Regnery Publishing, 2004), 13-14.

8. David Horowitz, "The sick mind of Noam Chomsky," *Salon,* September 26, 2001, https://www.salon.com/2001/09/26/treason_2/.

9. Brian Flood, "New York Times deletes 9/11 tweet after backlash: 'Airplanes took aim and brought down the World Trade Center,'" *Fox News,* September 11, 2019, https://www.foxnews.com/media/new-york-times-9-11-tweet-deleted-airplanes.

10. David Horowitz, *Dark Agenda: The War to Destroy Christian America* (West Palm Beach, FL: Humanix Books, 2018), 131.

11. Horowitz, *Unholy Alliance*, 34.

12. Dennis Prager, "If you believe that people are basically good…," *Jerusalem World Review*, December 31, 2002, http://jewishworldreview.com/0103/prager123102.asp.

13. See Paul Marshall and Nina Shea*, Silenced: How Apostasy and Blasphemy Codes Are Choking Freedom Worldwide* (New York: Oxford University Press, 2011), 174.

14. Horowitz, *Dark Agenda*, 59-60.

15. Thomas D. Williams, PhD, "7th Graders in Tennessee Made to Recite 'Allah Is the Only God' in Public School," *Breitbart,* September 10, 2015, https://www.breitbart.com/politics/2015/09/10/7th-graders-in-tennessee-made-to-recite-allah-is-the-only-god-in-public-school/.

16. Robert Spencer, *Stealth Jihad: How Radical Islam Is Subverting America without Guns or Bombs* (Washington, DC: Regnery Publishing, 2008), 190.

17. Spencer, *Stealth Jihad*, 195.

18. Spencer, *Stealth Jihad*, 206.

19. Horowitz, *Dark Agenda*, 61.

20. Boykin et al., *Shariah*, 125-126.

21. *Shariah: The Threat to America: Abridged*, 16.

22. Stephen Coughlin, *"Bridge Building" to Nowhere: The Catholic Church's Study in Interfaith Delusion* (Washington, DC: The Center for Security Policy, 2015), 8.

23. Muhammad Shafiq and Mohammed Abu-Nimer, *Interfaith Dialogue: A Guide for Muslims* (Herndon, VA: The International Institute of Islamic Thought, 2011).

24. Shariq and Abu-Nimer, *Interfaith Dialogue*, 43.

25. Shariq and Abu-Nimer, *Interfaith Dialogue*, 108.

Chapter 9—Vilify! Vilify! Vilify!

1. Saul D. Alinsky, *Rules for Radicals: A Pragmatic Primer for Realistic Radicals* (New York: Vintage Books, 1989), 130.

2. Ellis Washington, "Alinsky, Obama: Lies, lies, lies," *WorldNetDaily*, September 16, 2011, https://www.wnd.com/2011/09/345625/.

3. "Homosexuality and psychology," Wikipedia, https://en.wikipedia.org/wiki/Homosexuality_and_psychology.

4. Jeffrey Satinover, *Homosexuality and the Politics of Truth* (Grand Rapids, MI: Baker Books, 1996), 33.

5. David Horowitz, *Dark Agenda: The War to Destroy Christian America* (West Palm Beach, FL: Humanix Books, 2018), 92.

6. Thomas Messner, "The Price of Prop 8," *The Heritage Foundation*, October 22, 2009, https://www.heritage.org/marriage-and-family/report/the-price-prop-8.

7. David Crary and Rachel Zoll, "Mozilla CEO resignation raises free-speech issues," *USA Today*, April 4, 2014, https://www.usatoday.com/story/news/nation/2014/04/04/mozilla-ceo-resignation-free-speech/7328759/.

8. K. Allan Blume, "'Guilty as charged,' Cathy says of Chick-fil-A's stand on biblical & family values," *Baptist Press*, July 16, 2012, http://www.bpnews.net/38271/guilty-as-charged-cathy-says-of-chickfilas-stand-on-biblical-and-family-values.

9. Annie Martin and Leslie Postal, "Lawmakers, voucher advocates meet on private schools' anti-LGBTQ policies," *Orlando Sentinel*, February 6, 2020, https://www.orlandosentinel.com/news/education/os-ne-school-scholarship-protests-20200206-bwclm26yy5abflbfc7l5z2dony-story.html.

10. George Orwell, *1984* (New York: Signet Classics, 1977), 267.

11. Jonathon Van Maren, "Protest at public library shows LGBT movement won't stop until it dominates everything," *LifeSite*, October 30, 2019, https://www.lifesitenews.com/blogs/feminist-argues-at-public-library-males-cant-become-female-lgbt-movement-rampages.

12. Van Maren, "Protest at public library shows LGBT movement won't stop until it dominates everything."

13. Jon Street, "Incoming Texas freshmen threatened with doxxing if they join conservative campus groups," *Campus Reform*, June 21, 2019, https://www.campusreform.org/?ID=13363.

14. Heather Mac Donald, *The Diversity Delusion* (New York: St. Martin's Press, 2018), 20-22.

15. Mac Donald, *The Diversity Delusion*, 4.

16. Mac Donald, *The Diversity Delusion*, 22.

17. Stewart Weiss, "The looting—and muting—of America," *The Jerusalem Post*, June 18, 2020, https://www.jpost.com/opinion/the-looting-and-muting-of-america-631909.

18. Gregor Strasser, "Thoughts about the Tasks of the Future," June 15, 1926, see Wikiquote: https://en.wikiquote.org/wiki/Gregor_Strasser.

19. WND Staff, "Antifa revealed! Free exposé of alt-left" *WorldNetDaily*, January 23, 2018, https://www.wnd.com/2018/01/antifa-revealed-free-expose-of-alt-left/.

20. Soeren Kern, "A Brief History of Antifa: Part 1," *Gatestone Institute*, June 12, 2020, https://www.gatestoneinstitute.org/16104/antifa-history.

21. "Video Shows NYC Protesters Chanting for 'Dead Cops,'" *NBC New York,* December 15, 2014, https://www.nbcnewyork.com/news/local/eric-garner-manhattan-dead-cops-video-millions-march-protest/2015303/.

22. Ross Barkan and Jillian Jorgensen, "Elected Officials, Sharpton React to Killing of Two Police Officers in Brooklyn," *Observer,* December 20, 2014, https://observer.com/2014/12/elected-officials-sharpton-react-to-killing-of-two-police-officers-in-brooklyn/.

23. Joe Carter, "How LGBT Pride Month Became a Religious Holiday," *The Gospel Coalition,* June 26, 2019, https://www.thegospelcoalition.org/article/lgbt-pride-month-became-religious-holiday/.

24. Horowitz, *Dark Agenda,* 32-33.

25. Horowitz, *Dark Agenda,* 33.

26. Horowitz, *Dark Agenda,* 33.

27. Horowitz, *Dark Agenda,* 34.

28. KOMU and Missourian Staff, "Sermon at The Crossing leads to call for boycott of local businesses," *Missourian,* October 18, 2019, https://www.columbiamissourian.com/news/local/update-sermon-at-the-crossing-leads-to-call-for-boycott-of-local-businesses/article_adb47a54-f151-11e9-87aa-eb41f6d01b0c.html.

29. Voltaire, Letter to Étienne Noël Damilaville (May 16, 1767), https://en.wikiquote.org/wiki/Voltaire.

Chapter 10—Wake Up! Strengthen What Remains!

1. Barna Group, "Almost Half of Practicing Christian Millennials Say Evangelism Is Wrong," February 5, 2019, https://www.barna.com/research/millennials-oppose-evangelism/.

2. Portions of this section are adapted from my book *The Church in Babylon* (Chicago: Moody Publishers, 2018).

3. Emma Green, "Rachel Held Evans, Hero to Christian Misfits," *The Atlantic,* May 6, 2019, https://www.theatlantic.com/politics/archive/2019/05/rachel-held-evans-death-progressive-christianity/588784/.

4. Nadia Bolz-Weber, *Shameless: A Case for Not Feeling Bad About Feeling Good (About Sex)* (New York: Crown Publishing Group, 2019), 71.

5. Bolz-Weber, *Shameless,* 133.

6. Bolz-Weber, *Shameless,* back cover.

7. Daron Roberts, "The Church Boy Who Never Grew Up," *The Cripplegate,* July 2, 2020, https://thecripplegate.com/the-church-boy-who-never-grew-up/.

8. Eleanor Busby, "Social media sites are damaging children's mental health, headteachers warn," *Independent,* March 9, 2018, https://www.independent.co.uk/news/education/education-news/headteachers-social-media-children-mental-health-school-association-college-a8246456.html; See also June Eric Udorie, "Social media is harming the mental health of teenagers. The state has to act," *The Guardian,* September 16, 2015, https://www.theguardian.com/commentisfree/2015/sep/16/social-media-mental-health-teenagers-government-pshe-lessons.

9. Robert Payne, *Life and Death of Lenin* (New York: Simon & Schuster, 1964), 209.

10. Quoted in J.S. Conway, *The Nazi Persecution of the Churches 1933–1945* (New York: Basic Books, 1968), v.

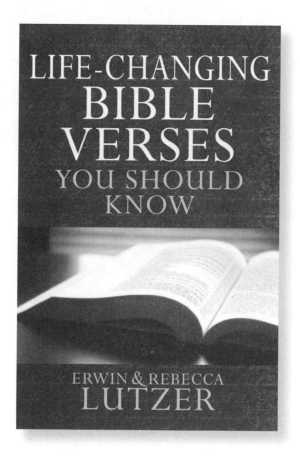

Life-Changing Bible Verses You Should Know

Do you desire to experience the life-changing power of God's Word? Do you long to hide God's Word in your heart, but don't know where to start?

In this book, Bible teacher Erwin Lutzer and his wife, Rebecca, have carefully selected more than 100 Bible verses that speak directly to the most important issues of life, and explained the very practical ways those verses can encourage and strengthen you.

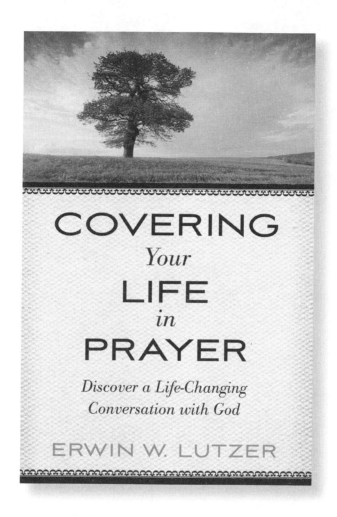

Covering Your Life in Prayer

Every Christian longs for a better and more intimate prayer life. And one of the most effective ways you can grow more powerful in prayer is to learn from the prayers of others. In this book you'll discover new ways to pray—new requests, concerns, and thanksgivings you can bring to God's throne of grace. A wonderful resource for expanding your prayer horizons and enriching your relationship with God.

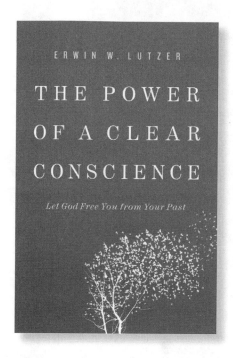

The Power of a Clear Conscience

Do you struggle with feelings of guilt about your past? Or are you bogged down by a conscience that haunts or imprisons you?

This is not how God intends for you to live. Your conscience was not created to hold you prisoner, but to guide you and point you to freedom from guilt and bad habits. Longtime pastor Erwin Lutzer shares what it means to live in the power of a clear conscience as you

- learn how to deal with guilt and replace it with joy
- discover how the truth that can hurt you can also heal you
- realize the incredible extent of God's forgiveness and love for you

You'll find yourself encouraged by the truths that no failure is permanent and no life is beyond God's power to bring about change.